Tolstoy

PLAYS

Tolstoy

PLAYS: VOLUME TWO, 1886–1889

Leo Tolstoy

Translated by Marvin Kantor

with Tanya Tulchinsky

Introduction by Andrew Baruch Wachtel

Northwestern University Press

Evanston, Illinois

Northwestern University Press

Evanston, Illinois 60208–4210

Copyright © 1996 by

Northwestern University Press.

All rights reserved.

Printed in the United States of America

ISBN cloth 0-8101-1394-5

   paper 0-8101-1395-3

Library of Congress

Cataloging-in-Publication Data

Tolstoy, Leo, graf, 1828–1910.

   [Plays. English]

   Tolstoy : plays / Leo Tolstoy ; translated by

   Marvin Kantor with Tanya Tulchinsky;

   introduction by Andrew Baruch Wachtel.

      p. cm. — (European drama classics)

      Contents: v. 1. 1856–1886. — v. 2. 1886–1889

      v. 1. ISBN 0-8101-1109-8. — ISBN 0-8101-1110-1

   (pbk). — v. 2. ISBN 0-8101-1394-5 (cloth).

   — ISBN 0-8101-1395-3 (paper)

      1. Tolstoy, Leo, graf, 1828–1910 — Translations into

English.   I. Kantor, Marvin.   II. Tulchinsky, Tanya.

III. Wachtel, Andrew Baruch.   IV. Title.

V. Series.

PG3366.A19   1994

891.72´3—dc20   94-22919

                                      CIP

Contents

Introduction

Among the burning, "accursed" questions that racked Russian society in the nineteenth century, the peasant question was perhaps the most important. At around the time of the emancipation proclamation of 1861, it was thought that the problem had been solved, but within a few years it became clear that the legal liberation of the serfs itself was no panacea. As one expert on the subject has written, "Serfdom was gone, but poverty remained: the mark of it was stamped upon the bodies of the people."[1] To this one might add that if serfdom's mark was visible on the peasant's body, it was even more deeply stamped on his brain. As it quickly became clear that emancipation had done little to improve the lot of the former serf, the energies of Russia's intellectual classes, which before 1861 had been concentrated on the matter of liberation, turned to the more important question of amelioration.

The most visible movement regarding the peasants among the Russian intelligentsia in the 1860s and 1870s was dubbed populism. The populists tended to idealize the Russian peasant, believing that the primitive socialism of the peasant village commune contained the seeds for a future revolutionary movement that would destroy the old order in the country. Of course, the fact that most populists were from urban families and had, therefore, almost no real experience of peasant life made such idealization easier. Young people were urged to go to the villages to learn from the people, as well as to incite them to revolutionary activity. The summer of 1874 marked the high point of this movement, as thousands of young populists attempted to "go to the people." The peasants themselves proved uninterested, however, and in most cases happily turned the agitators over to the authorities.

Although he was no populist, Tolstoy had a soft spot in his heart for the Russian peasant. In many of his works, peasants are founts of homespun knowledge and provide examples of ethical behavior which serve as lessons for the better-born characters as well as Tolstoy's readers. One only needs to mention Platon Karataev in *War and Peace*, the peasant Fyodor at the end of *Anna Karenina*, or the servant Gerasim in "The Death of Ivan Ilich." What is more, we know that Tolstoy himself tended to wear peasant garb (see the famous portrait by Ivan Kramskoy) and that he would do peasant work, particularly after his "conversion" in 1879. Nevertheless, Tolstoy lived among the Russian peasants daily, and although he appreciated their good qualities, he knew their darker sides too well to idolize them completely. Nowhere is this contradictory attitude toward the peasant better expressed than in his greatest drama, *The Realm of Darkness* (1886).

The initial stimulus for the play is generally regarded to have been Tolstoy's acquaintance with a trial that took place in 1880. Although it is well known that courts and trials were extremely important stimuli for Dostoevsky, it is less frequently recognized that a number of Tolstoy's later works, including the novel *Resurrection* and the play *The Living Corpse*, are also creative reworkings of criminal proceedings. In the instance of *The Realm of Darkness*, the connection to the actual events of the trial of Efrem Koloskov and Martha Ionova appears to be quite close. As Tolstoy put it in an 1896 interview: "The subject of *The Realm of Darkness* was almost exactly taken by me from an actual criminal case that took place in the Tula court. I was informed of the details by my good friend, Davydov, who was then the prosecutor and is now the judge of that court. . . . Just as it was presented in *The Realm of Darkness*, the case dealt precisely with the murder of a child who had been born to a stepdaughter, and, what is more, the murderer confessed publicly in just the same way at the marriage of his stepdaughter."[2] As it happens, Davydov was not Tolstoy's only source of knowledge of the case. The author himself went to the Tula jail and interviewed the convicted murderer Koloskov sometime in 1881.

Nevertheless, as is usually true in such cases, the actual facts of a murder case were but one of the subtexts underlying Tolstoy's work. Indeed, the pattern of illicit sex, murder of a helpless victim (usually a child), and public confession that seems to link the actions of Koloskov and Tolstoy's Nikita is a paradigm that had been employed by Russian literature well before 1881. Although Tolstoy appears not to have been consciously aware of what he was doing, his reworking of the Koloskov trial is simultaneously a revisitation and reinterpretation of a pattern that had first surfaced in Russian literature in a play by Alexei Pisemsky entitled *A Bitter Fate* (1859). That work begins with the arrival in his home village of a peasant named Anany who has been working in the big city for a number of years. He discovers that in the meantime his wife Lizaveta has been having an affair with his and her owner, the landlord Cheglov-Sokovin (i.e., illicit sex). As opposed to most stories of such liaisons, that of Lizaveta and Cheglov-Sokovin is not one of exploitation but of mutual love. Lizaveta was forced to marry her husband against her will and she and her owner now have a true relationship. Her husband, however, cannot accept the situation, and, after fruitless negotiations with the weak landowner, he returns to his hut where he seizes and murders the child that had been born to Lizaveta and Cheglov-Sokovin (i.e., murder). After the murder he escapes, but he eventually returns to the village to confess—"You can run away and hide from human judgment but you can't escape God's."[3] In addition to containing the sex/murder/confession paradigm, this drama also features extensive use of peasant dialect. This was something completely unheard of in Russian drama at the time, and it would be used even more extensively by Tolstoy in *The Realm of Darkness.*

As one might expect, Tolstoy was aware of Pisemsky's drama. When it first came out, he said, "I liked Pisemsky's drama very, very much: wonderful, wonderful, strong and true to life, not invented."[4] Interestingly enough, when he reread the work in 1890, he came to a rather different conclusion, as a diary entry attests: "Read Pisemsky's drama *A Bitter Fate.* Bad."[5] Of course, a comparison of the two plays makes the reasons for Tolstoy's changed opinion of Pisemsky's work clear. One interesting fact about Tolstoy's reading practice is that he often read for potential, seeing in works only what he wanted to see. When he read Pisemsky's drama in 1859, he must have seen in it the linguistic wealth and the power of the murder and confession scenes. What is more, he probably would have recognized the potential strength of the conflict within Amany's mind before, during, and after the murder, something that Pisemsky does not bring out in his drama. In rewriting Pisemsky's drama (keeping in mind his knowledge of the court case), Tolstoy dropped completely characters from the gentry sphere, narrowing the focus to the peasants. He banished the love element represented by Lizaveta and the landowner, and, in addition, he eliminated a farcical investigation scene that almost ruins Pisemsky's fifth act. Instead, he focused on the gradual psychological disintegration of Nikita and created strong evil women characters (Matryona, Akulina, and Anisya) alongside him. Finally, in the characters of Akim and Mitrich, he created a certain counterweight to the play's blackness. After having accomplished all these revisions, Tolstoy was, presumably, incapable of recognizing anything of value in Pisemsky's play, for in his own mind he had now realized its potentials while avoiding its failures.

Nor was *A Bitter Fate* the only literary work that might have provided Tolstoy with ideas about how to craft his play. It seems likely that his reading of Dostoevsky's *Crime and Punishment* might have played a role as well. As I stated above, one potential aspect of the dramatic situation that clearly interested Tolstoy was the disintegration of the mind of the murderer. This, of course, is central to Dostoevsky's great novel. And while the story of Raskolnikov lacks the illicit sex segment of the paradigm that links Tolstoy's play to Pisemsky's and to Koloskov's trial (actually, illicit sex is present in the novel in the aborted "incestuous" relationship between Raskolnikov's double Svidrigailov and his sister Dunya), it contains an abundance of material relating to the mind of the murderer as well as a scene of public confession. As in the case of Pisemsky's play, however, Dostoevsky's novel is not as unremittingly dark as Tolstoy's play, balancing as it does the murder with the sentimentality of Marmeladov and the love story of Raskolnikov and Sonya.[6] It was Tolstoy's achievement to take the paradigm provided by literature and life and to make of it a play that would fully capture the darkest sides of Russian peasant existence.

Interestingly enough, Tolstoy's play was not the final Russian literary work to employ the paradigm I have been discussing. In 1900, Anton Chekhov published a longish story entitled "In the Ravine" ("V ovrage") which covers the same ground. In that story we see the collapse of the Tsybukin family of merchants. The eldest son is a forger who is eventually arrested and sent to prison. He was married to Lipa, with whom he had a child. The second son is a simpleton whose wife, Akulina(!), cheats on him with various neighbors (i.e., illicit sex). In a fit of rage, she murders Lipa's child by throwing a tub full of boiling water on him (the scene is one of the most brutal in Russian literature). Chekhov breaks the paradigm, however, and darkens the story even further by eliminating the expected confession scene. Instead, Akulina eventually pushes her father-in-law out of his house and appears to live happily ever after.

The period of the 1880s was one in which, in principle, Tolstoy had renounced literary activity in favor of spiritual and educational products. Nevertheless, literature was a constant temptation, and when Tolstoy received a letter asking for support from M. V. Lentovsky, director of the Moscow people's theater "Skomorokh," he responded by beginning work on *The Realm of Darkness*. He worked intensively in the second half of 1886, producing no less than seven drafts of the play. The extent to which the work drew him in despite himself can be felt in a letter to his secretary and assistant Vladimir Chertkov: "I worked on the calendar and then on the drama. It seems that I sinned with the latter, polishing it a lot."[7] Despite a certain amount of trouble with the censors, the drama was published in 1887. The title, interestingly enough, was added at the last moment. In all the manuscripts the play is called by its present subtitle—"If a Claw Gets Stuck, the Bird is Lost." In previous translations, the title has been rendered as *The Power of Darkness*. The word "power," however, tends to connote some kind of outside force, whereas what Tolstoy seems to have had in mind was that evil can be inherent in human nature. Thus, his focus is on the entire enclosed world in which the crimes described in this play were committed rather than on any external power. That is why we have opted for "realm" here.

Although Tolstoy succeeded in having the drama published, getting it staged proved a great deal more complicated. Under the tsars, Russia had two separate censorships for publication and performance, the latter being even more demanding. In the case of *The Realm of Darkness* the process of getting approval for staging was hideously difficult. Initially, the play was to have been performed at the Aleksandrinsky Theater in Saint Petersburg under the direct patronage of Tsar Alexander III. The tsar had been present at a reading of Tolstoy's play and had pronounced it a "wonderful thing."[8] However, Alexander's all-powerful minister, Konstantin Pobedonostsev, talked the tsar out of approving the play for performance. In a long and furious letter Pobedonostsev wrote: "I have just finished reading the new drama of L. Tolstoy and I can hardly recover from horror. . . . I know of nothing similar in any literature. Even Zola has not descended to such a level of coarse realism as has Tolstoy. The author's art is amazing, but what an insult to art! What an absence—even more—a renunciation of the ideal, what an insult to moral feeling, what a slur to taste."[9] In response to this outburst the tsar retreated and the play was banned from performance. Not until 1895, during the reign of Nicholas II, was the play permitted on the Russian stage.

The creation and fate of Tolstoy's next play, *The Fruits of Enlightenment*, were in marked contrast to *The Realm of Darkness*. In 1889 Tolstoy's eldest daughter asked her father to write a play to be performed at home by her friends and the Tolstoy family. The author responded joyfully and, as had happened the last time he had written a play for his family's entertainment (the dramatic fragment *The Nihilist* of 1866; see volume one of this edition, pp. 137–51), the result was a comedy, although by no means a farce, which was performed for the first time in Tolstoy's home on December 30, 1889. The tutor of the Tolstoys' younger children, A. M. Novikov, left a description of the preparations for the domestic production that provides a wonderful portrait of the Tolstoy household at one of its happiest moments: "An ecstatic group of young people wrote out the parts in the morning, rehearsed in the evening—and almost every day after they finished Tolstoy would collect the parts and again redo the play. It was created directly for the performers and was redone and rewritten some twenty or thirty times, although the final polishing was done after the performance, in January, 1890."[10]

Tolstoy's central comic target in *The Fruits of Enlightenment* are the Zvezdintsevs, an upper-class Russian family who are the direct descendants of the Pribyshevs in his earlier play *The Infected Family* (see volume one of this edition, pp. 37–135). The diseases from which they suffer, however, are as different as the 1880s were from the 1860s. In the earlier play, the diseases were political and social, outgrowths of the radicalization of Russian society at around the time of the great reforms of Alexander II. By the late 1880s, under the reign of Alexander III, reaction had set in, and the new obsessions of Russia's empty-headed aristocrats were spiritualism, health, and the preservation of class privileges (represented in the play by Leonid, his wife, and his son, respectively).

Of course, the central target of Tolstoy's play was the modish fascination with spiritualism ("the belief in the continued existence of the dead and in the ability of the living to communicate with them through a sensitive or medium"[11]) that swept Europe from the 1850s and arrived in Russia soon thereafter. The play was not the first time that Tolstoy, ever the rationalist, had skewed his contemporaries' fondness for mysticism: in part 7 of *Anna Karenina*, for example, he provides an unsympathetic portrait of the half-witted medium Landau in order to lambaste some of his more inane aristocratic characters. In *The Fruits of Enlightenment*, his target is so-called scientific spiritualism, which, "regardless of its 'occult' trappings, was essentially positivistic in its insistence that various Spiritualist phenomena were indeed consistent with modern science and would eventually be explained according to the laws of nature."[12]

The attack on the gullibility of characters like Leonid Zvezdintsev and his spiritualist friends is, of course, pure farce. What gives the play a certain level of seriousness is the coexistence of the secondary plot involving the peasants' desire to buy land and Tanya's successful attempts to help them and herself. When describing the peasant world in *The Realm of Darkness*, Tolstoy was clearly able to recognize its problematic aspects. Here, however, his peasants are consistently idealized, shown to be more clever, more sympathetic, and more deserving in every respect than the addle-headed aristocrats for whom they work. Even the farmers from Kursk, who are by no means educated and whose speeches can sound comic, are meant to seem sympathetic, as can be seen by Tolstoy's own comments after witnessing a performance of the play by Moscow's famous Maly Theater in 1891: "After all, in the peasants' speeches one can hear constant complaints, sometimes even attempts at protest. In my opinion, their words should elicit sympathy toward their hopeless position, and certainly not laughter."[13] While this division into inept aristocrats and clever peasants may not be entirely believable, it does have the virtue of providing dramatic balance as well as a few positive roles in what would otherwise be a completely negative play.

The two plays presented in this volume show Tolstoy at the height of his powers as a dramatist. *The Fruits of Enlightenment* is a more or less standard stage comedy, written in a light-hearted moment, yet it has important things to say about the disintegration of the society in which it was written. It is easy to see, for example, why aristocrats like the Zvezdintsevs were unable to put up serious resistance when revolutionary movements swept their country in 1905 and 1917. *The Realm of Darkness* is one of the grimmest evocations of the world of the Russian peasant, a world that Tolstoy knew well and frequently admired, but one whose evils were also clear to him. With its constant use of peasant dialect and its shocking violence, *The Realm of Darkness* stands practically alone in the Russian dramatic tradition. Taken together, the plays reveal that even in his post-*Confession* period, after having renounced literary activity entirely, Tolstoy could not avoid being a writer, could not avoid using the written word to speak unpleasant truths to his society.

Andrew Baruch Wachtel
Evanston, Ill.

Translators' Preface

Beside wearing peasant garb and doing peasant work, as is mentioned in the Introduction, Tolstoy was also acquainted with the language of the peasant, and utilized it in works of prose that appeared between 1850 and 1870. However, it was not until the 1880s that he became engrossed in the study of the peasantry. Having now mastered this idiom, in particular the use of regional dialect, he gave it broad literary expression in two of his so-called peasant plays, *The Realm of Darkness* and *The Fruits of Enlightenment*.

Tolstoy's extensive use of substandard language and dialect, as well as proverbs and corruptions, in these two plays has made translation into English a daunting task. We chose not to follow the path of previous translators, who have, without exception, rendered these plays into more or less standard, colorless, literary English. Such use of English ensures that the flavor and tone of the original will be utterly lost. Therefore, we have attempted an explicit "colloquial" rendition, one that is unmarked as to regional, ethnic, or racial origin. The dialect "transcription" we utilize emphasizes the way the plays should *sound*. This choice has resulted in a potential problem: it takes some getting used to, since as a piece of English writing the transcription *looks* affected and "kinda" awful on the page. To some extent this is also true of the original scripts for Russian readers, who have to make their way through a maze of corruptions, dialectisms, and distortions. It is our hope that our transcription will not prove to be too much of a burden on the readers of this volume.

It should be noted that we have preserved the scene divisions of Tolstoy's scripts. For lack of a better word, we use "scene" to designate also the tiny units—sometimes only several words long—Tolstoy considers scenes. They are not as developed as the traditional scene, and function as intersections of events, which are important and lend balance in reading the plays.

Finally, we would like to extend especial thanks to Andrew Wachtel, Marina Kamenskaya, and Géza von Molnár for their invaluable help in the preparation of our translation, and to Caryl Emerson for her critical comments.

The Realm of Darkness

or

"If a Claw Gets Stuck, the Bird Is Lost"

A Drama in Five Acts

> But I say unto you, That whosoever looketh on a woman to lust after her hath committed adultery with her already in his heart.
> And if thy right eye offend thee, pluck it out, and cast it from thee: for it is profitable for thee that one of thy members should perish, and not that thy whole body should be cast into hell.
>
> Matthew 5:28, 29

Dramatis personae

Pyotr [Ignatich]
  a rich peasant, 42, married for the second time, and ailing
Anisya [Anisyushka]
  his wife, 32, a dressy woman
Akulina [Akul, Akulka]
  *Pyotr's daughter from his first marriage, 16, hard of hearing, and
  simple-minded*
Anyutka [Anna Petrovna]
  his other daughter, 10
Nikita [Akimych Chilikin, Mikita, Mikit, Mikitka, Mikishka,
  Mikitushka, Nikitka, Nikitushka]
  their hired hand, 25, a sharp dresser
Akim
  Nikita's father, 50
  a plain-looking, God-fearing peasant
Matryona
  his wife, 50
Marina [Marinka, Marinushka, Marishka]
  an orphan girl, 22

This dramatis personae is for Act I. Throughout the volume, additional information
has been provided in brackets.

ACT I

The action takes place in the fall in a large village. The set depicts PYOTR *'s spacious cottage.* PYOTR *is sitting on a bench and mending a horse collar.* ANISYA *and* AKULINA *are spinning.*

SCENE 1

PYOTR, ANISYA, *and* AKULINA. *The latter are singing a duet.*

PYOTR (*looks out the window*). Again the horses're loose. Now you watch, they'll kill the colt. Mikita, hey, Mikita! Gone deaf! (*Listens. To the women.*) Nuff o' that, can't hear a thing.

NIKITA (*his voice from the yard*). What?

PYOTR. Get the horses back.

NIKITA (*his voice*). I'll get 'em, just hold on.

PYOTR (*shaking his head*). Boy, these hired hands! If I was aw right, I wouldn't keep'em aroun' for nothin'. Just grief with 'em... (*Stands up and sits down again.*) Hey Mikit!... Ain't no use callin'. How 'bout one o' yuh, go on. Akul, go, get 'em back.

AKULINA. What, the horses?

PYOTR. What else?

AKULINA. Right away. (*Exits*).

SCENE 2

PYOTR *and* ANISYA.

PYOTR. That guy's a real goof-off, worthless. Now he'll do it, now he won't.

ANISYA. Yuh're no speed demon yuhself, only good at goin' from yer sack on the stove t'yer bench. Just know how t'boss others.

PYOTR. If no one bossed yuh, there'd be no house in a year. Ah, what people!

ANISYA. Yuh want ten things done at a time, an' then cuss. It's easy t'give orders from the stove.

PYOTR (*sighing*). Ah, if this sickness didn't put me on my back, I wouldn't keep 'im for a day.

AKULINA (*her voice*). Gee up, gee up, gee up... (*Sound of the colt neighing, and the horses running through the gate. The gate creaks.*)

PYOTR. Bullshitin', that's all he does. Really, I wouldn't keep 'im aroun'.

ANISYA (*mimicking him*). Won't keep 'im aroun'. Try doin' it yuhself, then yuh could talk.

SCENE 3

THE SAME *and* AKULINA.

AKULINA (*enters*). I barely got 'em in. It's always the roan...

PYOTR. So where's Mikita?

AKULINA. Mikita? Standin' outside.

PYOTR. What's he standin' for?

AKULINA. What for? He's standin' roun' the corner, an' gabbin'.

PYOTR. Can't get any sense out of 'er. Who's he gabbin' with?

AKULINA (*does not hear*). What? (PYOTR *waves his hand at* AKULINA; *she sits down to spin.*)

SCENE 4

THE SAME *and* ANYUTKA.

ANYUTKA (*runs in. To her mother*). Mikitka's father an' mother've come. They're takin' 'im home, cross my heart.

ANISYA. Yuh're kiddin?

ANYUTKA. No! Strike me dead! (*Laughs.*) I'm walkin' by an' Mikita says: "Good-bye now," he says, "Anna Petrovna. Come dance at my weddin'. I'm leavin' yuh," he says, an' just laughs.

ANISYA (*to her husband*). Yuh're not much needed, are yuh. There now, he's gettin ready t'take off on his own... "I'll kick 'im out!", he says...

PYOTR. Let 'im go; as if I can't find someone else.

ANISYA. An' what about the money yuh gave 'im up front?.. (ANYUTKA *comes up to the door, listens to what they are saying, and exits.*)

SCENE 5

NISYA, PYOTR, *and* AKULINA.

PYOTR (*frowning*). The money—if need be, he'll work it off in the summer.

ANISYA. Sure yuh're happy t'let 'im go—one less mouth t'feed. But in the winter I'll have t'do it all myself, like some horse. That girl o' yers ain't much for work, an' yuh'll be lyin' on the stove. I know yuh.

PYOTR. Yuh didn't hear nothin', so why're yuh waggin' yer tongue.

ANISYA. The yard's full o' livestock. Yuh didn't sell the cow, an' yuh brought all the sheep in for the winter. It takes all yuh can do t'feed an' water 'em—an' yuh want t'let the hired hand go. I ain't gonna do no man's work! I'll just lie on the stove like you—the hell with it all. You do as yuh like.

PYOTR (*to* AKULINA). Go get the fodder, will yuh. It's time.

AKULINA. The fodder? Okay. (*Puts on her coat and takes a rope.*)

ANISYA. I ain't gonna work for yuh. Nuff, I won't. Work yuhself.

PYOTR. Nuff o' that. Whacha ravin' 'bout, like a crazed sheep?

ANISYA. Yuh're a mad dog yuhself! There ain't no work from yuh, an' no joy. Yuh're just a nag. A stumblin' dog, that's what.

PYOTR (*spits and gets dressed*). Damn yuh! God forgive me! I'll go find out what's what. (*Exits.*)

ANISYA (*after him*). Rotten horn-nosed devil!

SCENE 6

ANISYA *and* AKULINA.

AKULINA. Whacha cussin' at Pa for?

ANISYA. Get lost, stupid, shut up.

AKULINA (*going to the door*). I know why yuh're cussin'. Yuh're stupid yuh-self, yuh bitch. I'm not 'fraid o' yuh.

ANISYA. What's with yuh? (*Jumps up and looks for something to hit her with.*) Watch out, yuh'll get it with the prongs.

AKULINA (*opening the door*). Yuh're a bitch, a witch, that's what yuh are! Witch, bitch, bitch, witch! (*Runs out.*)

SCENE 7

ANISYA *alone.*

ANISYA (*becomes thoughtful*). "Come t'my weddin'," he says. What a thing t'come up with! Get 'im married? Watch out, Mikitka: if that's yer idea, I'll... I can't live widout 'im. I won't let 'im go.

SCENE 8

ANISYA *and* NIKITA.

NIKITA (*enters and looks around; seeing that* ANISYA *is alone, he goes up to her quickly; whispers*). Well, my dear friend, there's trouble. Father's come, wants t'take me back—tells me t'come home. Once'n for all, he says, we're gonna get yuh married, an' you live at home.

ANISYA. So, get married. What's it t'me?

NIKITA. That's it, eh. I'm thinkin' how t'do this best, an' look at 'er: tells me get married. What's up? (*Winks.*) Maybe yuh've forgotten?...

ANISYA. Go get married, I don't care...

NIKITA. Whacha in a huff about? Look at that, she won't even let me touch 'er... What's wrong?

ANISYA. What's wrong is yuh wanna dump me... Yuh wanna dump me, so I don't need yuh either. That's it in a nutshell!

NIKITA. Nuff, Anisya. Do I really want t'forget yuh? Not on yer life. Once'n for all, I'll never dump yuh, yuh know. I'm thinkin' like this: even if they marry me, I'll come back t'yuh anyway; if only he don't take me home.

ANISYA. A lot a need I got for yuh married.

NIKITA. What's t'do, my dear friend—there's really no way o' gettin' aroun' what Father wants.

ANISYA. Yuh're dumpin' on yer father, but it's all yer idea. Yuh've long been makin' up t'that broad o' yers, Marinka. She's broadsided yuh. No wonder she came runnin' here t'other day.

NIKITA. Marinka? Much need I have for her!... Ain't there nuff of 'em hangin' roun' me!...

ANISYA. So why'd yer father come for? You told 'im to! Yuh've been cheatin' on me!... (*Cries.*)

NIKITA. Anisya! D'ya believe in God or not? I never even dreamt of it. Once'n for all, I dunno nothin', nothin' at all. My ol' man thought it all up.

ANISYA. If you don't wanna yuhself, is someone gonna pull yuh, like on a rope?

NIKITA. Well, I'm thinkin' yuh can't go 'gainst yer father. Even though I don't wanna.

ANISYA. Put yer foot down, that's all.

NIKITA. One guy did, so they gave 'im a good thrashin' at the county seat. That was it. I don't want that either. They say it tickles...

ANISYA. Nuff o' yer jokin'. You listen, Mikita: if yuh get hitched t'Marina, I dunno what I'll do t'myself... I'll kill myself! I've sinned, I've broken my vows, so there's no goin' back. You just leave me, an' I'll...

NIKITA. Why should I leave? If I wanted t'leave, I'd've left long ago. T'other day Ivan Semyonych begged me t'be his coachman... What a great life! But I didn't go. Cuz, I'm thinkin', everyone likes me. If yuh didn't love me, it'd be different.

ANISYA. You just remember. The ol' man'll die one o' these days, I figger—
we'll cover up all our sins. I'll take new vows, I've been figgerin', an' you'll
be boss.

NIKITA. Why think 'bout the future. What's it t'me? I work like I'm doin'
it for myself. The boss likes me, an' his woman likes me, yuh know. An'
if the women like me, it's not my fault—that's it.

ANISYA. Will you keep on lovin' me?

NIKITA (*hugs her*). An' how! An' yuh'll stay in my heart...

SCENE 9

THE SAME *and* MATRYONA (*enters, and crosses herself before the icons
for a long time;* NIKITA *and* ANISYA *move away from each other*).

MATRYONA. I saw nothin', I heard nothin'. Yuh've been playin' aroun' with
the little woman—so what? Even a calf, yuh know, even it plays aroun'.
Why not have some fun? That's what young's for. Now, Sonny, the boss
is in the yard lookin' for yuh.

NIKITA. I came for the ax.

MATRYONA. I know, I know, my dear, what kinda ax. That ax is by the
women most o' the time.

NIKITA (*bends over and takes the ax*). So, Ma, do yuh actually wanna get
me married? I'm thinkin', there's no reason to. Besides, I'm not much
for it.

MATRYONA. Hey, darlin', why should I wanna? Keep on doin' what yer
doin'. It's all the ol' man. Go 'head, my dear, we'll work things out widout yuh.

NIKITA. That's really amazin': first get married, then don't. Once'n for all,
I can't make nothin' out. (*Exits.*)

ANISYA *and* MATRYONA.

ANISYA. So, Ma Matryona, d'ya actually wanna get 'im married?

MATRYONA. Marry with what, pumpkin! Yuh know how much we got. It's all just my ol' man babblin' for nothin': get married an' get married. That's none o' his business. Horses, yuh know, don't run from oats, you just let well nuff alone. That's what the deal's here. Don't I see (*winks*) how things're goin'?

ANISYA. Why would I wanna hide it from yuh, Ma Matryona. Yuh know all about it. I've sinned, I've fallen for yer son.

MATRYONA. So that's news! As if Ma Matryona didn't know. Eh, little girl, Mother Matryona's been aroun' an' aroun', an' aroun' again. I'll tell yuh, pumpkin, Ma Matryona can see an arm's length underground. I know it all, pumpkin! I know why young wives need sleepin' powders. I brought some. (*Unties a knot in her kerchief, and takes out powder wrapped in paper.*) What I have to, I see, what I don't have to, I dunno nothin', nothin' at all. That's it. Ma Matryona was young once too. I also had t'know how t'get on with my fool, yuh see. I know all seventy seven moves. Pumpkin, I see yer ol' man's dryin' up, dryin' up. What's he livin' on? Yuh couldn't draw blood from 'im with a pitchfork. See if yuh won't be buryin' im by spring. Yuh'll need someone for the farm. Why not my son as yer man? He's no worse'n others. So what would I gain by takin' 'im away from a good thing? Why should I stand in my kid's way?

ANISYA. If only he don't leave us.

MATRYONA. But he won't leave, kitten. It's a bunch o' rubbish. Yuh know my ol' man. He's a real scatterbrain, but at times he'll get somethin' into his noggin' that sticks so's yuh can't knock it out.

ANISYA. So how'd this thing get started?

MATRYONA. Yuh see, pumpkin, yuh know yuhself how the boy's with women, he's also a looker, yuh can't say no. Well, yuh know, he was workin' at the railway, an' there was an orphan girl workin' there as a cook. So she begun chasin' after 'im, this girl did.

ANISYA. Marinka?

MATRYONA. That's the one, let 'er drop dead. Well, was there somethin' or not, but my ol' man happened t'hear 'bout it. Maybe from others or she herself complained to 'im!...

ANISYA. What a brassy bitch!

MATRYONA. So my ol' man, the numskull, gets all worked up: get 'im married, he says, get 'im married t'cover up the sin. Let's take the kid home, he says, an' get 'im married. I talked my head off. Got nowhere! Well, I think, okay. Let me try somethin' else. Them fools, pumpkin, yuh gotta play along with. Make like yuh agree. But when it gets right down to it, then yuh turn it yer way. Fallin' from a stove, a woman's got seventy seven thoughts 'fore she hits the ground, yuh know, so how's he t'figger it out. Well, I says, ol' man, it's a good thing. We just gotta think 'bout it. Let's go t'Sonny, I says, an' talk it over with Pyotr Ignatich. What'll he have t'say? So here we are.

ANISYA. O-oh, Ma Matryona, how'll things be? What if his father tells 'im to?

MATRYONA. Tells 'im? Yuh can shove it up a dog's rear end. You just don't worry, it won't happen. I'll now run the whole thing through a fine strainer for yer ol' man, so's nothin'll be left. I came here with 'im just t'make it look good. If my Sonny's livin' happily, an' lookin' for happiness, will I go make a match with a whore? Am I stupid, or what?

ANISYA. She also came arunnin' to 'im here, that Marinka. Would yuh believe it, Ma Matryona, when I heard yuh wanted 'im t'get married, it was like my heart was cut with a knife. I thought he loves 'er.

MATRYONA. Hey, pumpkin, is he stupid, or what? He wouldn't love a homeless slut. Mikishka, yuh know, he's a smart kid. He knows who t'love. So don't you worry, pumpkin. We won't take 'im away for nothin'. An' we won't get 'im married. Just give us a little cash, an' let 'im stay.

ANISYA. It's like, if Mikita leaves, I won't go on livin'.

MATRYONA. Of course, when yuh're young 'tain't easy! You, a woman with the juices aflowin', livin' with such a carcass...

ANISYA. Would yuh believe it, Ma Matryona, I'm sick'n tired of 'im, really sick'n tired, can't stand the sight of 'im, the horn-nosed dog.

MATRYONA. Yep, that's how it is. Look here. (*Says in a whisper, looking around.*) Yuh know, I was at that ol' man's place for powders—he gave me two different drugs. Take a look here. This, he says, is sleepin' powder. Give 'im this one—he'll fall into such a deep sleep yuh could even step on 'im. An' that one, he says, is the kind o' drug if, he says, yuh give it t'someone t'drink, there's no taste but it's real strong. It's for seven times, he says, a pinch at a time. Give it seven times, an' she'll be free soon enough, he says.

ANISYA. O-o-oh... What is it?

MATRYONA. It don't leave a trace, he says. Charged a rouble, he did. Can't do it for less, he says. Cuz, yuh know, it's tricky gettin' 'em. Paid out me own money, pumpkin. Maybe she'll take 'em, I'm thinkin', if she won't, I'll give 'em t'Mikhailovna.

ANISYA. O-oh! But can't somethin' bad happen from 'em?

MATRYONA. What bad can happen, pumpkin? It'd be one thing if yer man was hearty, but as it is, he only looks alive. He won't make it, yuh know. There're a lot like 'im.

ANISYA. Oh, oh, my poor achin' head! I'm afraid, Ma Matryona, there could be a sin in it. No, I dunno.

MATRYONA. I could take 'em back.

ANISYA. What d'ya do, dissolve 'em in water, like the others?

MATRYONA. Betta, he says, in tea. Yuh can't tell a thing, he says, no taste, nothin'. The man's real clever.

ANISYA (*takes the powder*). Oh, oh, my poor achin' head. I'd never do such things if my life wasn't a livin' hell.

MATRYONA. Now don't forget the rouble, I promised t'drop it off t'the ol' man. He put hisself out.[1]

ANISYA. It goes widout sayin'. (*Goes to her trunk and hides the powder.*)

MATRYONA. An' you, pumpkin, hide it real good so's no one finds out. If, God forbid, it comes t'it, say it's for cockroaches... (*Takes the rouble.*) It's also good on cockroaches... (*cuts herself short.*)

SCENE 11

THE SAME, PYOTR, *and* AKIM. AKIM *enters and crosses himself in front of the icons.*

PYOTR (*enters and sits down*). So what's it gonna be, Pa Akim?

AKIM. What's best, Ignatich, how's best, d'ya, what's best... Cuz, it's no good. I mean, it's tomfoolery. I'd like, d'ya... I mean, I'd like right for the boy. But if yuh, I mean, d'ya, then maybe. Whatever's best...

PYOTR. Okay, okay. Sit down, let's talk it over. (AKIM *sits down.*) So what's up? Yuh wanna get 'im married, or what?

MATRYONA. We can wait a bit with the marryin', Pyotr Ignatich. Yuh know we're broke, Ignatich. Where's marryin' t'come from. We're hardly makin' it ourselves. So where's marryin' from!...

PYOTR. Do what's best.

MATRYONA. Now there's no rush with marryin'. It's that kind o' thing. 'T'aint a raspberry that'll fall if not picked.

PYOTR. Well, if yuh get 'im married—it'd be a good thing.

AKIM. I'd like, I mean, d'ya... Cuz for me, I mean, d'ya... a job turned up in town, a good job, I mean...

MATRYONA. Some job! Cleanin' cesspools. He came home t'other day an' I heaved my guts out, dammit!

AKIM. It's true, at first it's like, d'ya, the smell, I mean, really hits yuh, but when yuh get used t'it, 'tain't bad, like slops, an', I mean, d'ya, it's aw right... An' the smell, I mean, d'ya... it's not for us t'complain. Yuh just change yer clothes. I'd like, I mean, Mikitka at home. Let 'im take care o' things, I mean. Let 'im take care o' things at home. An' me, I'll, d'ya, make some money in town.

PYOTR. Yuh wanna keep yer son at home, that's right. But what about the money yuh took?

AKIM. That's true, true, Ignatich, just as yuh say, I mean, d'ya, cuz if he hired on an' took money—he's gotta finish up, I mean... But it's only, d'ya, t'get married—for a little while, I mean, let 'im go, if need be.

PYOTR. Well, I could do that.

MATRYONA. But this thing ain't yet settled 'tween us. I'll open up t'yuh, Pyotr Ignatich, just as I would t'God. Maybe yuh can judge 'tween me an' my ol' man. He keeps on harpin', get 'im married an' get 'im married. But yuh ask 'im, marry t'who! If there was a proper bride, I wouldn't stand in my kid's way, but this girl ain't no good...

AKIM. Now that ain't right. 'Tain't right, d'ya, bein' hard on that girl. 'Tain't right. Cuz she, that there girl, was wronged by my son, wronged, I mean. That girl, I mean.

PYOTR. Wronged, how so?

AKIM. It's cuz, I mean, d'ya, with my son Nikitka. With Nikitka, I mean, d'ya.

MATRYONA. You just wait, let me tell it, my tongue ain't got no bumps. Before comin' here, yuh know, that boy of ours was workin' at the railway. An' a girl there latches on to 'im, yuh know, a real simp called Marinka—worked there in the gang as a cook. So that there girl, she ups an' accuses our son, as if he, Mikita, like bamboozled 'er.

PYOTR. There's nothin' good 'bout this.

MATRYONA. But she's no damn good 'erself, she's a tramp. Kind of a whore.

AKIM. Again yuh, I mean, ol' woman, yuh ain't, d'ya, an' yuh keep on, yuh ain't, d'ya, an' yuh keep on, I mean, yuh ain't, d'ya...

MATRYONA. Now them there's the only words yuh get from my hero here—d'ya, d'ya, d'ya, an' what's d'ya, he dunno 'imself. An' you, Pyotr Ignatich, don't ask me, ask other folks 'bout the girl, they'll all tell yuh the same thing. She's just a homeless tramp.

PYOTR (*to* AKIM). Well, Pa Akim, if that's how things are, there's no sense in gettin' 'im married. A daughter-in-law's not like an ol' shoe, yuh can't just chuck 'er out.

AKIM (*flaring up*). The ol' woman, I mean, she's lyin' 'bout the girl, d'ya, she's lyin'. Cuz the girl's, d'ya, real nice, a real nice girl, I mean. I feel sorry, I mean, sorry for that girl.

MATRYONA. Yuh're like Mary who for the world grieves, but widout eats her children leaves. Yuh're sorry for the girl, but not for yer son. Tie 'er on t'yer neck an' carry 'er aroun'. Stop talkin' gibberish.

AKIM. 'Tain't gibberish.

MATRYONA. Don't butt in, lemme talk.

AKIM (*interrupts*). 'Tain't gibberish. I mean, yuh turn things yer way, 'bout the girl, 'bout yuhself—yuh turn things yer way, however's best for yuh, but God'll, I mean, d'ya, turn it His way. That's what's gonna be.

MATRYONA. Oh, yuh just wear yer tongue out talkin' t'yuh.

AKIM. The girl's hard-workin', upstandin' an', I mean, d'ya, a pleasin'... I mean. An' cuz we're poor, that's just, d'ya, what we need, I mean: an' the weddin' ain't much. But what's much is the girl's been wronged, I mean, d'ya, the girl's an orphan, that's what. An' there's a wrong.

MATRYONA. Any o' them girls'll say this...

ANISYA. Just you listen t'us women, Pa Akim. We'll tell yuh a story!

AKIM. An' God, how 'bout God! Ain't she a person, that girl? I mean, she's also, d'ya, a person t'God. What do yuh think?

MATRYONA. Ah, he's off...

PYOTR. Yuh know what, Pa Akim, yuh really can't believe them girls. The kid's still aroun'. He's right here! Let's get hold of 'im an' ask straight out, is it true? He won't give up his soul. Call the kid! (ANISYA *gets up.*) You tell 'im his father wants 'im. (ANISYA *exits.*)

SCENE 12

THE SAME *without* ANISYA.

MATRYONA. That's it, my dear, yuh've settled it an' doused the fire. Let the kid speak for 'imself. Yuh know, nowadays yuh just can't force kids t'get married. Yuh gotta ask the kid too. He'd never wanna marry 'er, an' shame 'imself. The way I see it, let 'im stay with yuh, an' have yuh as his boss. There ain't no reason t'take him for the summer; we can hire someone. Just give us a tenner an' let 'im stay.

PYOTR. Yuh're ahead o' yuhself, gotta do things in order. Finish one thing before beginnin' another.

AKIM. I'm, I mean, sayin' it cuz, Pyotr Ignatich, cuz, I mean, d'ya, it's happened. Yuh try t'do, I mean, what's best for yuhself, but, d'ya, yuh forget 'bout God; yuh want what's best for yuhself...yuh turn things yer way, an' look out, it all comes tumblin' down on yuh, I mean. Yuh've wanted what's best, but it comes out much worse widout God.

PYOTR. That goes widout sayin'! Yuh gotta keep God in mind.

AKIM. Look aroun', it's worse, but when it's right, an' God's way, it's all kind o', d'ya, it makes yuh happy. Yuh wanna do it, I mean. So I figgered, I mean, I'll get, I mean, the kid married, so there's no sin, I mean. He'll be at home, I mean, d'ya, as is only right, an' I, I mean, d'ya, I'll be workin' in town. It's a good job. Suits me. God's way, I mean, d'ya, is much betta. An' then she's an orphan. Like last year they took wood from the foreman that way. Figgered they'd fool 'im; an' they fooled the foreman, but God, I mean, d'ya, they didn't fool. Well, so...

SCENE 13

THE SAME, NIKITA, *and* ANYUTKA.

NIKITA. Did'ya want me? (*Sits down and takes out his tobacco.*)

PYOTR (*quietly, reproachfully*). What's with yuh, don't yuh know how t'act. Yer father wants t'talk t'yuh, an' yuh sit down an' fiddle aroun' with yer tobacco. Get up, come over here! (NIKITA *goes up to the table, leans against it smugly, and smiles.*)

AKIM. It turns out, I mean, d'ya, like there's a complaint 'gainst yuh, Mikishka, a complaint, I mean.

NIKITA. A complaint, from who?

AKIM. A complaint? From a girl, an orphan girl, I mean, there's a complaint. From her, I mean, there's a complaint 'gainst yuh, from that there Marina, I mean.

NIKITA (*chuckling*). That's amazin', really. What kind o' complaint? An' who told yuh this, she did?

AKIM. Now I'm, d'ya, doin' the askin', an' yuh'll, I mean, d'ya, do the answerin'. Did'ya get mixed up with the girl, I mean, like, mixed up with 'er, I mean?

NIKITA. Once'n for all, I don't get what yuh're askin'.

AKIM. I mean, monkey business, d'ya, monkey business, I mean, did'ya have some monkey business with 'er, I mean?

NIKITA. All sorts o' stuff. When yuh're bored yuh joke a bit with the cook, yuh play the accordion a little an' get 'er t'dance. What's the other monkey business?

PYOTR. Don't talk back, Mikita, you answer properly what yer father's askin'.

AKIM (*solemnly*). Mikita! Yuh can hide from men, but yuh can't hide from God. Just you, Mikita, I mean, d'ya, think, don't yuh dare lie! She's an orphan girl, I mean, an' it's easy t'wrong 'er. An orphan girl, I mean. You talk straight.

NIKITA. Well, there's nothin' t'say. Once'n for all, I said it all already, so there's nothin' mo' t'say. (*Becoming excited.*) What won't she say. Go on an' say what yuh want, like speakin' 'bout the dead. Why didn't she say somethin' 'bout Fedka Mikishkin? An' what's it supposed t'mean, nowadays can't yuh even joke aroun' a bit? But she can say what she wants.

AKIM. Eh, Mikishka, be careful! A lie'll out. Is it yes or no?

NIKITA (*aside*). Boy, they're really on me. (*To* AKIM). I'm tellin' yuh, I dunno nothin'. There was nothin' 'tween me'n her. (*Angrily*.) I swear t'Christ, may I drop on the spot. (*Crosses himself*.) I know nothin' 'bout nothin'. (*Silence. Becoming even more excited*.) An' what's the idea o' gettin' me t'marry 'er? It's really a cryin' shame. Yuh've no right nowadays t'get someone married by force. It's that simple. Besides, I swore, I know nothin' 'bout nothin'.

MATRYONA (*to her husband*). Yuh see now, you'n yer crazy, thick skull; whatever they fill 'im with, he believes it all. Yuh just put the kid t'shame for nothin'. It's best t'let 'im stay on here with his boss as before. His boss'll now help us out with a tenner. An' when the time comes, we'll get 'im married.

PYOTR. Well, what's it gonna be, Pa Akim?

AKIM (*clucks his tongue; to his son*). Watch out, Mikita, tears o' the wronged, d'ya, ain't shed for nothin', someone's gotta, d'ya, always answer. Watch out 'tain't so.

NIKITA. What's there t'watch out for, you watch out yuhself. (*Sits down*.)

ANYUTKA. Gotta go tell Momma. (*Runs out*.)

SCENE 14

PYOTR, AKIM, MATRYONA, *and* NIKITA.

MATRYONA (*to* PYOTR). That's always how it is, Pyotr Ignatich. That troublemaker o' mine, once he gets somethin' into his noggin, ain't no way o' knockin' it out; we just bothered yuh for nothin'. So let the kid stay on here same as before. Hold on t'the kid—he's yer man.

PYOTR. So what's it gonna be, Pa Akim?

AKIM. Why I, d'ya, didn't wanna force the kid, so long as nothin', d'ya. I wanted, I mean, d'ya...

MATRYONA. Yuh dunno yuhself what yuh're mixin' up. Let 'im stay on as before. The kid don't wanna leave either. An' what do we need 'im for, we'll manage by ourselves.

PYOTR. Just one thing, Pa Akim: if you take 'im away for the summer, I don't want 'im in the winter. If he stays, it's for the year.

MATRYONA. Then for the year he'll be beholden. At home we'll hire someone durin' the height o' the season if need be. So let the kid stay on, an' you now give us a tenner...

PYOTR. So what's it t'be, another year?

AKIM (*sighs*). Well, looks that way, d'ya, if it's so, I mean, looks that way, dya.

MATRYONA. For another year, startin' with St. Dmitry's day. Yuh'll be fair with the pay, just give us a tenner now. Help us out. (*Gets up and bows.*)

SCENE 15

THE SAME, ANISYA, *and* ANYUTKA. ANISYA *sits down on the side.*

PYOTR. Well? If that's it, that's it—lets go t'the tavern an' drink t'the deal. Come on, Pa Akim, we'll have some vodka.

AKIM. I don't drink liquor, nope I don't.

PYOTR. Well, yuh'll have some tea.

AKIM. Tea's my downfall. Tea sure is.

PYOTR. An' the women'll also have some tea. Look here, Mikita, move the sheep an' gather up the straw.

NIKITA. Okay. (*All exit except* NIKITA. *It gets dark.*)

SCENE 16

NIKITA *alone.*

NIKITA (*lights a cigarette*). Boy, they don't leave me alone, go on an' tell 'im how yuh fooled aroun' with the girls. It'd sure take a long time t'tell all them tales. Marry 'er, he says. If I marry 'em all, I'd have a pile o' wives.

Yeah, I really need t'get married, as if I'm not betta off than any married stiff, they all envy me. What a break that somethin' told me t'swear before the icon. Right away I put an end t'the whole mess. They say it's scary t'swear t'a lie. That's all alotta bunk. Nothin' but talk. Plain an' simple.

SCENE 17

NIKITA *and* AKULINA.

AKULINA (*enters, lays down a rope, takes off her coat, and goes into the pantry*). Yuh could've at least got the light on.
NIKITA. T'look at yuh? I can see yuh as is.
AKULINA. Get lost!

SCENE 18

THE SAME *and* ANYUTKA.

ANYUTKA (*runs in and whispers to* NIKITA). Mikita, come quick, someone's lookin' for yuh, cross my heart.
NIKITA. Who is it?
ANYUTKA. Marinka from the railway. Standin' aroun' the corner.
NIKITA. Yuh're kiddin'.
ANYUTKA. Cross my heart.
NIKITA. What's she want?
ANYUTKA. She wants yuh t'come. "I gotta," she says, "have a quick word with Mikita." I began askin', but she ain't sayin'. She only asked: is it true that he's leavin' yuh? An' I says: no it ain't, his father wanted t'take 'im away an' get 'im married, but he refused and'll stay with us another year. So then she says: "For God's sake, send 'im out t'me. I really gotta," she says, "have a word with 'im." She's been waitin' a long time already. Why don't yuh go to 'er.
NIKITA. The hell with 'er. What should I go for?

ANYUTKA. She says, if he don't come, I'll go t'his house myself. I'll come, she says, cross my heart.

NIKITA. She'll probably just hang aroun' a bit an' go 'way.

ANYUTKA. Or is it, she says, they wanna marry 'im t'Akulina?

AKULINA (*goes to get her spinning wheel by* NIKITA). Marry who t'Akulina?

ANYUTKA. Mikita.

AKULINA. Is that so? Who says?

NIKITA. Looks like lots o' folks say so. (*Looks at her and laughs.*) Well, Akulina, will yuh marry me?

AKULINA. Marry yuh? Maybe I woulda before, but I won't now.

NIKITA. Why won't yuh now?

AKULINA. Cuz yuh won't love me.

NIKITA. Why won't I?

AKULINA. They won't let yuh. (*Laughs.*)

NIKITA. Who won't?

AKULINA. My stepmother, that's who. She's bitchin' all the time an' watchin' yuh all the time.

NIKITA (*laughs*). You're really somethin'! Kept yer eyes open, eh.

AKULINA. Me? Do I hafta? What am I blind? She blew up at Pa today, really blew up. She's a fat-assed witch. (*Exits to the pantry.*)

ANYUTKA. Nikita, take a look! (*Looks out of the window.*) She's comin'. It's her, cross my heart. I'm leavin'. (*Exits.*)

SCENE 19

NIKITA, AKULINA *in the pantry, and* MARINA.

MARINA (*enters*). Whacha doin' t'me?

NIKITA. What'm I doin'? I'm doin' nothin'.

MARINA. D'ya wanna leave me?

NIKITA (*getting up, angrily*). Well, whacha doin' here anyway?

MARINA. Ah, Mikita!

NIKITA. Yuh're a strange lot, you broads. Why'd yuh come?

MARINA. Mikita!

NIKITA. Mikita what? That's my name. What d'ya want? Beat it, I'm tellin' yuh.

MARINA. So that's it, right, yuh wanna dump me an' forget?

NIKITA. An' what's there t'remember? You broads dunno yuhselves. Yuh waited aroun' the corner, yuh sent Anyutka for me, I didn't come t'yuh. Means, I don't need yuh, it's that simple. So, get outta here.

MARINA. Don't need me! Now yuh don't need me. I believed yuh, I thought yuh'd love me. An' now that yuh've ruined me, yuh don't need me.

NIKITA. There's no point at all t'what yer sayin', it's way off. An' yuh even told all this crap t'my father. Get outta here, how 'bout it.

MARINA. You know yuhself I never loved anyone but you. If yuh married me or didn't, I wouldn't be hurt. I didn't do no wrong t'yuh. Why did'ya stop lovin' me? Why?

NIKITA. What's the use of our wastin' time. Just get outta here. You dumb broads!

MARINA. I'm not hurt cuz yuh cheated on me, yuh promised t'marry me, but cuz yuh stopped lovin' me. An' I'm not so hurt that yuh stopped lovin' me, but that yuh left me for another—an' I know for who!

NIKITA (*goes up to her, angrily*). Eh! There's no speakin' t'you broads, yuh don't understand nothin'. Get outta here, I'm tellin' yuh, 'fore yuh come t'harm.

MARINA. T'harm? What, yuh gonna hit me? Go 'head, here. Why're yuh turnin' yer puss away? Ah, Nikita.

NIKITA. You know, someone'll come, it'll look bad. But why waste time talkin'.

MARINA. So that's it, then, what was ain't no mo'. Yuh're tellin' me t'forget! Just remember, Nikita. I was keepin' my honor like my life. Yuh ruined me for nothin', yuh lied t'me. Yuh didn't pity an orphan (*cries*), yuh left me. Yuh killed me, but I bear no grudge 'gainst yuh. God be with yuh. If yuh find someone betta—you'll forget me, if worse—you'll remember. You'll remember, Nikita. So, good-bye. I really loved yuh. Good-bye for the last time. (*Wants to embrace him, and takes his head in her hands.*)

NIKITA (*tearing himself away*). Eh! Talkin' t'you broads. If you don't wanna go, I'll go myself, you can stay here.

MARINA (*screams*). You beast! (*In the doorway.*) God won't grant yuh happiness! (*Exits crying.*)

SCENE 20

NIKITA *and* AKULINA.

AKULINA (*comes out of the pantry*). Yuh're a son of a bitch, Nikita.
NIKITA. What d'ya mean?
AKULINA. The way she screamed. (*Cries.*)
NIKITA. So what?
AKULINA. So what? Yuh wro...o...onged 'er... An' that's how you'll wrong me... You son of a bitch. (*Exits to the pantry.*)

SCENE 21

NIKITA *alone.*

NIKITA (*after a silence*). What a mess. I love them broads like candy; but if yuh go too far—there's trouble!

Curtain.

ACT II

Dramatis personae
Pyotr
Anisya
Akulina
Anyutka
Nikita
Matryona
Mavra*
   Anyutka's godmother and Anisya's neighbor
Marfa
   Pyotr's sister
Peasants

The set depicts a street and PYOTR*'s cottage. On the audience's left is the two-room cottage, the entranceway with the porch in the center; on the right is the gate and a corner of the yard. At the corner of the yard* ANISYA *is scutching hemp. Six months have passed since Act I.*

SCENE 1

ANISYA *alone.*

ANISYA (*stops and listens*). Again he's mumblin' somethin'. Musta climbed down from the stove.

---

*In the original text she is listed in the dramatis personae as GODMOTHER and A NEIGHBOR. We learn her name (MAVRA) later on in the act (II, 7). That name will be utilized for this character.

SCENE 2

ANISYA *and* AKULINA (*enters with buckets on a yoke*).

ANISYA. He's callin'. Go see what he wants. Oh... is he yellin'.
AKULINA. What about you?
ANISYA. Go 'head, I'm tellin' yuh. (AKULINA *goes into the cottage.*)

SCENE 3

ANISYA *alone.*

ANISYA. He's really worn me out. Don't open up where the money's at, an' that's it. T'other day he was in the entranceway, musta hid it there. Now I dunno myself where it's at. Thank God he's afraid o' partin' with it. At least it's in the house. I just have t'find it. It wasn't on 'im yesterday. Now I dunno myself where it's at. He's done worn me out.

SCENE 4

ANISYA *and* AKULINA (*enters tying on her kerchief*).

ANISYA. Where yuh goin'?
AKULINA. Where? He told me t'get Auntie Marfa. "Get," he says, "my sister t'me. I'm dyin'," he says, "I have t'have a word with 'er."
ANISYA (*to herself*). He wants his sister. Oh, my achin' head! Oh, oh! Must be he wants t'give it to 'er. What'll I do! Oh! (*To* AKULINA.) Don't go! Where yuh goin'?
AKULINA. For my aunt.
ANISYA. Don't go, I tell yuh, I'll go myself. An' you go down t'the river with the wash, or else yuh won't get it done 'fore dark.
AKULINA. But he told me to.
ANISYA. Go where I'm tellin' yuh. I'll get Marfa myself, I tell yuh. Take the shirts from the fence.

AKULINA. The shirts? But yuh probably won't even go. He told me to.

ANISYA. I said I'll go. Where's Anyutka?

AKULINA. Anyutka? She's mindin' the calves.

ANISYA. Send 'er here, they won't likely wander off. (AKULINA *picks up the wash and exits.*)

SCENE 5

ANISYA *alone.*

ANISYA. If I don't go—he'll get mad, if I go—he'll give his sister the money. All my work'll be for nothin'. I just dunno what t'do. My head's bustin'. (*She continues to work.*)

SCENE 6

ANISYA *and* MATRYONA (*enters with a walking stick and small bundle*).

MATRYONA. God bless yuh, pumpkin.

ANISYA (*looks around, drops her work, and throws up her hands with joy*). What a sight for sore eyes, Ma Matryona. God sent the right guest at the right time.

MATRYONA. Well, what's up?

ANISYA. I'm really goin' outta my mind. It's terrible!

MATRYONA. I hear he's alive, that so?

ANISYA. Don't even ask. Alive he's not, an' die he don't.

MATRYONA. He didn't give the money away t'someone?

ANISYA. He's now askin' for Marfa, his sister. Must be 'bout the money.

MATRYONA. Probably so. He didn't give the money away t'someone else?

ANISYA. Ain't no one. I've been watchin' 'im like a hawk.

MATRYONA. So where's it at?

ANISYA. He ain't tellin'. An' I can't find out nohow. He keeps on changin' hidin' places. An' I can't do much cuz of Akulka. She may be stupid, but she's also snoopin' an' watchin'. Oh, my achin' head! I'm all worn out.

MATRYONA. Eh, pumpkin, if the money gets into someone else's hands, yuh'll cry yer eyes out. They'll kick yuh outta here with nothin'. Yer whole life, poor dear, yuh've put up with'n put up with a husband yuh hate, an' now you'll end up a widow an' go beggin'.

ANISYA. Yuh don't hafta tell me that, Ma Matryona. I'm sick at heart, dunno what t'do, an' there's no one t'ask. I talked with Mikita. But he's scared an' don't wanna get mixed up in it. The only thing he did was tell me yesterday that it's in the floor.

MATRYONA. So, did'ya look?

ANISYA. Couldn't, he was there. I've noticed sometimes he has it with 'im, sometimes he hides it.

MATRYONA. You just remember, little girl, once yuh miss yer chance, you'll never get it again. (*In a whisper.*) Well, did'ya give 'im any o' that strong tea?

ANISYA. Oh, oh! (*Is about to answer, but sees her neighbor and stops.*)

SCENE 7

THE SAME *and* MAVRA (*walks by the cottage, listens to a shout from within; to* ANISYA).

MAVRA. Hey, Cousin![2] Anisya, hey Anisya! Yer man seems t'be callin'.

ANISYA. He keeps on coughin' so loud that it's like he's shoutin'. He's really bad.

MAVRA (*goes up to* MATRYONA). How d'ya do, Granny, where yuh comin' from, by God?

MATRYONA. Just from home, dear. Come t'see my kid. Brought 'im some clean shirts. Yuh feel for yer own kid, yuh know.

MAVRA. That goes widout sayin'. (*To* ANISYA.) Cousin, I wanted t'bleach linen but, I thought t'myself, it's too early. No one's begun yet.

ANISYA. What's the rush?

MATRYONA. So, did he take communion?

ANISYA. Sure, the priest was here yesterday.

MAVRA. I had a look at 'im yesterday also, my God, his life's hangin' on a thread. He's all wasted away. An' t'other day, my God, he near died, they even put 'im under the icons.[3] They'd already wailed over 'im, an' got ready t'lay 'im out.

ANISYA. He came to—got up. Now he's wanderin' aroun' again.

MATRYONA. Well, are yuh gonna give 'im last rites?

ANISYA. Folks're sayin' we should. If he stays alive, we'll be sendin' for the priest tomorrow.

MAVRA. Oh, it must be hard on yuh, Anisyushka. No wonder they say: sick an' in need makes others sick indeed.

ANISYA. It's pretty damn hard. If only it was one way or another.

MAVRA. That's right, t'aint easy, he's been dyin' for a whole year now. He's tied yuh up hand'n foot.

MATRYONA. It's tough bein' a widow also. It's okay when yuh're young, but who wants yuh when yuh get old. Ol' age's no fun. Just look at me. I didn't walk that far but I'm dead tired, can't feel my feet. So where's my kid?

ANISYA. He's plowin'. Why don't yuh come in, we'll get the samovar goin'. Tea's a good pick-me-up.

MATRYONA (sits down). I'm really dead tired, my dears. As for last rites—that's gotta be done. They say it's good for the soul.

ANISYA. We'll send for the priest tomorrow.

MATRYONA. That's it, it'll be betta. Yuh know, little girl, we had a weddin'.

MAVRA. How's that, in spring?[4]

MATRYONA. Well, just as the sayin' goes, when a poor man marries, the night's short. Semyon Matveyevich took Marinka for a wife.

ANISYA. So she's found happiness after all!

MAVRA. Must be a widower with kids.

MATRYONA. Four of 'em. What proper girl'd go for 'im! So, he took 'er. She's glad. Well, yuh know, they drank liquor from a flawed glass—an' it leaked.

MAVRA. Aha! So there's been talk? Well, does the guy have a bundle?

MATRYONA. So far they're livin' pretty good.

MAVRA. True enough, who'll go for a man with kids! Just look at our Mikhailo. My God, the man's...

MAN'S VOICE. Hey, Mavra, where the devil are yuh? Go get the cow. (MAVRA exits.)

SCENE 8

ANISYA *and* MATRYONA.

MATRYONA (*as* MAVRA *exits she speaks in her normal voice*). Well, little girl, we married 'er, an' took 'er from sin; at least my ol' fool won't be thinkin' no mo' 'bout Mikishka. (*Suddenly changes her voice to a whisper.*) She's gone! (*In a whisper.*) So, I'm askin', did'ya give 'im the tea?

ANISYA. Don't even ask. It'd be betta if he died by 'imself. He's not dyin' anyway, I've just sinned for nothin'. Oh, oh, my achin' head! Why on earth did'ya give them powders for?

MATRYONA. What 'bout the powders? Them're sleepin' powders, little girl, why not give 'em? Them won't do no harm.

ANISYA. I don't mean the sleepin' powder, but that there whitish stuff.

MATRYONA. That powder, pumpkin, is medicine.

ANISYA (*sighs*). I know, but I'm still scared. He's really worn me out.

MATRYONA. Well, did'ya use it a lot?

ANISYA. I gave it to 'im twice.

MATRYONA. Well, could he tell?

ANISYA. I took a sip o' the tea myself, was a little bitter. But he just drank it up an' says: "Even the tea tastes lousy t'me." I says, everything's bitter for the sick. An' I really felt horrible, Ma Matryona.

MATRYONA. Don't you think 'bout it. The mo' yuh think, the worse it is.

ANISYA. I wish yuh'd never given 'em t'me an' led me t'sin. Just thinkin' 'bout it tears me up. Why on earth did'ya give 'em t'me?

MATRYONA. Eh, pumpkin, what d'ya mean! God help yuh. Why're yuh layin' it off on me? Watch out, little girl, don't be layin' the blame on someone else. If it comes t'somethin', my hands're clean. I dunno nothin', nothin' at all; I'll swear on the cross I didn't give no powders, didn't see no powders, an' never even heard o' no kinda powders. Work it out yuhself, little girl. T'other day we were talkin 'bout yuh, what, we says, she's goin' through, the poor dear. Her stepdaughter's a dummy, an' her husband's rottin' away—she only got grief. With that kind o' life what wouldn't yuh do.

ANISYA. I sure ain't gonna deny it. Yuh wouldn't only do that with my kinda life, you'd either hang yuhself or strangle 'im. Is this a life?

MATRYONA. That's just it. Yuh can't stand aroun' with yer mouth open. Somehow yuh gotta find the money an' give 'im the tea.

ANISYA. O-oh, my poor achin' head! What t'do now I dunno myself, an' I'm really in a fright—it'd be betta if he died by 'imself. I don't wanna have it on my conscience neither.

MATRYONA (angrily). So how come he's not tellin' where the money is? What, he's gonna take it with 'im so's no one gets it? Is that right? God forbid such a bundle goes t'waste. Ain't that a sin? What's he doin'? Don't just look at 'im.

ANISYA. I dunno myself nomo'. He's done worn me out.

MATRYONA. What's not t'know. It's all very clear. Yuh miss yer chance now an' you'll be sorry the rest o' yer life. He'll give the money t'his sister an' yuh're out.

ANISYA. O-oh, he's already sent for 'er , yuh know—I gotta go.

MATRYONA. Just hold up with goin'; first get on with the samovar. We'll give 'im some tea, an' then the two of us'll look aroun' for the money— we'll sure dig it up.

ANISYA. O-oh! If only nothin'll go wrong.

MATRYONA. What else then, just look? What, you'll just make eyes at the money an' let it slip outta yer hands? Do somethin'.

ANISYA. So I'll go get the samovar goin'.

MATRYONA. Go on, pumpkin, do what yuh gotta do so's not t'cry over it later. That's it. (ANISYA turns to go but MATRYONA calls her back.) Just one thing: don't tell Mikitka 'bout all this. He's a silly-head. God forbid he finds out 'bout the powders. God knows what he'll do. He's so soft-hearted. Yuh know, he wouldn't even kill a chicken. Don't tell 'im. There'll be trouble, he won't understand. (Stops short in horror. PYOTR appears on the threshold.)

SCENE 9

THE SAME and PYOTR (leaning on the wall, drags himself to the porch and calls in a weak voice).

PYOTR. How come yuh don't answer? O-oh! Anisya, who's here? (*Falls onto the bench.*)

ANISYA (*enters from around the corner*). Why did'ya come out? Yuh shoulda stayed where yuh were.

PYOTR. Well, has the girl gone for Marfa?... It's bad... Oh, if it'd only end quickly!...

ANISYA. She's busy, I sent 'er down t'the river. Just hold on, I'll finish'n go myself.

PYOTR. Send Anyutka. Where's she? Oh, it's bad! Oh, I'm dyin'.

ANISYA. I've already sent for 'er.

PYOTR. Oh! So where's she?

ANISYA. I'll kill 'er, where's she?

PYOTR. Oh, I can't take it no mo'. My inside's afire. It's like a drill bit turnin'... Yuh just dumped me like a dog... no one t'even gimme a drink... Oh... Send Anyutka t'me.

ANISYA. Here she is. Anyutka, go t'yer father.

SCENE 10

THE SAME *and* ANYUTKA (*runs in;* ANISYA *exits around the corner*).

PYOTR. You go... oh... t'Aunt Marfa, tell 'er: father wants yuh, says t'come, needs yuh.

ANYUTKA. Okay.

PYOTR. Wait. Need 'er right now, tell 'er. Tell 'er—I'm gonna die. O-oh...

ANYUTKA. I'll just get my kerchief an' be off. (*Runs out.*)

SCENE 11

PYOTR, ANISYA, *and* MATRYONA.

MATRYONA (*winking*). Well, little girl, remember what yuh gotta do. Go into the house'n ransack it good. Look aroun' like a dog lookin' for fleas; go through everythin', an' I'll give 'im a goin' over.

ANISYA (*to* MATRYONA). Right away. Seems I'm less scared with you aroun'. (*Goes to the porch. To* PYOTR.) Shouldn't I get the samovar goin' for yuh? Ma Matryona's here t'see 'er son—yuh'll have tea with 'er.

PYOTR. Okay, get it goin'.

SCENE 12

PYOTR *and* MATRYONA. MATRYONA *goes to the porch.*

PYOTR. Howdy.

MATRYONA. How d'ya do, my good man. How dya do, my darlin'. Looks like yuh're still sick. My ol' man's also sorry for yuh. Go, he says, see how he's doin'. Sent his regards. (*Bows once again.*)[5]

PYOTR. I'm dyin'.

MATRYONA. Yes, Ignatich, I can see on yuh that pain sure hits men, not trees. I can see yuh've withered, withered away, poor dear. Sickness don't make yuh look good, no, it don't.

PYOTR. My end's come.

MATRYONA. Well, Pyotr Ignatich, it's God's will, yuh took communion, an' God willin', yuh'll get last rites. Yer wife's smart, thank God, an' yuh'll be buried'n remembered, as should be. Meanwhile my Sonny'll also help aroun' the house.

PYOTR. There's no one t'tell 'em what t'do! My wife's careless, busy with monkey business, I know, I know everythin', yuh know... My girl's a dope, an' besides, too young. I've put together a household, an' there's no one t'take care of it. It's a real pity. (*Sobs.*)

MATRYONA. Well, if there's money or somethin', yuh can tell 'em...

PYOTR (*to* ANISYA *in the entranceway*). Has Anyutka gone yet?

MATRYONA (*aside*). Damn, he remembered.

ANISYA (*from the entranceway*). She went right away. Why don't yuh go back t'the house, I'll take yuh.

PYOTR. Lemme sit here a spell for the last time. It's so stuffy inside. I feel bad... Oh, my heart's all afire... I wish I was dead...

MATRYONA. If God won't take 'way yer soul, it won't go 'way by itself. Life'n death're in God's hands, Pyotr Ignatich. Yuh can't tell when yuh'll die. Sometimes, yuh're up'n about again. Like back in our village a man there was as good as dead, an' then...

PYOTR. No. I feel I'm gonna die today. I feel it. (*Leans back and closes his eyes.*)

SCENE 13

THE SAME *and* ANISYA.

ANISYA (*enters*). Well, are yuh gonna come or not? Can't wait for yuh all day. Pyotr! Hey, Pyotr!

MATRYONA (*walks off and motions to* ANISYA *with her finger*). Well?

ANISYA (*walks down from the porch to* MATRYONA). Not there.

MATRYONA. But did'ya look through everythin? Under the floor too?

ANISYA. It's not there either. Maybe in the shed. He was pokin' aroun' there yesterday.

MATRYONA. Keep lookin', look for all yuh're worth. Scour the place clean. I can see already—he's gonna die today: his nail's blue'n his face's ashen. Is the samovar ready yet?

ANISYA. It's about t'boil.

SCENE 14

THE SAME *and* NIKITA (*comes from the other side—if possible, riding on horseback to the gate; does not see* PYOTR).

NIKITA (*to his mother*). Howdy, Momma! All well at home?

MATRYONA. Thank God, we're still alive'n kickin'.

NIKITA. Well, how's the boss?

MATRYONA. Hush up, he's sittin' over there. (*Points to the porch.*)

NIKITA. So what, let 'im sit. What's it t'me?

PYOTR (*opens his eyes*). Mikita, eh, Mikita, come 'eer. (NIKITA *goes up to him.* ANISYA *and* MATRYONA *whisper.*)

PYOTR. How come yuh're back early?

NIKITA. I'm finished plowin'.

PYOTR. Did'ya plow the strip on t'other side o' the bridge?

NIKITA. That's too far away.

PYOTR. Too far? It's even further from the house. Yuh'll have t'go special. Shoulda done 'em together. (ANISYA *listens in without showing herself.*)

MATRYONA (*walks up*). Ah, Sonny, why ain't yuh doin' yer best for the boss? The boss's sick, dependin' on yuh; so do like for yer own father, roll up yer sleeves, work like I've been tellin' yuh to.

PYOTR. So you, oh!... get the potatoes out, the women'll... oh!... sort 'em.

ANISYA (*to herself*). Ain't no way I'm gonna go. Again he wants t'get everyone away from 'im; must be the money's on 'im now. Wants t'hide it somewheres.

PYOTR. Otherwise, o-oh!... they'll be rotten when plantin' time comes. Oh, I can't take it. (*Gets up.*)

MATRYONA (*runs up on the porch, supports* PYOTR). Wanna go in?

PYOTR. Yeah. (*Stops.*) Mikita!

NIKITA (*angrily*). What now?

PYOTR. I won't be seein' yuh... I'm gonna die today... Forgive me,[6] for God's sake, forgive me if I've ever sinned 'gainst yuh... If I've ever sinned in word or deed... There's been a whole lot o' things. Forgive me.

NIKITA. What's there t'forgive, I'm also a sinner.

MATRYONA. Ah, Sonny, have some feelin'.

PYOTR. Forgive me, for God's sake. (*Cries.*)

NIKITA (*snivels*). God'll forgive yuh, Pa Pyotr. Why, I've got no cause t'-complain 'bout yuh. Yuh've never done me wrong. You forgive me. Maybe I've done worse t'yuh. (*Cries.* PYOTR *exits, sobbing.* MATRYONA *supports him.*)

SCENE 15

NIKITA *and* ANISYA.

ANISYA. Oh, my poor achin' head! He didn't do it for nothin'. He sure got somethin' in mind. (*Goes up to* NIKITA.) So, you said the money's under the floor—t'aint there.

NIKITA (*does not answer, cries*). He never done me no wrong, nothin' but good. An' look what I've gone an' done!

ANISYA. Well, nuff. Where's the money?

NIKITA (*angrily*). Who the heck knows? Go look yuhself.

ANISYA. Whacha so sorry for?

NIKITA. I'm sorry for 'im. So sorry for 'im! How he cried! E-eh!

ANISYA. Look at 'im, feelin' sorry, he don't deserve it! He kept on cussin' yuh, an' cussin', an' just now he was gonna have yuh kicked off the place. Yuh should be sorry for me.

NIKITA. Why should I be sorry for yuh?

ANISYA. He'll hide the money'n die...

NIKITA. No fear, he won't hide it...

ANISYA. Oh, Nikitushka! He's sent for his sister, yuh know, wants t'give it away to 'er. We're in trouble! How're we gonna live if he gives the money away? They'll boot me outta here! Really, yuh'd betta do somethin'. Did yuh say he was pokin' aroun' the shed last night?

NIKITA. I saw 'im comin' from there, but who the heck knows where he stuck it.

ANISYA. Oh, my achin' head, I'll go'n take a look there.

SCENE 16

THE SAME *and* MATRYONA (*comes out of the cottage, goes down to* ANISYA *and* NIKITA).

MATRYONA (*in a whisper*). Don't go nowhere, the money's on 'im—I felt aroun' for it, it's hangin' on a string.

ANISYA. Oh, my poor achin' head!

MATRYONA. Yuh lose it now, yuh'll wind up on a wild goose chase. Once the sister comes—just kiss it good-bye.

ANISYA. She'll come aw right, an' he'll give it away to 'er. What's there t'do? Oh, my achin' head!

MATRYONA. What's there t'do? Look here. The samovar's ready, go make tea'n give it to 'im (*in a whisper*), an' pour the rest outta the paper an' let 'im drink it. When he's finished the tea, just take it. No fear, he won't tell.

ANISYA. Oh, I'm scared!

MATRYONA. Don't talk now, just do it quickly'n I'll watch out for the sister, just in case. Don't goof. Pull out the money an' bring it here, Mikita'll hide it.

ANISYA. Oh, my achin' head! How am I gonna an'... an'...

MATRYONA. I'm tellin' yuh, don't talk; just do what I say. Mikita!

NIKITA. What?

MATRYONA. You stay here, sit down on the mound[7] in case o' somethin'.

NIKITA (*waving his hand*). The things these women think of! They'll twist yer head, once'n for all. The hell with yuh! I betta go'n get the potatoes out.

MATRYONA (*grabs him by the arm*). I'm tellin' yuh, wait.

SCENE 17

THE SAME *and* ANYUTKA (*enters*).

ANISYA. Well?

ANYUTKA. She was in her daughter's garden. Comin' right away.

ANISYA. She's comin', what'll we do?

MATRYONA (*to* ANISYA). Yuh'll make it, just do what I say.

ANISYA. I dunno—I dunno nothin', my head's a mess. Anyutka! Go t'the calves, sweetie, they've got loose. Oh, I don't dare.

MATRYONA. Go, really, the samovar's steamin', I'll bet.

ANISYA. Oh, my poor achin' head! (*Exits.*)

SCENE 18

MATRYONA *and* NIKITA.

MATRYONA (*goes up to her son*). Well now, Sonny. (*Sits down next to him on the mound.*) We gotta think yer business over real good.

NIKITA. What business?

MATRYONA. The business o' how yuh'll live yer life.

NIKITA. How'll I live my life? I'll live like everyone else does.

MATRYONA. The ol' man's probably gonna die today.

NIKITA. Yeah, he'll die, God rest his soul, what's it t'me?

MATRYONA (*keeps on glancing at the porch while talking*). Ah, Sonny. The livin' think 'bout life. Here yuh gotta have lots o' smarts, pumpkin. What d'ya think, I've been all over the place 'bout yer business, walked my feet off doin' things for yuh. So you remember, an' don't forget me later.

NIKITA. Doin' things 'bout what?

MATRYONA. 'Bout yer business, 'bout yer future, yers. If yuh don't do things beforehand, yuh'll get nothin'. Yuh know Ivan Moseich? I feel at home with 'im. I stopped by his place t'other day. I'd done somethin' for 'im, yuh know. So I was there'n we got t'talkin'. Ivan Moseich, I says, what d'ya make o' this business? Supposin', I says, a widower man, got 'imself hitched, supposin, t'another woman, an', supposin', the only children are a daughter by that first wife an' one by this one. So, I says, when this man dies, could another man marry the widow an' take over the homestead? Could this other man, I says, marry off the daughters an' stay on the homestead 'imself? "Yes, he could," he says, "only it takes lots o' effort. With money," he says, "yuh can arrange this business, widout money," he says, "ain't no point in tryin'."

NIKITA (*laughing*). So what's new, just give 'em money. Everybody needs money-o.

MATRYONA. So, pumpkin, I opened up to 'im 'bout everythin'. "First thing," he says, "yer sonny-boy's gotta get 'imself registered in that village. Yuh need money for that—t'buy rounds for the elders. Then, yuh see, they'll lend a hand. Everythin'," he says, "gotta be done with smarts." Look here (*takes a paper out of her kerchief*). He's written out this paper, read it, yuh're sharp, yuh know. (NIKITA *reads,* MATRYONA *listens.*)

NIKITA. The paper's simply a rulin'. 'Tain't nothin' too clever 'bout it.

MATRYONA. You just listen, this is what Ivan Moseich said. "The main thing," he says, "look out, Matryona, that the money don't slip away. If she don't grab the money," he says, "they won't give 'er their blessings.[8] Money's the key," he says, "t'the whole business." So look out. The time's now, Sonny.

NIKITA. What's it t'me? The money's hers, so let 'er do it.

MATRYONA. The way you think, Sonny! Can a woman really figger things out? Even if she takes the money, how's she gonna figger things out—a woman's for woman's business, but yuh're a man. I mean, yuh can hide it, an' all that. After all, yuh've got mo' sense, when it comes right down to it.

NIKITA. Ah, you women don't see things the right way!

MATRYONA. Why not the right way! Yuh just snatch the money. Then the woman'll be in yer hands. If she happens t'get in a snit or somethin', yuh can always cut 'er short.

NIKITA. The hell with the both o' yuh, I'm gone.

SCENE 19

NIKITA, MATRYONA, *and* ANISYA (*pale, runs out of the cottage and around the corner to* MATRYONA).

ANISYA. It was on 'im aw right. Here it is. (*Points under her apron.*)

MATRYONA. Give it t'Mikita, he'll hide it. Mikita, take it an' hide it somewheres.

NIKITA. Aw right, gimme.

ANISYA. O-oh, my achin' head. I'd betta do it myself. (*Goes toward the gate.*)

MATRYONA (*grabs her by the arm*). Where're yuh goin'? They'll be lookin' for yuh; there's the sister comin'. Give to 'im, he knows how. What a dummy!

ANISYA (*stops, indecisive*). Oh, my achin' head!

NIKITA. Go ahead, gimme, I'll stick it somewheres.

ANISYA. Where'll yuh stick it?

NIKITA. What, yuh scared? (*laughs*).

SCENE 20

THE SAME *and* AKULINA (*comes with the wash*).

ANISYA. O-oh, my poor achin' head! (*Hands over the money.*) Look out, Mikita.

NIKITA. Whacha afraid o'? I'll bury it so's I won't find it myself. (*Exits.*)

SCENE 21

MATRYONA, ANISYA, *and* AKULINA.

ANISYA (*in a fright*). O-oh! What if he...

MATRYONA. So, is he dead?

ANISYA. I think so. He didn't move when I was takin' it off 'im.

MATRYONA. Go inside, here's comes Akulina.

ANISYA. I've sinned, an' what if he does somethin' with the money...

MATRYONA. Nuff, go inside, here comes Marfa too.

ANISYA. Well, I trusted 'im. What'll happen? (*Exits.*)

SCENE 22

MARFA, AKULINA, *and* MATRYONA.

MARFA (*comes from one side*, AKULINA *from the other; to* AKULINA). I woulda come before, but I went t'my daughter. So, how's the ol' man? He fixin' t'die?

AKULINA (*puts down the wash*). Who the heck knows? I was at the river.

MARFA (*points to* MATRYONA). Who's that?

MATRYONA. I'm from Zuyevo, I'm Mikita's mother, from Zuyevo, dearie. How d'ya do. He's fadin', fadin, the poor dear, yer brother. He came out here. "Get me my sister," he says, "cuz," he says... Oh, I think maybe he's dead?

SCENE 23

THE SAME *and* ANISYA.

ANISYA (*runs out of the cottage with a scream, grabs a post, and begins to wail*). O-o-oh, an' who-o-o've yuh left me to an' o-o-oh an' who-o-o've yuh forsa-aken me to o-o-oh... a miserable widow... for ever'n ever... closed his bright eyes...[9]

SCENE 24

THE SAME *and* MAVRA. MAVRA *and* MATRYONA *hold her by the arms.* AKULINA *and* MARFA *go into the cottage. A crowd gathers.*

VOICE FROM THE CROWD. Get the ol' ladies, gotta lay 'im out.
MATRYONA (*rolls up her sleeves*). Is there some water in the kettle? Maybe there's some left in the samovar. It wasn't all poured out. I'll pitch in too.

Curtain.

ACT III

Dramatis personae

   Akim

   Nikita

   Akulina

   Anisya

   Anyutka

   Mitrich

     an old man, hired hand, and ex-soldier

   Mavra

     Anisya's neighbor [and Anyutka's godmother]

PYOTR*'s cottage. Winter. Nine months have passed since Act II.* ANISYA, *simply dressed, sits at a loom, weaving.* ANYUTKA *is on the stove.* MITRICH, *an old hired hand, enters slowly.*

SCENE 1

MITRICH (*undresses*). Oh, Lord have mercy! So, the boss ain't back yet?

ANISYA. What?

MITRICH. Mikita's not back from town?

ANISYA. Nope.

MITRICH. Must be on a binge. Oh, Lord!

ANISYA. Did'ya clean up the threshin' floor?

MITRICH. Sure nuff. Got it all cleaned up right proper'n covered in straw. Don't like things half-assed. Oh, Lord! Gracious Nicholas! (*Picks at his calluses.*) Yep, it's 'bout time he was back already.

ANISYA. What's he gotta rush for? He's got money, probably havin' a good time with the girl...

MITRICH. He's got money, so why not have a good time? But what'd Akulina go t'town for?

ANISYA. You ask 'er what the devil took 'er there.

MITRICH. Why t'town? Lots o' things in town, as long as yuh got somethin'. Oh, Lord!

ANYUTKA. Momma, I heard it myself. "I'll buy yuh," he says, "a short wrap," cross my heart, "I will," he says; "yuh can pick it out yuhself," he says. An' she got 'erself all dressed up: put on a velveteen vest an' a French kerchief.

ANISYA. Her girlish shame only goes up t'the door, once she's out—it's gone'n forgotten. She's really shameless!

MITRICH. Go on! Where's the shame in it? Yuh got money, go'n have a good time. Oh, Lord! Still too early for supper, ain't it? (ANISYA *is silent.*) I'll go'n warm up a bit meanwhile. (*Climbs onto the stove.*) O, Lord, Holy Mother o' God, Saint Nicholas!

SCENE 2

THE SAME *and* MAVRA.

MAVRA (*enters*). Looks like yer man ain't back yet, huh?

ANISYA. Nope.

MAVRA. Should be. Wonder if he stopped by our tavern. My sister, Fyokla, was sayin', honey, there's lots o' sleighs there from town.

ANISYA. Anyutka! Hey, Anyutka!

ANYUTKA. What?

ANISYA. Run over t'the tavern, sweetie, see if he didn't stop by there drunk.

ANYUTKA (*jumps off the stove, gets dressed*). Okay.

MAVRA. An' he took Akulina with 'im?

ANISYA. No need t'go otherwise. It's cuz of 'er he's got things t'do. "Gotta go t'the bank,"[10] he says, "gotta get dough." She's just got 'im all mixed up.

MAVRA (*shakes her head*). What can yuh say. (*Silence.*)

ANYUTKA (*in the doorway*). If he's there, what should I say?

ANISYA. You just take a look, see if he's there.

ANYUTKA. Okay, I'll be back in a jiffy. (*Exits.*)

ANISYA, MITRICH, *and* MAVRA. *A long silence.*

MITRICH (*booms out*). Oh, Lord, gracious Nicholas.

MAVRA (*shudders*). Oh, yuh scared me. Who's that?

ANISYA. It's Mitrich, our hired hand.

MAVRA. Oh, how he startled me! I'd plumb forgotten. So I hear tell, Cousin, they're matchmakin' for Akulina.

ANISYA (*gets up from the loom and goes to the table*). They were 'bout t'have a go at it from Dedlovo, but word musta got there, too—'bout t'have a go, but then nothin'; so the whole thing fell through. Who'd want to anyway?

MAVRA. What about the Lizunovs from Zuyevo?

ANISYA. Matchmakers were here, but it also came t'nothin'. He wouldn't even meet with no one.

MAVRA. Yuh should really marry 'er off.

ANISYA. We sure should. I can hardly wait, Cousin, t'get 'er outta here, but things just ain't workin' out. He don't wanna. She don't wanna either. He ain't yet lived it up enough with that beauty of his, yuh see.

MAVRA. E-e-eh, what sins! Can't even think 'bout it. An' him bein' her stepfather.

ANISYA. Ah, Cousin. I can't even tell yuh how easily they set me up, just took me in. Fool that I was, I noticed nothin', suspected nothin', an' so I married 'im. Didn't guess a single thing, but they were already in ca-hoots.

MAVRA. O-oh, what a mess!

ANISYA. An' it got worse, I see they started hidin' from me. Ah, Cousin, I'm in real misery, my life's been misery. If only I didn't love 'im.

MAVRA. What can yuh say.

ANISYA. It hurts me, Cousin, t'put up with such humiliation from 'im. Oh, it hurts!

MAVRA. I hear tell he's also gotten free with his hands, that right?

ANISYA. Does it all. Used t'be he was easygoin' when drunk. He poured it down before, too, but he liked me then; now when he gets tanked up, he climbs all over me, wants t'stomp me. T'other day he got me by the hair,

I barely got loose. An' the girl's worse'n a snake, I dunno how the earth bears such rotten creatures.

MAVRA. O-o-oh! Yuh poor thing, Cousin, I can see it on yuh! That's tough; yuh took in a beggar, an' now he's tauntin' yuh. Why don't yuh cut him short?

ANISYA. Oh, my dear Cous! What can I do with my heart? My departed was pretty strict, but still I could twist 'im aroun' any way I wanted; but here I can't, Cous. Soon's I lay eyes on 'im, my heart just melts. I can't get up no courage 'gainst 'im. When he's aroun' I'm like a wet hen.

MAVRA. O-oh, Cousin! Seems a spell's been put on yuh. I hear tell, Matryona does them things. It must be her.

ANISYA. That's what I think myself, Cousin. Cuz I'm so mad at times, I could tear 'im t'pieces. But soon's I lay eyes on 'im, I don't have it in my heart no mo'.

MAVRA. Plain as day, spell's been cast. It don't take long, honey, t'ruin a person. When I look at yuh, where's yer ol' self!

ANISYA. My legs've gotten thin like sticks. Now look at that dummy, at Akulina. The girl was a filthy slob, an' look at 'er now. Somethin' happened to 'er. Besides, he dressed 'er up. She's all decked out'n puffed up like a soap bubble. A dummy she is, but she's gotten into 'er head: "I'm the mistress here," she says, "the house's mine. Pa wanted 'im t'marry me." An' she's real nasty, God help us. She'll get so mad she'll tear the thatch off the roof.

MAVRA. O-oh, I see what yer life's like, Cousin. An' still people envy yuh. "They're rich," they say. But, honey, seems riches don't keep back the tears.

ANISYA. Like there's somethin' t'envy. An' it'll all just go up'n smoke. He throws money aroun' like crazy.

MAVRA. Well, Cousin, why'd yuh make it so easy for 'im? It's yer money.

ANISYA. If yuh only knew everythin'. I did make one mistake.

MAVRA. If I was you, Cousin, I'd go straight t'the man in charge, the main one. It's yer money. How come he's throwin' it aroun'? He don't have no right to.

ANISYA. Nowadays they pay that no mind.

MAVRA. Ah, Cousin, just look at yuh. Yuh've gottten so weak.

ANISYA. Weak is right, dear, really weak. He's made me weary. I dunno nothin' no mo' myself. O-oh, my poor achin' head!

MAVRA. Ain't that someone comin'? (*Listens. The door opens, enter* AKIM.)

SCENE 4

THE SAME *and* AKIM.

AKIM (*crosses himself, knocks the snow off his bast shoes, and undresses*). Peace t'this house. Yuh all doin' well? Howdy, little woman.

ANISYA. How d'ya do, Pa. Comin' from home? Come in, take off yer coat.

AKIM. Thought, d'ya, lemme, I mean, go see, d'ya, my sonny, go t'my sonny. Didn't leave early, had my dinner, I mean, then left; but it's so snowy, d'ya, it's hard, walkin', it's hard, that's why, d'ya, I'm late, I mean. My sonny home? I mean, is my sonny home?

ANISYA. Nope, in town.

AKIM (*sits down on the bench*). Got some business with 'im, I mean, d'ya, some business. Told 'im, I mean, t'other day, d'ya, I mean, told 'im what I need, the ol' horse's done for, I mean, the ol' horse. Gotta, d'ya, come up with some kind o' horse, a horse. That's why, d'ya, I've come, I mean.

ANISYA. Mikita told me. When he comes, you'll talk. (*Goes to the stove.*) Have some supper, an' he'll come. Mitrich, come have supper, hey Mitrich!

MITRICH (*waking, booms out*). What?

ANISYA. Supper.

MITRICH. Oh, Lord, gracious Nicholas!

ANISYA. Come have supper.

MAVRA. I'll be goin' now. 'Bye. (*Exits.*)

SCENE 5

AKIM, ANISYA, *and* MITRICH.

MITRICH (*climbs down from the stove*). Didn't even notice I fell asleep. Oh, Lord, Saint Nicholas! Howdy, Pa Akim.

AKIM. Hey! Mitrich! Whacha doin' here, I mean, d'ya?

MITRICH. I'm workin' here, for Mikita, for yer son.

AKIM. That's really somethin'! I mean, d'ya, workin' for my son. That's really somethin'!

MITRICH. I used t'work for a merchant in town, but drank everthin' away there. So I came out t'the village. Don't have a place o' my own, so I hired on. (*Yawns.*) Oh, Lord!

AKIM. What's, d'ya, if, d'ya, what's Mikishka do? Is he got, I mean, some business that he's hired a hand for, I mean, d'ya, a hand for?

ANISYA. What business? He used t'manage 'imself, but now his head's somewheres else, so he took on a hand.

MITRICH. He's got the money, so why shouldn't he...

AKIM. That's, d'ya, wrong. Now that's all, d'ya, wrong. That's wrong. It's spoilin', I mean.

ANISYA. He's spoilt, real spoilt, that's the trouble.

AKIM. That's it, d'ya, yuh think it'd be betta, d'ya, but it's, I mean, worse. A man gets spoilt by riches, spoilt he gets.

MITRICH. Fat livin' even makes a dog go batty. Sure hard not bein' spoilt by fat livin'! Boy did I go on a bender cuz o' fat livin'. Drank for three weeks widout stoppin'. Drank away my last pair o' britches. Had nothin' left, so I quit. I've sworn off it now. The hell with it.

AKIM. An' yer ol' lady, I mean, where's she?

MITRICH. My ol' lady's in 'er right place, pal. Hangs aroun' the bars in town. She's a real beaut too—one eye's knocked out, t'other's black 'n 'er snout's off t'one side. She ain't never sober, cocksucker![11]

AKIM. O-oh! Why's that?!

MITRICH. What else's there for a soldier's wife? She's doin' the only thing she can do. (*Silence.*)

AKIM (*to* ANISYA). So did Nikita take, d'ya, somethin' t'town, t'sell, I mean, take somethin'?

ANISYA (*sets the table and serves*). Went empty. Went for money, t'the bank t'get money.

AKIM (*eats supper*). How come yuh're gettin' it, d'ya, the money, yuh wanna do somethin' with the money?

ANISYA. No, we ain't touchin' it. Just twenty or thirty roubles; it's come, gotta take it.

AKIM. Gotta take it? Why're yuh takin' it, d'ya, the money? Today, I mean, d'ya, yuh'll take, tomorrow, I mean, you'll take—an' you'll go through it, d'ya, all of it, I mean.

ANISYA. We get this extra. The money's all there.

AKIM. All there? How come, d'ya, all there? Yuh take it, an' it's, d'ya, all there. How come? You go, d'ya, fill a bin, d'ya, or barn, an' all that, with flour, I mean, an' then you go take some flour from there—what, it'll all, d'ya, be there? That, I mean, ain't, d'ya. They're cheatin'. Yuh'd betta find this out, or else they'll cheat. How come it's all there? Yuh, d'ya, take it'n it's all there.

ANISYA. I really dunno. Ivan Moseich told us to that time. "Put yer money," he says, "in the bank—it'll all be there, an' you'll get interest."

MITRICH (*finishes supper*). That's right. I used t'work for a merchant. They all do it like that. Put money in then lie on the stove an' collect.

AKIM. That's, d'ya, odd talk. How come, d'ya, collect; yuh, d'ya, collect, but from who do they, I mean, d'ya, collect? The money?

ANISYA. They give money from the bank.

MITRICH. What's that? A woman, she can't figger it out. You look here, I'll explain the whole thing t'yuh. Listen up. Supposin' yuh've got money, an', supposin', spring's come'n my land's lyin' fallow, got nothin' t'sow with, or tax's due, whatever. So, yuh know, I come t'yuh: "Akim," I says, "gimme a tenner, I'll return it by Intercession Day when I'll have my field harvested, an' I'll do yer couple o' acres for the favor." Now, supposin', yuh see I've still got somethin' yuh can squeeze outta me: an ol' horse or cow, an' yuh say: it'll be two, three roubles for the favor, that's it. I'm really in a bind, can't do widout it. Okay, I says, I'll take the tenner. I turn things aroun' in the fall, bring the dough, an' yuh screw me outta three roubles.

AKIM. But that's, I mean, d'ya, what crooked peasants do, d'ya, only someone who, d'ya, forgot God, I mean. That's, I mean, not right.

MITRICH. Just wait. She'll wind up doin' the same thing aw right. Listen up. Now, I mean, yuh've done this thing, skinned me, I mean, an', supposin', Anisya's got money lyin' aroun'. She dunno what t'do with it, an', bein' she's a woman, dunno where t'put it. So she comes t'yuh; "Can't yuh," she says, "make some profit on my money too." "Sure can," yuh say. An' now yuh wait. I come again 'fore summer. "Gimme," I say, "another tenner, an' I'll make up the favor..." So now yuh do some figgerin': if my hide ain't all gone'n yuh can skin me some mo', yuh gimme Anisya's money. But if, supposin', I ain't got nothin', not even some grub, yuh take, yuh know, note of it, yuh see there ain't no skin left, an' right away yuh say: "Move on, pal, God be with yuh," an' yuh look for someone else t'give to again, lend yer own an' Anisya's money, an' skin that guy. That's what the bank's all about. That's how it goes roun'n roun'. Pretty fuckin' smart, pal.

AKIM (*excitedly*). What's that? That's, d'ya, I mean, filthy business. That's what, d'ya, peasants do, but even peasants, I mean, know it's, d'ya, a sin. That's, d'ya, not lawful, not lawful, I mean. It's filthy business. How come learned people, d'ya...

MITRICH. That's the thing they like best, pal. Listen here. Whoever's stupid, or a woman, an' can't do somethin' with his money 'imself, he brings it t'the bank, an' they grab it an' fleece people with this money, cocksuckers! Pretty fuckin' smart.

AKIM (*sighing*). Ah, I see, d'ya, it's trouble, d'ya, widout money, an' twice as much, d'ya, with money. What's that? God commanded us t'work. But yuh, I mean, d'ya, put money in the bank an' go t'sleep, an' the money'll, I mean, d'ya, feed yuh while yuh're lyin' aroun'. That's filthy business, I mean, 'tain't lawful.

MITRICH. 'Tain't lawful? They don't care about that nowadays, pal. They'll just clean yuh out. That's how it is.

AKIM (*sighs*). It seems, d'ya, the end's at hand. Also had a look, I mean, at the outhouses in town. What don't they come up with. Spiffy, so spiffy, I mean, smart. Made up like a tavern. An' it's for nothin'. It's all for nothin'. Oh, God's been forgotten. Forgotten, I mean. We've forgotten, forgotten God, God. Thanks, dear, I'm full, happy. (*Leaves the table; MITRICH climbs onto the stove.*)

ANISYA (*takes away the dishes and eats*). If only his father would straighten 'im out, but I'm ashamed t'tell 'im.

AKIM. What?

ANISYA. Just talkin' t'myself.

SCENE 6

THE SAME *and* ANYUTKA (*enters*).

AKIM. There's a good girl! Always busy! Got cold, I'll bet?

ANYUTKA. Yeah, awfully cold. Hi, Grampa.

ANISYA. So? Is he there?

ANYUTKA. Nope. Only Andriyan's there from town, says he saw 'em back in town, in a tavern. He says Dad's dead drunk.

ANISYA. Yuh wanna eat? Here.

ANYUTKA (*goes to the stove*). Oh, it's so cold. My hands're numb. (AKIM *takes his bast shoes off;* ANISYA *washes the spoons.*)

ANISYA. Pa!

AKIM. What is it?

ANISYA. So, is Marishka doin' well?

AKIM. Not bad. Doin' fine. She's, d'ya, a smart, quiet little woman, doin' fine, I mean, d'ya, she tries. Not bad. She's, I mean, a decent little woman, an' all, d'ya, hard-workin' an', d'ya, listens. The little woman's, I mean, not bad, I mean.

ANISYA. What's this I hear tell, someone from yer village, kinfolk o' Marinka's husband, wanted t'arrange a marriage t'our Akulina. Have yuh heard 'bout it?

AKIM. Who, the Mironovs? The women were blabbin' 'bout it. Paid it no mind, I mean. That's right, I mean, dunno, d'ya. The ol' ladies were sayin' somethin'. I just don't remember things, don't remember, I mean. Well, the Mironovs, d'ya, I mean, they're nice folks, d'ya.

ANISYA. I can't wait t'marry 'er off.

AKIM. Why?

ANYUTKA (listens). They've come.

SCENE 7

THE SAME *and* NIKITA (*enters drunk with a sack and a bundle under his arm, and some packages wrapped in paper; opens the door and stops*).

ANISYA. Well, don't be botherin' 'em. (*Keeps on washing the spoons and does not turn her head when the door opens.*)

NIKITA. Anisya, wife! Who's come? (ANISYA *glances at him and turns away. She remains silent.*)

NIKITA (*threateningly*). Who's come? Maybe yuh've forgotten?

ANISYA. Cut yer clownin'. Come in.

NIKITA (*even more threateningly*). Who's come?

ANISYA (*goes up to him and takes him by the arm*). Okay, my husband's come. Come into the house.

NIKITA (*refuses to move*). Right, husband. An' what's the husband's name? Say it right.

ANISYA. Oh, go t'hell—Mikita.

NIKITA. Right! Yuh hick—say the middle name.

ANISYA. Akimych. So!

NIKITA (*still in the doorway*). Right. No, you tell me, what's the last name?

ANISYA (*laughs and pulls him by the arm*). Chilikin. Yuh're really loaded!

NIKITA. Right. (*Holds on to the door jamb.*) No, you tell me, what foot does Chilikin step in with?

ANISYA. Oh, cut it out—yuh lettin' the cold in.

NIKITA. Tell me, what foot? Yuh're gonna have t'say.

ANISYA (*to herself*). He's gettin' t'me now. Okay, left. C'mon in.

NIKITA. Right.

ANISYA. Look who's here.

NIKITA. Father? Okay, I can face Father. I can pay respect t'Father. Howdy, Pa. (*Bows to him and puts out his hand.*) My respects t'yuh.

AKIM (*not answering*). Liquor, liquor, I mean, what it does. Nasty!

NIKITA. Liquor? Yuh mean I'm drunk? Once'n for all, guilty. Drank with a buddy, wished 'im well.

ANISYA. Why don't yuh go lie down.

NIKITA. Wife, say, where'm I standin'?

ANISYA. Okay, just go lie down.

NIKITA. No, I'm first gonna drink a samovar with father. Get the samovar goin'. Akulina, c'mon in.

SCENE 8

THE SAME *and* AKULINA.

AKULINA (*all dressed up, carrying packages; to* NIKITA). Why did'ya throw everythin' aroun'? Where's the yarn?

NIKITA. Yarn? The yarn's there. Hey, Mitrich! Where're yuh? Asleep? Go put away the horse.

AKIM (*does not see* AKULINA *and looks at his son*). What it does? The ol' man's, I mean, d'ya, dead tired, I mean, been threshin', an' he's, d'ya, loaded. "Put away the horse." Phew! Nasty!

MITRICH (*climbs off the stove, puts on his felt boots*). Oh, gracious Lord! Is the horse out in the yard? Dead tired, I bet. How d'ya like that, soused t'the gills, let 'im bust! Oh, Lord, Saint Nicholas! (*Puts on a fur coat and goes out to the yard.*)

NIKITA (*sits down*). Forgive me, Pa. I'm drunk, that's true, so what's t'do? Even a chicken drinks. Ain't that so? You forgive me. Y'know, Mitrich— he won't be offended, he'll take care of it.

ANISYA. D'ya really want me t'get the samovar goin'?

NIKITA. Yeah. Father's come, I wanna talk with 'im, have tea with 'im. (*To* AKULINA). Did'ya bring in all the packages?

AKULINA. Packages? I took mine, the rest's in the sleigh. Here, this one ain't mine. (*Throws a package on the table and puts the others into her trunk.* ANYUTKA *watches her put them away;* AKIM *does not look at his son and puts his leg wraps and bast shoes on the stove.*)

ANISYA (*exiting with the samovar*). The trunk's already full—an' he buys mo'.

SCENE 9

AKIM, AKULINA, ANYUTKA, *and* NIKITA.

NIKITA (*tries to appear sober*). Don't be mad at me, Pa. Yuh think I'm
drunk. I can absolutely do it all. Yuh can drink, but don't lose yer head.
I can talk with yuh now, Pa. I remember all that business. Yuh told me
'bout the money, the ol' horse bein' done for—I remember. That's all
doable. That's all in my hands. If the amount o' money wanted's real big,
it'll have t'wait a bit; otherwise I can do it all! Here it is!

AKIM (*continues to fuss with the lacing*). Eh, Sonny, d'ya, I mean, a muddy
lane, d'ya, ain't no road...

NIKITA. Whacha mean by that? Ain't there no words for talkin' with a
drunk? Now don't you fret. We'll have some tea. An' I can do it all, can
absolutely fix the whole thing up.

AKIM (*shakes his head*). Eh, eh, eh!

NIKITA. Here's the money. (*Reaches into his pocket, gets his wallet, flips
through the bills, takes a ten-rouble note.*) Take it, buy yuhself a horse.
Take it, buy yuhself a horse, I can't forget my father. Sure won't let yuh
down. Cuz yuh're my father. Here, take it. It's that simple. I don't mind.
(*Comes up and shoves the money at* AKIM. AKIM *does not take the
money.*)

NIKITA (*grabs his hand*). Take it, I'm tellin' yuh, while I'm givin', I don't
mind.

AKIM. I can't, I mean, d'ya, take it, an' I can't, d'ya, talk with yuh, I mean.
Cuz, d'ya, yuh ain't in God's image, I mean.

NIKITA. I won't let yuh go. Take it. (*Shoves the money into* AKIM*'s hand.*)

SCENE 10

THE SAME *and* ANISYA.

ANISYA (*enters and stops*). Yuh'd betta take it. He won't let off, yuh know.

AKIM (*takes it, shaking his head*). Eh, the liquor! Not a man, I mean...

NIKITA. Now that's betta. If yuh give it back—yuh give it back, if yuh don't—let it go. That's how I am! (*Sees* AKULINA.) Akulina, show 'em yer presents.

AKULINA. What?

NIKITA. Show 'em yer presents.

AKULINA. The presents, why show em? I've already put 'em away.

NIKITA. Get 'em, I tell yuh. Anyutka would really like t'see 'em. Show 'em t'Anyutka, I tell yuh. Open the one with the short wrap. Bring it here.

AKIM. O-oh, makes me sick! (*Climbs onto the stove.*)

AKULINA (*gets the presents and puts them on the table*). So there, what's t'look at?

ANYUTKA. Oh how pretty! It's as good as Stepanida's.

AKULINA. Stepanida's? Where does Stepanida's come t'this! (*Becoming animated and opening the presents.*) Look here, real quality... French.

ANYUTKA. What a neat print! Mashutka has one like it, only lighter, with a sky-blue background. That's awfully pretty.

NIKITA. That's right. (*Angry,* ANISYA *goes to the pantry, returns with the pipe for the samovar and a tablecloth, and goes up to the table.*)

ANISYA. Damn yuh, cluttered things up.

NIKITA. Take a look here!

ANISYA. What's for me t'look at! D'ya think I haven't seen 'em? Take 'em away. (*Brushes the short wrap onto the floor.*)

AKULINA. Whacha throwin' things aroun' for?... Throw yer own things aroun'. (*Picks it up.*)

NIKITA. Anisya! Watch out!

ANISYA. Watch out for what?

NIKITA. Yuh think I forgot yuh? Look here. (*Shows her a package and sits down on it.*) Present for yuh. Just gotta earn it. Wife, where am I sittin'?

ANISYA. Stop pushin' me aroun'. I ain't 'fraid o' yuh. Whose money yuh havin' a good time with'n buyin' yer tub o' lard presents? Mine.

AKULINA. What d'ya mean, yers! Yuh wanted t'steal it, but yuh couldn't. Get outta here! (*Wants to go by; shoves her.*)

ANISYA. Why're yuh shovin'? I'll teach yuh t'shove

AKULINA. Yuh'll teach me? Okay, c'mon. (*Presses against her.*)

NIKITA. Hey, you two. Cut it out! (*Stands between them.*)

AKULINA. Who's she t'poke her nose in. Yuh'd betta shut up, just keep things t'yuhself. Yuh think nobody knows?

ANISYA. Knows what? Out with it, out with what they know!

AKULINA. I know somethin' 'bout yuh.

ANISYA. Yuh're a slut, livin' with someone else's husband.

AKULINA. An' you did yers in.

ANISYA (*rushes at* AKULINA). Liar.

NIKITA (*restrains her*). Anisya! Have yuh forgotten?

ANISYA. Wanna scare me? I ain't 'fraid o' yuh.

NIKITA. Get out! (*Turns* ANISYA *around and pushes her out.*)

ANISYA. Where'll I go? I ain't leavin' my own house.

NIKITA. Out, I tell yuh. An' don't yuh dare come back.

ANISYA. I ain't goin'. (NIKITA *pushes her. Clinging to the door,* ANISYA *cries and screams.*) What's goin' on, are they thrown me the hell outta my own house? Whacha doin', yuh monster? Yuh think yuh can get away with it? You just wait!

NIKITA. Well, well!

ANISYA. I'll go t'the elder, t'the policeman.

NIKITA. Out, I tell yuh! (*Pushes her out.*)

ANISYA (*from behind the door*). I'll hang myself.

SCENE 11

NIKITA, AKULINA, ANYUTKA, *and* AKIM.

NIKITA. Like hell.

ANYUTKA. O-o-oh! Mommy dear. (*Cries.*)

NIKITA. Yeah, I'm real scared of 'er. Whacha cryin' for? She'll be back, no sweat! Go check the samovar. (ANYUTKA *exits.*)

SCENE 12

NIKITA, AKIM, *and* AKULINA.

AKULINA (*gathers her packages and puts them away*). Look what a mess she's made, the slob! You just wait, I'll cut up her vest. I sure will.

NIKITA. I kicked 'er out, what else d'ya want?

AKULINA. She got my new wrap all dirty. What a bitch! If she hadn't o' left, I'da poked both 'er eyes out.

NIKITA. Stop bein' mad. Whacha so mad about? As if I loved 'er.

AKULINA. Loved 'er? That cow, what's there t'love? Yuh shoulda dumped 'er then, an' that woulda been it. Yuh shoulda kicked 'er the hell outta here. The house's mine anyway, an' the money's mine. Says she's the boss, the boss, what kind o' boss is she over her husband? She's a killer, that's what. An' she'll do the same t'you.

NIKITA. Ah, yuh just can't shut women up. Yuh're blabbin', an' dunno yuhself 'bout what.

AKULINA. Yes I do. I won't live with 'er. I'll kick 'er outta here. She can't live with me. Some boss. She's no boss, she's a jailbird.

NIKITA. Oh, stop it. What d'ya have t'share with 'er? Don't pay 'er no mind. I'm the one. I'm the boss. I do what I want. I don't love 'er no mo', I love you. I love who I want. My will. She's nil, jail bait. Here's where I got 'er. (*Points under his feet.*) Ah, pity I don't have my accordion! [*Sings.*]

> Loaves on the stove,
> Gruel's there, too,
> We'll give life a run,
> We'll have our fun,
> But when death'll come,
> We'll all be done.
> Loaves on the stove,
> Gruel's there, too...

SCENE 13

THE SAME *and* MITRICH (*enters, undresses, and climbs onto the stove*).

MITRICH. Looks like the women been fightin' again. Got in each other's hair. Oh, Lord! Gracious Nicholas.

AKIM (*sits on the edge of the stove; takes his leg wraps and bast shoes and puts them on*). Hop up, hop into the corner.

MITRICH (*climbs up*). They just can't get along, I reckon. Oh, Lord!

NIKITA. Get out the liqueur. We'll have some with tea.

SCENE 14

THE SAME *and* ANYUTKA.

ANYUTKA (*enters; to* AKULINA). Sis, the samovar's boilin' over.

NIKITA. Where's yer mother?

ANYUTKA. She's standin' in the entranceway cryin'.

NIKITA. That's it. Call 'er, tell 'er t'bring in the samovar. Akulina, take out the cups.

AKULINA. The cups? Okay. (*Sets the table.*)

NIKITA (*takes out the liqueur, crackers, and herring*). So, that's for me, this yarn's for the wife, kerosene's in the entranceway. An' here's the money. Wait. (*Takes the abacus*). I'll figger it right out. (*Counts.*) Wheat flour, eighty kopecks, vegetable oil... T'Pa, ten roubles. Pa! Come have some tea. (*Silence.* AKIM *sits on the stove lacing up his bast shoes.*)

SCENE 15

THE SAME *and* ANISYA.

ANISYA (*brings in the samovar*). Where should I put it?

NIKITA. On the table. So, have yuh been t'the elder's? That's it, watch what yuh say. Well, quit bein' mad. Sit down, have a drink. (*Pours her a shot.*) Here's a little present for yuh. (*Hands her the package on which he was sitting.* ANISYA *silently takes it, shaking her head*)

AKIM (*climbs down from the stove and puts on his fur coat; goes over to the table and puts the bill on it*). Here's yer money. Put it away.

NIKITA (*does not see the bill*). Where're yuh headin' all dressed?

AKIM. I'm leavin', leavin', I mean; for God's sake, forgive me. (*Takes his hat and belt.*)

NIKITA. How d'ya like that! Whe're yuh goin' in the middle o' the night?

AKIM. I can't, I mean, d'ya, I can't, d'ya, I mean, stay in yer house, can't stay, forgive me.

NIKITA. Why're yuh goin' 'fore havin' tea?

AKIM (*puts on his belt*). I'm leavin' cuz, I mean, 'tain't, I mean, d'ya, 'tain't right in yer house, Mikishka, t'aint. I mean, yuh're livin' bad, Mikishka, bad. I'm leavin'.

NIKITA. Nuff o' this talk. Sit down an' have some tea.

ANISYA. What's goin' on, Pa, yuh'll shame us before everyone. Whacha offended at?

AKIM. Nothin' at all, d'ya, nothin's offended me, I mean, it's just that, d'ya, I see, I mean, my son goin' t'ruin, I mean, my son, t'ruin, I mean.

NIKITA. What ruin? Just show me.

AKIM. Ruin, ruin, yuh're all the way in ruin. What'd I tell yuh last year?

NIKITA. Yuh told me a lotta things.

AKIM. I told yuh, d'ya, 'bout the orphan girl, that yuh wronged the orphan girl, Marina, I mean, wronged.

NIKITA. Look what he remembered! Let sleepin' dogs lie. That's over'n done with.

AKIM (*angrily*). Over? No, pal, 'tain't over. Sin, I mean, latches onto sin an' pulls yuh along, an' yuh're stuck in sin, Mikishka. Yuh're stuck in sin, I see. Yuh're stuck, yuh've sunk in it, I mean.

NIKITA. Sit down an' have some tea, nuff o' this talk.

AKIM. I can't, I mean, d'ya, drink no tea. Cuz yer nasty ways, I mean, d'ya, make me sick, mighty sick. I can't, d'ya, drink no tea with yuh.

NIKITA. Ah, diddlin' aroun'. C'mom, sit down.

AKIM. Yuh're caught in riches, d'ya, like in a net. Yuh're in a net. Ah, Mikishka, yuh need a soul!

NIKITA. What real right d'ya have t'scold me in my own house? Why're yuh on me anyhow? I ain't a kid for you t'pull my hair! That ain't done nowadays.

AKIM. That's right, I heard nowadays that, d'ya, that fathers're pulled by their beards, I mean, but that's ruin, ruin, I mean.

NIKITA (*angrily*). We're managin', don't ask yuh for nothin', an' it's you who's come t'us with wants.

AKIM. The money? Yer money's over there. I'll go, d'ya, beggin', but not, d'ya, wont take it, I mean.

NIKITA. Nuff o' that. Whacha gettin' mad for, upsettin' the gatherin'! (*Holds him back by the arm.*)

AKIM (*shrieks*). Lemme go, I won't stay. Betta I spend the night under some fence than in this filth o' yers. Phew, God forgive me! (*Exits.*)

SCENE 16

NIKITA, AKULINA, ANISYA, *and* MITRICH.

NIKITA. I'll be!

SCENE 17

THE SAME *and* AKIM.

AKIM (*opens the door*). Come t'yer senses, Mikita. Yuh need a soul. (*Exits.*)

SCENE 18

NIKITA, AKULINA, ANISYA, *and* MITRICH.

AKULINA (*takes the cups*). So, should I pour the tea? (*All are silent.*)

MITRICH (*booms out*). Oh Lord, have mercy upon me, a sinner! (*All start.*)

NIKITA (*lies down on the bench*). Oh, I'm down, down, Akulka! Where's my accordion?

AKULINA. Accordion? Now yuh miss it. Yuh sent it out t'be fixed. I poured the tea, have some.

NIKITA. I don't wanna. Put out the light... Oh, I'm down, so down! (*Cries.*)

Curtain.

ACT IV

Dramatis personae
Nikita
Matryona
Anisya
Anyutka
Mitrich
Neighbor
  a woman
Mavra
Ivan*
  the groom's father, a gloomy man

Fall. Evening. The moon is shining. The interior of the yard. The entranceway is in the middle, to the right is the heated part of the cottage and a gate, to the left is the unheated part of the cottage and the cellar. Talking and drunken shouts are heard from inside the cottage. The NEIGHBOR *woman comes out of the entranceway and motions to* MAVRA, ANYUTKA*'s godmother.*

SCENE 1

MAVRA *and* NEIGHBOR.

NEIGHBOR. How come Akulina didn't show up?
MAVRA. How come she didn't show up? She'd be glad to, but she ain't got the time, yuh know. The groom's relatives came t'look the bride over, but, honey, she's lyin' there in the cold part o' the house an' don't even poke 'er nose out, poor dear.

---

*In the original text he is listed in the dramatis personae as the GROOM'S FATHER. We learn his name (IVAN) later on in the act (IV, 3). That name will be utilized for this character.

NEIGHBOR. Why's that?

MAVRA. It's a spell, she says, a bellyache.

NEIGHBOR. Yuh don't say!

MAVRA. That's it aw right. (*Whispers in her ear.*)

NEIGHBOR. My goodness! Now that's a sin. An' the groom's relatives'll find out.

MAVRA. There's no way they'll find out. They're all drunk. Besides, they're mostly after the dowry. Just imagine, honey, with the girl they're given two fur coats, six silk gowns,[12] a French wrap, also a lotta linen, an', I hear tell, some money, two hundred in cash.

NEIGHBOR. Well, the way it is, yuh won't be happy for the money. Just a disgrace.

MAVRA. Shhh... His father's comin', I think. (*They stop talking and go into the entranceway.*)

SCENE 2

IVAN *alone, comes out of the entranceway, hiccups.*

IVAN. I'm all sweated up. It's hot as hell. Lemme cool off a bit. (*Stands still breathing deep.*) God only knows what... somethin' ain't right, it don't make me happy... Well, I'll leave t'my ol' lady...

SCENE 3

IVAN *and* MATRYONA.

MATRYONA (*comes out of the entranceway also*). An' I'm wonderin': where's the father? Where's the father? Here's where yuh are, my dear... Well, dearie, thank the Lord, everything's how it should be. Matchmakin' ain't for boastin'.[13] I've never been one t'boast. But as yuh've come here t'get a good thing done, with God's help, you'll be forever thankin' me. Such a bride's a rare find, yuh know. There ain't another girl like 'er in the district.

IVAN. That's true, but we oughtn't let the money slip away.

MATRYONA. Don't yuh worry none 'bout the money. She still got everythin' her folks gave 'er. And hundred'n a half nowadays ain't hay.

IVAN. We ain't compainin', but it's our kid. Wanna do the best we can.

MATRYONA. I'm tellin' yuh the truth, friend: if not for me, yuh'd never find one like 'er. They also got a look-see from the Kormilins, but I stuck up for yuh. And 'bout the money—I'll tell yuh true: when the departed, rest his soul, was dyin', he left word that the widow should take Mikita in. I know all this from my son, and the money, yuh know, should go t'Akulina. Another might've took advantage o' this, yuh see, but Mikita's givin' it away, all of it. That kinda money ain't hay.

IVAN. Folks're sayin' there was mo' money left to 'er. The boy's pretty sharp too.

MATRYONA. Oh, goodness gracious. The grass's always greener on t'other side; she's gettin' what was there. I'm tellin' yuh, stop all yer figgerin'. Firm up the deal. What a girl, good as gold.

IVAN. That's so. There's one thing the ol' lady an' me's been wonderin' 'bout the girl. How come she didn't show up? We're thinkin', maybe she's sick?

MATRYONA. Ah, ah... She? Sick? There ain't none like 'er in the district. The girl's so solid there's nothin' t'pinch. Yuh saw 'er t'other day. Works like a demon. She's a little deaf, that's true. But then, a little wormhole don't spoil the whole apple. An' why she didn't show up, that's cuz of a spell, yuh see. Somethin's been done to 'er. An' I know the bitch that done it. Yuh see, they knew 'bout the betrothal so they done it. But I know how t'undo it. The girl'll be up'n about tomorrow. Don't you worry none 'bout the girl.

IVAN. Well, okay, the thing's settled.

MATRYONA. That's it, yuh've agreed, so no backin' out. An' don't forget me, I did a lotta work too. Don't you forget...

WOMAN'S VOICE (*from the entranceway*). It's time t'go, c'mon, Ivan.

IVAN. Comin'. (*Exits. A crowd of people gather in the entranceway and make ready to leave.*)

SCENE 4

ANISYA *and* ANYUTKA.

ANYUTKA (*runs out of the entranceway and motions to* ANISYA). Momma!

ANISYA (*from the entranceway*). What?

ANYUTKA. Mommy, come here, or they'll hear. (*Goes off with her to the shed.*)

ANISYA. What is it? Where's Akulina?

ANYUTKA. She went into the barn. What she's doin' there, awful! Cross my heart, "I can't take it," she says, "I'll scream," she says, "as loud as I can." Cross my heart.

ANISYA. She can wait. Let's see our guests off.

ANYUTKA. Oh, Mommy! It's so hard for 'er. An' she's mad too. "No use," she says, "in them toastin' me. I ain't," she says, "gettin' married, I'm," she says, "gonna die." Mommy, supposin' she dies! I'm awfully scared!

ANISYA. No sweat, she won't die; an' don't you go near 'er. Get goin'. (ANISYA *and* ANYUTKA *exit.*)

SCENE 5

MITRICH (*alone; comes from the gate and begins picking up the scattered hay*). Oh, Lord, gracious Nicholas! The liquor they've guzzled. An' the stink they've made. It even stinks in the yard. No, I don't want it, the hell with it! Look at all the hay they threw aroun'! Eat, they don't eat—just pick at it. Yuh blink an' a bale's gone. An' the stink! It's like right under yer nose. The hell with it! (*Yawns.*) Time t'go t'sleep. But I don't feel like goin' into the house. It just hangs roun' yer nose. The goddam stuff really stinks. (*The guests are heard leaving.*) Finally they're goin'. Oh, Lord, gracious Nicholas! Look at 'em staggerin' an' bullshittin' each other. An' all for nothin'.

SCENE 6

MITRICH *and* NIKITA.

NIKITA (*enters*). Mitrich! Get up on the stove, I'll clean up.

MITRICH. Okay; throw it t'the sheep. So, yuh saw 'em off?

NIKITA. Yeah, but things're bad. Dunno what t'do.

MITRICH. Shit happens! But nothin' to it. There's the Fundlings'[14] for such things. Just drop a kid off there, they'll take it in. Yuh can bring as many as yuh wanna, they don't ask questions. They even give yuh money. Yuh just gotta become a wet nurse. It's simple these days.

NIKITA. Yuh betta watch out, Mitrich, don't blab too much.

MITRICH. What's it t'me? Cover yer tracks anyway yuh wanna. Yuh sure reek o' liquor! I'm goin' in. (*Exits, yawning.*) Oh, Lord!

SCENE 7

NIKITA *is silent for a long time; sits down on the sleigh.*

NIKITA. What a mess!

SCENE 8

NIKITA *and* ANISYA.

ANISYA (*enters*). Where're yuh now?

NIKITA. Here.

ANISYA. Whacha sittin' for? There's no time t'wait. Gotta get it outta there now.

NIKITA. What're we gonna do?

ANISYA. I told yuh what. So go do it.

NIKITA. Maybe yuh should take it t'the Foundlings'.

ANISYA. Go'n take it there, if yuh wanna. Yuh're good at doin' dirty things, but a wimp at gettin' out of 'em, I see.

NIKITA. So what's t'do?

ANISYA. I'm tellin yuh, go t'the cellar an' dig a hole.

NIKITA. Couldn't yuh do it some other way?

ANISYA (*mimicking him*). Some other way? There just ain't no other way. Yuh shoulda thought 'bout that before. Go where yuh're told.

NIKITA. Ah, what a mess, what a mess!

SCENE 9

THE SAME *and* ANYUTKA.

ANYUTKA. Mommy! Grandma's callin'. Sis musta had a baby, cross my heart, it cried.

ANISYA. I'll kill yuh, whacha makin' up? Them're kittens whinin'. Get into the house an' go t'sleep, or I'll let yuh have it.

ANYUTKA. Mommy, dear, it's true, I swear...

ANISYA (*threatens her*). I'll let yuh have it! Get outta my sight! (ANYUTKA *runs out.*)

ANISYA (*to* NIKITA). Go on, do what yuh're told. Or else watch out! (*Exits.*)

SCENE 10

NIKITA *alone, is silent for a long time.*

NIKITA. What a mess! Oh, these women! A real fix! Says yuh shoulda thought 'bout that before. Think when before? Think when? That Anisya latched on t'me last year. So, what? Am I a monk? The boss died, an' so I covered up the sin, like was proper. Ain't no way I'm t'blame here. Don't that happen all the time? Now them powders. Did I put 'er up t'that? If I knew, I woulda killed 'er right then, the bitch! Really, woulda killed 'er! She made me a partner in these dirty doins, the trash! An' I couldn't stand 'er from then on. Soon's my mother told me, I couldn't stand 'er, couldn't stand 'er no mo', can't even look at 'er. So how could I live with 'er? An' so it started!... This girl began hangin' aroun'. So why not? If not me, someone else would. Now this's what it's come to. Once again, ain't no way I'm t'blame here. Oh, what a mess!... (*Sits there, becomes thoughtful.*) These women got guts—look what they thought of. But I won't go along with it.

SCENE 11

NIKITA *and* MATRYONA (*enters hastily with a lantern and a shovel*).

MATRYONA. Why're yuh sittin' like a chicken on eggs? What'd yer wife tell yuh t'do? Get things ready.

NIKITA. Whacha gonna do?

MATRYONA. We know what t'do. You do yer part.

NIKITA. Yuh're gettin' me into trouble.

MATRYONA. What? Yuh thinkin' o' backin' out? It's come t'this, an' yuh're backin' out.

NIKITA. But what a thing! Yuh know, it's a livin' bein'.

MATRYONA. Eh, a livin' bein'! It's hardly livin' at all. So what can we do with it? Go'n take it t'the Foundlings'—it'll die anyway, an' talk'll start, folks'll spread it an' the girl'll remain on our hands.

NIKITA. An' what if they find out?

MATRYONA. In our own home how could we miss? We'll do it widout leavin' a trace. Just do what I say. Ain't no way we women can do it widout a man. Here, take the shovel, get down there an' get things ready. I'll hold the light.

NIKITA. Get what ready?

MATRYONA (*in a whisper*). Dig a hole. Then we'll bring it down there an' cover it up quick. There, she's callin' again. Go on! I'll go to 'er.

NIKITA. But is it dead?

MATRYONA. Sure, it's dead. Only yuh gotta hurry up. Folks ain't asleep yet. They may hear or see—they gotta know everythin', the bastards. An' last evenin' the policeman stopped by. So this's what yuh do. Crawl down into the cellar. (*Hands him the shovel.*) Dig a hole in the corner, the ground's soft there, an' then yuh'll smooth it out again. Mother Earth won't tell a soul, she'll wipe it clean as a whistle. Go on. Go, my dear.

NIKITA. Yuh're gettin' me into trouble. The hell with the both o' yuh. Really, I'm gettin' outta here. Do it yuhselves like yuh wanna.

SCENE 12

THE SAME *and* ANISYA.

ANISYA (*from the doorway*). So, did he get it dug?

MATRYONA. Why'd yuh leave? Where'd yuh put it?

ANISYA. I covered it with burlap. No one'll hear. So, did he get it dug?

MATRYONA. He don't wanna!

ANISYA (*flies through the door in a rage*). Don't wanna! An' does he wanna feed lice in jail?! I'll go right now an' tell the police everythin'. We'll all be done for. I'll tell eveythin' right now.

NIKITA (*taken aback*). What'll yuh tell?

ANISYA. What? Everythin'! Who took the money? You! (NIKITA *is silent.*) An' who gave the poison? I did! But you knew, you knew, you knew! We did it together!

MATRYONA. Nuff o' that. Mikishka, why're yuh so stubborn? Well, what's there t'do? Yuh gotta do some work. C'mon, pumpkin.

ANISYA. Look at'im, the goody two-shoes! Don't wanna! Yuh've wronged me enough. Yuh've been ridin' me, an' now it's my turn. Go, I'm tellin' yuh, or I'll do what I said!... Here, take the shovel, take it! Go on!

NIKITA. Cut it out; why're yuh buggin' me? (*Takes the shovel, but hesitates.*) If I don't wanna—I won't go.

ANISYA. Won't go? (*Begins to shout.*) Hey, neighbors! Hey!

MATRYONA (*covers* ANISYA*'s mouth*). What's with yuh! Yuh nuts! He'll go... C'mon, Sonny, go, my dear.

ANISYA. I'm gonna call for help.

NIKITA. Stop it! Ah, these people. You hurry up now. Let's get it done. (*Goes toward the cellar.*)

MATRYONA. That's how it is, pumpkin: yuh knew how t'fool aroun', now yuh gotta know how t'cover up the traces.

ANISYA (*still excited*). He's been makin' fun o' me with that Miss Cuddles o' his! Nuff o' that! I ain't gonna be the only one. Let 'im be a killer also. He'll find out how it feels.

MATRYONA. Now, now, yuh're all worked up. Don't you get mad, little girl, take it slow'n easy, that's best. Go t'the girl now. He'll do the job. (*Follows him with a lantern.* NIKITA *crawls into the cellar.*)

ANISYA. I'll also make 'im choke his dirty little brat. (*Still excited.*) I've worried myself sick all alone, pullin' the life outta Pyotr's bones. Let 'im feel that too. I won't spare myself; I said, I won't!

NIKITA (*from the cellar*). Gimme some light!

MATRYONA (*holds up the lantern; to* ANISYA). He's diggin'. Go'n get it.

ANISYA. Stay with 'im, or he'll leave, the bastard. I'll go get it.

MATRYONA. Look, don't forget t'put a cross on it. Or I can do it. D'ya have a cross?

ANISYA. I'll find one, I know how. (*Exits.*)

SCENE 13

MATRYONA *alone and* NIKITA (*in the cellar*).

MATRYONA. The woman really lost 'er cool. But what's t'say, she's hurtin'. Well, with God's help, we'll cover up this business an' that'll be the end of it. We'll shove the girl off widout trouble. An' my sonny'll rest easy. They're livin' high on the hog, thank God. An' he won't forget me either. Where'd they be widout Matryona? They couldn't think nothin' up. (*Calls down into the cellar.*) Sonny, ready yet?

NIKITA (*crawling up, his head shows*). What's goin' on there? C'mon on, bring it! Why're yuh screwin' aroun'? If yuh gonna do it, do it.

THE SAME *and* ANISYA. MATRYONA *goes to the entranceway and meets* ANISYA. ANISYA *comes out with a baby wrapped in rags.*

MATRYONA. So, did'ya put the cross on it?

ANISYA. What d'ya think? It was tough gettin' it—she wouldn't let go. (*Comes up to* NIKITA *and hands him the baby.*)

NIKITA (*does not take it*). Bring it down yuhself.

ANISYA. Here, take it, I'm tellin' yuh. (*Throws the baby to him.*)

NIKITA (*catches it*). It's alive! Oh, my God, it's movin'! It's alive! What am I gonna...

ANISYA (*snatches the baby out of his arms and throws it into the cellar*). Choke it quick an' it won't be alive. (*Pushes* NIKITA *down.*) It's yer doin', now you do away with it.

MATRYONA (*sits down on the porch step*). He's soft-hearted. It's hard on 'im, poor dear. Well, so what! It's also his fault. (ANISYA *stands over the cellar.* MATRYONA *sits on the porch step, looks at her, and talks.*) E-e-eh, how scared he was. Well, so what? Even if it's hard, yuh can't get aroun' it. Whacha gonna do with it? An' just think o' the times folks pray for kids! But look, God don't grant 'em; they always have dead ones. Just take the priest's wife. Now here it ain't wanted, an' here it's alive. (*Looks toward the cellar.*) He musta finished. (*To* ANISYA.) Well, is he?

ANISYA (*looking into the cellar*). He's covered it with a board an' sat down on it. Musta finished.

MATRYONA. O-oh! Yuh'd be happy not sinnin', but what can yuh do?

NIKITA (*crawls out, shaking all over*). It's still alive! I can't! It's alive!

ANISYA. If it's alive, where're yuh off to? (*Tries to stop him.*)

NIKITA (*rushes at her*). Get outta here! I'll kill yuh! (*Grabs her by the arm; she breaks away; he runs after her with the shovel.* MATRYONA *rushes toward him and stops him.* ANISYA *runs onto the porch.* MATRYONA *tries to take the shovel away. To his mother.*) I'll kill yuh, I'll kill yuh too, get away! (MATRYONA *runs out to* ANISYA *on the porch.* NIKITA *stops.*) I'll kill yuh. I'll kill yuh all!

MATRYONA. It's cuz he's scared. That's nothin', it'll pass.

NIKITA. What've they done? What've they done t'me? How it whimpered... How it crunched under me. What've they done t'me! An' it's still alive, it's really alive! (*Keeps silent and listens.*) It's whimperin'... There, it's whimperin'. (*Runs to the cellar.*)

MATRYONA (*to* ANISYA). Here he goes, he must wanna bury it. Mikita, yuh should take the lantern.

NIKITA (*not answering, listens by the cellar*). Don't hear nothin'. Just imagined it. (*Walks away and stops.*) An' how its little bones crunched under me. Crr... Crr... What've they done t'me! (*Listens again.*) There, it's whimperin' again, it's really whimperin'. What is that? Momma, hey, Momma! (*Goes up to her.*)

MATRYONA. What, Sonny?

NIKITA. Oh, Momma, sweet Momma, I can't no mo'. Can't do nothin'. Momma, sweet Momma, have pity on me!

MATRYONA. Oh, yuh got so scared, poor dear. Go on, go on, have a drink, what d'ya say, for grit.

NIKITA. Oh, Momma, sweet Momma, it musta got t'me. What've yuh done t'me? How them little bones crunched, an' how it whimpered!... Momma, sweet Momma, what've the two o' yuh done t'me! (*Walks away and sits down on the sleigh.*)

MATRYONA. Go on, my dear, have a drink. It's true, its scary at night. Just wait a bit, day'll come, an' then, yuh know, a couple mo' days'll pass, an' yuh'll forget all about it. Wait a bit, we'll marry the girl off an' forget the whole thing. So have a drink, go on, have a drink. I'll clean up in the cellar myself.

NIKITA (*shaking himself*). Any liquor left in there? Maybe I'll wind up drinkin'?! (*Exits.* ANISYA, *who all this time stood by the entranceway, silently moves aside.*)

SCENE 15

MATRYONA *and* ANISYA.

MATRYONA. Go 'head, go, pumpkin, I'll do it myself. I'll crawl in an' bury it. Where'd he throw the shovel? (*Finds the shovel and goes down halfway into the cellar.*) Anisya, come here, gimme some light, will yuh?

ANISYA. What about him?

MATRYONA. He's too scared. Yuh've been too hard on 'im. Leave 'im alone, he'll come aroun'. Forget about 'im, I'll do it myself. Put the lantern over here. I can see then. (*Disappears into the cellar.*)

ANISYA (*toward the door where* NIKITA *exited*). So, have yuh fooled aroun' enough? Yuh had yer fling, now you wait, yuh'll find out how it feels. Yuh'll cool down.

SCENE 16

THE SAME *and* NIKITA (*runs out of the entranceway and heads for the cellar*).

NIKITA. Momma, hey, Momma!

MATRYONA (*pokes her head out of the cellar*). What, Sonny?

NIKITA (*listening*). Don't bury it, it's alive. Don't yuh hear? It's alive! There... it's whimperin'. There, clearly...

MATRYONA. How could it whimper? Yuh made it flat as a pancake. Yuh smashed its little head t'bits.

NIKITA. What's that? (*Stops his ears.*) It's still whimperin'! My life's finished. Finished! What've they done t'me?! Where can I go? (*Sits down on the step.*)

Curtain.

VARIANT

The following variant of Act IV may be read in place of Scenes 12–14, 15, and 16.[15]

PART 2

The cottage of Act I.

SCENE 1

ANYUTKA, *undressed, lies on a bench covered with a coat.* MITRICH *sits in the loft and smokes.*

MITRICH. Gee! What a stink they've made, cocksuckers! They've been spillin' the good stuff. Can't even kill it with tobacco. It gets right up yer nose. Oh, Lord! Time t'turn in, I guess (*Goes over to the lamp to turn it out.*)

ANYUTKA (*quickly sits up*). Gramp,[16] don't put it out, please Gramps!

MITRICH. Why not?

ANYUTKA. What a ruckus they were makin' in the yard. (*Listens.*) They've went t'the barn again, d'ya hear?

MITRICH. What's it t'yuh? Ain't no one askin' yuh, sure ain't. Lie down an' sleep. An' I'll turn out the light. (*Starts turning it.*)

ANYUTKA. Gramp, sweet Gramps! Don't put it out all the way. Leave it just a teensy-weensy, or it's creepy.

MITRICH (*laughs*). Aw right, aw right. (*Sits down beside her.*) Now what's so creepy?

ANYUTKA. It's real creepy, Gramp! The way Sis was poundin'. She kept poundin' her head 'gainst the step. (*Whispers.*) I know... She's gonna have a baby... Maybe she had it already...

MITRICH. What a busybody, get bucked by a bullfrog. Yuh gotta know everythin'. Just lie down an' go t'sleep. (ANYUTKA *lies down*). That's it. (*Covers her.*) That's it. Yuh know, curiosity killed the cat.

ANYUTKA. Are yuh gonna get up on the stove?

MITRICH. Where else? Look at yuh, how silly yuh are. She's gotta know everythin'. (*Covers her up again and gets up to go.*) That's it, just lie there an' sleep. (*Goes to the stove.*)

ANYUTKA. It cried just once, an' now yuh can't hear it.

MITRICH. Oh, Lord, gracious Nicholas... What can't yuh hear?

ANYUTKA. The baby.

MITRICH. There ain't none, so yuh can't hear it.

ANYUTKA. But I heard it, cross my heart, I did. So wee-ak.

MITRICH. Yeah, yuh heard a lot. An' if yuh did, then it was a little girl just like you that the bogeyman put into his sack, an' that was it for her.

ANYUTKA. What bogeyman?

MITRICH. Just a plain ol' bogeyman. (*Climbs onto the stove.*) The stove's so good today, warm. Nice! Oh, Lord, gracious Nicholas!

ANYUTKA. Gramp! Yuh gonna sleep?

MITRICH. What'd yuh think—I'm gonna sing? (*Silence.*)

ANYUTKA. Gramp, hey, Gramp! They're diggin'! Honest t'God, they're diggin' in the cellar, d'ya hear! Cross my heart, they're doin' it!

MITRICH. What she won't think up. Diggin' at night. Who's diggin'? That's a cow scratchin' itself, an' yuh say—they're diggin'! Go t'sleep, I tell yuh, or I'll put the light out right now.

ANYUTKA. Gramp, sweet Gramps, don't put it out. I'll stop. Honest t'God, I'll stop, cross my heart, I will. I'm scared.

MITRICH. Scared? Don't be 'fraid o' nothin', an' yuh won't be scared. It's she herself that's afraid an' then says she's scared. How can't yuh be scared if yuh're afraid? What a silly little girl. (*Silence. A cricket sounds off.*)

ANYUTKA. Gramp! Hey, Gramp! Yuh asleep?

MITRICH. Well, what now?

ANYUTKA. What's the bogeyman like?

MITRICH. He's like he is. When he catches someone like you, who don't sleep, he comes with a sack an' throws the little girl into it, an' he dives head first into the the sack, lifts her nightie an' gives 'er a spankin'.

ANYUTKA. An' what's he spank 'er with?

MITRICH. He takes a broom along.

ANYUTKA. But he can't see there, in the sack.

MITRICH. Don't worry, he sees aw right.

ANYUTKA. But I'll bite 'im.

MITRICH. No, little friend, yuh can't bite 'im.

ANYUTKA. Gramp, someone's comin'! Who is it? Oh my God! Who is it?

MITRICH. So what if someone's comin'. What's with yuh? It's probably yer mother.

SCENE 2

THE SAME *and* ANISYA (*enters*).

ANISYA. Anyutka! (ANYUTKA *pretends to be asleep.*) Mitrich!

MITRICH. What?

ANISYA. Why're yuh keepin' the light on? We're gonna sleep in the unheated side.

MITRICH. Just finished up. I'll put it out.

ANISYA (*looking in the trunk and grumbling*). Whenever yuh need somethin' yuh can never find it.

MITRICH. Whacha lookin' for?

ANISYA. For a cross. Gotta put one on it. God forbid it'll die! Unchristened! That's a sin, yuh know.

MITRICH. That's right, sure, gotta do it right... So, did'ya find it?

ANISYA. Yeah. (*Exits.*)

SCENE 3

MITRICH *and* ANYUTKA.

MITRICH. Good, or I'da given 'er mine. Oh, Lord!

ANYUTKA (*jumps up, trembling*). O-oh, Gramp! Don't go t'sleep, for God's sake. It's so scary!

MITRICH. What's so scary?

ANYUTKA. The baby'll probably die, won't it? Granny christened Auntie Arina's like that—an' it died.

MITRICH. If it dies—they'll bury it.

ANYUTKA. Maybe it wouldn't die, but Granny Matryona's here. Yuh know, I heard what she said, cross my heart, I did.

MITRICH. What'd yuh hear? Go t'sleep, I tell yuh. Pull the covers over yer head, an' that's that.

ANYUTKA. If it lived, I'd take care of it.

MITRICH (*booms out*). Oh, Lord!

ANYUTKA. Where'll they put it?

MITRICH. They'll put it where they gotta. None o' yer business. Go t'sleep, I tell yuh. Wait tell yer mother comes—she'll let yuh have it! (*Silence.*)

ANYUTKA. Gramp! That little girl yuh were tellin' 'bout, she didn't get killed, did she?

MITRICH. That one? Oh, that little girl really made it.

ANYUTKA. Gramp, how'd yuh say she was found?

MITRICH. She was just found, that's it.

ANYUTKA. But where? Tell me.

MITRICH. In their own house, that's where. We came to a village an' the soldiers began goin' through the houses; suddenly—there's that same little girl lyin' on 'er belly. They were gonna kill 'er, but I felt bad 'bout it an' picked 'er up. Yuh know, she didn't stand for it. She became heavy like weighin' two hundred pounds, an' grabbed hold o' whatever she could with 'er hands so that yuh couldn't tear 'er loose no way. Well, I held 'er an' began pattin' 'er head, just pattin' 'er head. It was shaggy like a hedgehog. I patted 'er an' patted—an' she calmed down. I soaked some hardtack an' gave it to 'er. She understood finally, an' nibbled on it a bit. What could we do with 'er? We took 'er with us. Took 'er an' began feedin' 'er an' feedin' 'er, an' she got so used t'us that we took 'er along on the march: an' she just went with us. A nice little girl she was.

ANYUTKA. So she wasn't christened?

MITRICH. Who knows. They were sayin', not properly, cuz them people wasn't ours.

ANYUTKA. Germans?

MITRICH. Yuh're somethin': Germans. Not Germans, Asians. They're just like Kikes, but not Kikes, no. Poles, but Asians. Krudlys... Kruds was their handle.[17] I've forgotten now. We called the little girl Sashka. Sashka was so nice. I've forgotten everythin' else, yuh know, but it's like I'm lookin at that little girl right now, cocksucker! Outta all o' my time in the service that's all I remember. How they flogged me, I remember, an' I remember that little girl. She'd hang roun' yer neck, an' yuh'd carry 'er. What a nice little girl, yuh couldn't find one betta even if yuh wanna. We gave 'er away later on. The company commander's wife adopted 'er. An' she made it. How sorry the soldiers felt lettin' 'er go!

ANYUTKA. Yuh know, Gramp, I can remember when Dad was dyin'. Yuh weren't livin' with us then. So, he called Mikita in an' says to 'im: "Forgive me, Mikita," he says, an' he began t'cry. (*Sighs.*) I felt sorry too.

MITRICH. Yeah, that's it, that's how it is...

ANYUTKA. Gramp, hey Gramp. They're makin' that noise again in the cellar. Oh, my God, dear God! Oh, Gramp, they'll do somethin' t'it. They'll do it in. It's so little... Oh! Oh! (*Covers her head and cries.*)

MITRICH (*listening*). They're really up t'somethin' dirty, let 'em bust! What dirty creatures them women are! Yuh can't say much for the men, but the women... They're like wild beasts. Ain't 'fraid o' nothin'.

ANYUTKA (*gets up*). Gramp, hey, Gramp!

MITRICH. Well, what now?

ANYUTKA. T'other day a traveler spent the night here; he was sayin' that when a baby dies its little soul goes straight t'heaven. Is that true?

MITRICH. Who knows, must be. Why?

ANYUTKA. I wish I would die too. (*Sobs.*)

MITRICH. If yuh die, yuh'll be gone.

ANYUTKA. Up t'ten yuh're still a baby, an' yer soul might go t'God, but then you'll go bad, yuh know.

MITRICH. An' how! How could the lot o' yuh not go bad? Who teaches yuh? What'll yuh see? What'll yuh hear? Nothin' but foul things. I ain't had much schoolin', but I know a thing or two. Not a lot, but I ain't like no hick woman. What's a hick woman? Just muck. There's many millions o' yer kind in Russia, an' yuh're all like blind moles—yuh dunno nothin'. How t'plow cattle disease under, all sorts o' spells, an' how t'cure kids by takin' 'em t'the chicken coop an' puttin' em under the roosts—that's what they know.

ANYUTKA. Mommy used t'take me.

MITRICH. That's it, that's how it is. There's so many millions o' you women an' girls, an' yuh're all like wild beasts. How she grew up is how she'll die. Sees nothin', hears nothin'. A man—even in a bar, or maybe even in prison, or soldierin', like me, he learns somethin'. But a woman? Never mind 'bout God, she don't even know 'bout Good Friday, what it's all about. Friday, Friday, but ask 'er what's Friday, she dunno. They go aroun' like blind pups stickin' their heads into dung. All they know is their stupid songs: ho-ho, ho-ho. But what's ho-ho, they dunno themselves...

ANYUTKA. But, Gramp, I know half the Our Father.

MITRICH. A lot yuh know! But then yuh can't ask much o' yuh. Who teaches yuh? Only a drunken man who'll lay the reins on yuh. That's all the teachin'. I dunno who'll answer for yuh. For recruits yuh can hold the drill instructor or sergeant responsible. But there ain't nobody responsible for yer kind. Like an unattended herd o' cattle, the wildest kind, them women. Yuh're the stupidest bunch. The most useless bunch.

ANYUTKA. So what can yuh do?

MITRICH. Nothin'. Just cover up yer head an' go t'sleep. Oh, Lord! (*Silence. A cricket sounds off.*)

ANYUTKA (*jumps up*). Gramp! Someone's screamin', somethin's wrong. Honest t'God, really, screamin'. Gramp, dear, someone's comin'.

MITRICH. Cover yer head, I tell yuh.

SCENE 4

THE SAME, NIKITA, *and* MATRYONA.

NIKITA (*enters*). What've they done t'me? What've they done t'me?

MATRYONA. Have a drink, pumpkin, have some liquor. (*Gets the liquor and puts it on the table.*) What's the matter?

NIKITA. Give it here. Maybe I'll wind up drinkin'?

MATRYONA. Quiet! They ain't asleep. Here, have some.

NIKITA. What's that? Why'd yuh think this up? Yuh shoulda took it somewheres.

MATRYONA (*in a whisper*). Just sit here awhile, have another drink or have a smoke. It'll take yer mind off things.

NIKITA. Oh, sweet Momma, it musta got t'me. How it whimpered, an' how them little bones crunched—crr... crr..., I ain't a man no mo'.

MATRYONA. E-eh! Yuh're talkin' such nonsense. It's true—it's scary at night, but wait, day'll come, a couple mo' days'll pass, and yuh'll forget all about it. (*Goes up to* NIKITA *and puts her hand on his shoulder.*)

NIKITA. Get away from me. What've yuh done t'me?

MATRYONA. C'mon, Sonny, really. (*Takes him by the hand.*)

NIKITA. Get away from me! I'll kill yuh! I don't care 'bout nothin' now. I'll kill yuh!

MATRYONA. Ah, ah, you got really scared! Maybe yuh should go t'sleep now.

NIKITA. Got nowhere t'go. I'm finished!

MATRYONA (*shaking her head*). Oh, oh, gotta get things cleaned up, an' let 'im sit here awhile, it'll pass. (*Exits.*)

SCENE 5

NIKITA, MITRICH, *and* ANYUTKA.

NIKITA (*sits, his face covered with his hands;* MITRICH *and* ANYUTKA *are very still*). It's whimperin', really whimperin', there, there, clearly. She'll bury it, really, bury it! (*Runs to the door.*) Momma, don't bury it, it's alive...

SCENE 6

THE SAME *and* MATRYONA.

MATRYONA (*returns, in a whisper*). Calm down, God help yuh! What don't yuh dream up. How can it be alive! All its little bones're smashed t'bits.

NIKITA. Gimme some mo' liquor. (*Drinks.*)

MATRYONA. Go on, Sonny. Yuh'll fall asleep now, it's aw right.

NIKITA (*stands, listens*). It's still alive... there... it's whimperin'. Can't yuh hear? There!

MATRYONA (*in a whisper*). No it's not!

NIKITA. Oh, sweet Momma! My life's finished. What've yuh done t'me! Where can I go? (*Runs out of the cottage and* MATRYONA *follows him.*)

SCENE 7

MITRICH *and* ANYUTKA.

ANYUTKA. Gramp, dear Gramps, they choked it!

MITRICH (*angrily*). Go t'sleep, I tell yuh. Ah, you, get bucked by a bullfrog! I'll let yuh have it with the broom! Go t'sleep, I tell yuh.

ANYUTKA. Gramp, sweet Gramps, someone's grabbin' my shoulders, someone's grabbin' me with its paws. Gramp, dear, cross my heart, I'll go right away. Gramp, sweet Gramps, lemme come up on the stove! Lemme, please, oh God... It's grabbin'... grabbin... A-ah! (*Runs to the stove.*)

MITRICH. Look how they've frightened the kid. Them rotten women, let 'em get bucked by a bullfrog. Aw right! Climb on up.

ANYUTKA (*climbs on the stove*). Don't you go away.

MITRICH. Where'll I go? C'mon, c'mon. Oh, Lord, gracious Nicholas, Holy Mother o' Kazan... How they frightened the kid. (*Covers her up.*) You silly little girl, yuh're really silly... They frightened 'er, them trashy women, really, cocksuckers!

Curtain.

ACT V

Dramatis personae
Nikita
Anisya
Akulina
Akim
Matryona
Anyutka
Marina
Marina's husband
First girl
Second girl
Policeman
Coachman
Best man
Groom's mother
Akulina's fiance
Elder
Guests, Women, Girls, people at the wedding.

PART 1

The threshing floor. In the foreground a grain rick, on the left the thresh-ing platform, on the right the barn. The barn doors are open; there is straw in the doorway. The yard can be seen in the background, and songs and chimes can be heard. Two girls are walking along the path past the barn to-ward the cottage.

SCENE 1

Two GIRLS.

FIRST GIRL. Now yuh see how we got through, didn't even get our bootees dirty, but goin' through the village's bad!—muddy... (*They stop and wipe their feet on the straw. The* FIRST GIRL *looks at the straw and sees something.*) What's this here?

SECOND GIRL (*takes a close look*). It's Mitrich, their hired hand. Look at that, got 'imself plastered.

FIRST GIRL. He didn't drink, did he?

SECOND GIRL. Not until he was offered, it seems.

FIRST GIRL. Just look, he musta came for some straw. See, he's still got a rope in his hands, an' just like that fell asleep.

SECOND GIRL (*listens*). They're still singin' praises t'the bride an' groom.[18] Probably didn't bless 'em yet. They were sayin' Akulina didn't even do no wailin'.[19]

FIRST GIRL. Mommy was sayin' she's marryin' 'gainst 'er will. Her stepfather threatened 'er, or else she'd never do it. There was, yuh know, lots o' talk 'bout 'er!

SCENE 2

THE SAME *and* MARINA (*catches up to the girls*).

MARINA. Hi, girls!

GIRLS. Hi, Ms. Marina.

MARINA. You kids goin' t'the weddin'?

FIRST GIRL. It's about over. Just gonna have a look.

MARINA. How 'bout gettin' hold o' my ol' man, Semyon from Zuyevo. Yuh know 'im, don't yuh?

FIRST GIRL. Sure do. He's the groom's relative.

MARINA. Yeah, the groom's my mister's nephew.

SECOND GIRL. Why don't yuh go yuhself? Can't imagine not goin' to a weddin'.

MARINA. Don't wanna, dear, an' don't have the time either. Gotta get goin'. We weren't fixin' t'come t'the weddin'. We're takin' oats t'town. Stopped t'only feed the horses, an' they dragged my ol' man in.

FIRST GIRL. Whose place did'ya stop at? Fyodoroch's?

MARINA. Yep. So I'll stay here, an' you, dear, get hold o' my ol' man. Get 'im, darlin'. Say: "Yer missus, Marina, is tellin' yuh it's time t'go; the guys're hitchin' up."

FIRST GIRL. Well, okay, if yuh won't go yuhself. (*The girls exit along the path toward the yard. Songs and chimes can be heard.*)

SCENE 3

MARINA *alone.*

MARINA (*becomes thoughtful*). I could go aw right but don't wanna, cuz I haven't seen 'im since that time he turned me down. It's mo' than a year ago. Still, I'd like t'have a look at how he's gettin' on with his Anisya. People're sayin' they don't get along. She's as common as dirt an' head-strong t'boot. He's probably remembered me mo' 'n once. He had a yen for the easy life. Swapped me for it. Well, God help 'im, I don't bear no grudge. Back then it hurt. Oh, was it painful! But now it's worn off—an' I've forgotten. Only, I'd like t'have a look at 'im... (*Looks toward the yard and sees* NIKITA.) Look at that! What's he comin' for? Now did the girls tell 'im? What'd he leave his guests for? I'd betta leave.

SCENE 4

MARINA *and* NIKITA (*at first walks with his head down, waving his arms and muttering*).

MARINA. How gloomy he looks!

NIKITA (*sees* MARINA, *recognizes her*). Marina! Dear friend, Marinushka! Why're yuh here?

MARINA. I've come for my ol' man.

NIKITA. Why didn't yuh come t'the weddin'? Coulda had a look, coulda laughed at me.

MARINA. What's there for me t'laugh at? I came for my mister.

NIKITA. Eh, Marinushka! (*Tries to embrace her.*)

MARINA (*moves away angrily*). You stop it, Mikita. What's been is gone. I came for my mister. He's at yer place, right?

NIKITA. Don't remember bygones, is that it? Yuh don't want me to?

MARINA. No use rememberin' bygones. What's been is gone.

NIKITA. An' it won't come back, is that it?

MARINA. No, it won't. So what'd yuh leave for? Yuh're the host, an' yuh've left the weddin'.

NIKITA (*sits down in the straw*). Why'd I leave? Eh, if yuh only knew, if yuh only knew!... I'm down, Marina, so down, my eyes don't wanna look. Got up from the table'n just left. Left the people so's not t'see no one.

MARINA (*comes closer to him*). Why's that?

NIKITA. Cuz I can't eat it away, drink it away, sleep it away. I feel sick, so sick! But mostly I feel sick, Marinushka, cuz I'm alone an' got no one t'tell my troubles to.

MARINA. Yuh can't live life widout troubles, Mikita. I cried mine away.

NIKITA. That was about what's past, bygones, Eh, my friend, yuh cried yers away, but now it's hit me!

MARINA. So why's that?

NIKITA. Cuz I'm sick o' life. I'm sick o' myself. Eh, Marina, yuh couldn't hold on t'me, yuh ruined me, an' yuhself too! What, is this a life?

MARINA (*stands by the barn, cries and tries to hold back her tears*). I ain't complainin' 'bout my life, Nikita. May God grant everyone a life like mine. I ain't complainin'. I told my ol' man all 'bout it then. He forgave me. An' he don't hold it 'gainst me. There's nothin' wrong with my life. My ol' man's easygoin' an' he likes me. I take good care o' his kids. An' he looks after me as well. So what's there t'complain. Must be the way God willed it. An' what's wrong with yer life? Yuh're rich...

NIKITA. My life!... I just don't wanna upset the weddin', or I'd take this here rope (*takes hold of a rope from the straw*), an' I'd toss it right over that crossbeam. Then I'd tie a noose real good, an' I'd climb up there an' put my head in it. That's what my life's like!

MARINA. Nuff, God help yuh!

NIKITA. Yuh think I'm kiddin'? Think I'm drunk? I ain't drunk. Liquor don't even get t'me these days. But grief, grief's eaten me t'the bone. It's swallowed me up so, that I don't care for nothin'! Eh, Marinushka, the only life I had was with you, remember how we killed the nights at the railway?

MARINA. Don't touch where it hurts, Mikita. I've taken vows, an' you have too. My sin's been forgiven, so don't stir up the past...

NIKITA. What am I do with my heart? Where am I t'turn?

MARINA. What's there t'do? Yuh got a wife, don't make eyes at others, but take care of yer own. Yuh loved Anisya, so go on lovin' 'er.

NIKITA. Ah, that Anisya's bitter like wormwood t'me, an' she's coiled roun' my legs like poison ivy.

MARINA. Whatever she is—she's yer wife. But what's the use o' talkin'! Yuh'd betta go t'yer guests, an' get hold o' my husband for me.

NIKITA. Oh, if only yuh knew... But what's the use o' goin' on 'bout it!

SCENE 5

NIKITA, MARINA, *her* HUSBAND, *and* ANYUTKA.

HUSBAND (*comes out to the yard, flushed and drunk*). Marina! Missus! Ol' Lady! Are yuh here?

NIKITA. There's yer mister comin', callin' for yuh. Go 'head.

MARINA. An' what about you?

NIKITA. Me? I'll lie down here for awhile. (*Lies down in the straw.*)

HUSBAND. So where's she?

ANYUTKA. Over there, mister, by the barn.

HUSBAND. Whacha standin' there for? Come t'the weddin'! The hosts say yuh gotta come, do 'em the honor. The weddin' party'll be takin' off right away, an' then we'll get goin'.

MARINA (*comes toward her* HUSBAND). I didn't wanna.

HUSBAND. C'mon, I tell yuh. Yuh'll have a drink'n toast that swindler Petrunka. The hosts're expectin' yuh. We'll have nuff time t'tend t'our business. (MARINA'S HUSBAND *embraces her and exits with her, staggering.*)

NIKITA *and* ANYUTKA.

NIKITA (*sits up in the straw*). Ah, seein' 'er makes me feel worse'n ever. The only life I really had was with her. I wasted my days for nothin', nothin' at all. I ruined myself! (*Lies down.*) Where'll I turn? Ah! I wish the earth'd open an' swallow me!

ANYUTKA (*sees* NIKITA *and runs over to him*). Daddy, hey Daddy! They're lookin' for yuh. Everybody's blessed 'em already, even the godfather. Cross my heart, they've blessed 'em. They're gettin' mad.

NIKITA (*to himself*). Where'll I turn?

ANYUTKA. What? What'd yuh say?

NIKITA. I didn't say nothin'. Whacha buggin' me for!

ANYUTKA. Daddy! Ain't yuh comin'? (NIKITA *is silent.* ANYUTKA *pulls him by the hand.*) Dad, come'n bless 'em! They're really gettin' mad, they're cussin'.

NIKITA (*pulls his hand away*). Leave me alone!

ANYUTKA. C'mon!

NIKITA (*threatens her with the reins*). Go 'way, I tell yuh. I'll let yuh have it.

ANYUTKA. Then I'll get Mommy. (*Runs off*).

SCENE 7

NIKITA *alone.*

NIKITA (*gets up*). How can I go? How can I touch the holy icon? How can I look 'er in the eyes? (*Lies down again.*) Oh, if there was a hole in the ground, I'd jump in. People wouldn't see me, I wouldn't see no one. (*Gets up again.*) No, I ain't goin'... Let 'em go t'hell. Ain't goin'. (*Takes off his boots and picks up a rope; makes a noose and puts it around his neck.*) That's it.

NIKITA *and* MATRYONA. NIKITA *sees his mother, removes the rope from his head, and lies down again in the straw.*

MATRYONA (*rushes up to him*). Mikita! Hey, Mikita! Look at 'im, he don't even answer. Mikita, what's with yuh, yuh drunk, or what? C'mon, Mikitushka, c'mon, c'mon, pumpkin. Folks're tired o' waitin'.

NIKITA. Oh, what've yuh done t'me? I ain't a man no mo'.

MATRYONA. But what's with yuh? C'mon, my dear, give 'em yer blessin', as is proper, an' yer all through. Folks're waitin', yuh know.

NIKITA. How can I bless 'em?

MATRYONA. The usual way. Don't yuh know how?

NIKITA. I know how, I know. But who am I gonna bless? What'd I do to 'er?

MATRYONA. What'd yuh do? Of all things t'think of! Nobody knows: not a cat, not a mouse, not a soul in the house. The girl's willin' t'get married.

NIKITA. Why's she willin'?

MATRYONA. She's willin' outta fear, naturally. But she's willin'. What else's there t'do? She shoulda thought 'bout it then. She can't fight it now. An' there's no offense for his kinfolk either. They looked the girl over twice, an' they're gettin' some money with 'er too. It's all covered'n clean.

NIKITA. But what's there in the cellar?

MATRYONA (*laughs*). What's in the cellar? Cabbage, mushrooms, potatoes, I'll bet. Whacha rememberin' the past for?

NIKITA. I'd be glad t'forget. But I can't. Soon's I start thinkin', I can hear it. Oh, what've yuh done t'me?

MATRYONA. Whacha makin' trouble for anyway?

NIKITA (*turns face down*). Momma! Don't you be botherin' me. I've had it up t'here.

MATRYONA. Still, yuh gotta do it. As it is folks're talkin', and here the father's gone off, stays away, an' ain't got the gumption t'give the blessin'. Pretty soon they'll be puttin' two'n two together. Soon's yuh get scared they'll begin guessin'. Don't act shook, yuh won't be taken for a crook.

Or you'll be jumpin' from the fryin' pan t'the fire. Most of all, don't show it, don't be scared, Sonny Boy, or else they'll find out all the mo'.

NIKITA. Ah, yuh got me into trouble!

MATRYONA. Nuff, let's go. Just go an' bless 'em; everything's right proper, an' that's the end of it.

NIKITA (*lies face down*). I can't.

MATRYONA (*to herself*). What's happened? Everything was fine, fine, and all of a sudden, wham. It must be a curse. Mikitka, get up! Look, there's Anisya comin', she's left the guests alone.

SCENE 9

NIKITA, MATRYONA, *and* ANISYA.

ANISYA (*dressed up, flushed and tipsy*). It's so nice, Momma, so nice, proper! An' how the folks're enjoyin' it. So where's he?

MATRYONA. Right here, pumpkin, right here. He's layed 'imself down in the straw an' just lays there. Won't move.

NIKITA (*looks at his wife*). See, drunk too! Lookin' at 'er turns my stomach. How can yuh live with 'er? (*Turns face down.*) I'll kill 'er some day. She'll get it.

ANISYA. Lookee where, holed up in the straw. The booze got yuh, huh? (*Laughs.*) I'd lay here with yuh a bit, but there's no time. C'mon, I'll take yuh. It's so nice in the house now! It's a pleasure t'see. And the accordion! The women're singin', it's so nice. Everyone's drunk. It's right proper, it's so nice!

NIKITA. What's so nice?

ANISYA. The weddin', it's a fun weddin'. Everyone's sayin' it's not often that there's a weddin' like this. It's so proper, everything's nice. Yuh gotta come. We'll go together... I've had a bit, but I'll take yuh. (*Takes him by the hand.*)

NIKITA (*pulls his hand back with disgust*). Go by yuhself. I'll come.

ANISYA. Whacha all gloom'n doom for? We've got rid o' all our troubles, we've got rid o' the one that stood 'tween us, we can just live an' be happy now. Everything's right proper, by the book. I'm so happy, I can't even

tell yuh. It's like I'm marryin' yuh all over again. E-e, how the folks're enjoyin' it! They're all thankin' us. And the guests're all so nice. And Ivan
Moseich—and the policeman too. They've been singin' praises also.

NIKITA. So go stay with 'em—why'd yuh come?

ANISYA. Right, I should go back. Or else what's it gonna look like? The
hosts go an' leave the guests alone. And the guests're all so nice.

NIKITA (*gets up, brushes off the straw*). You two go, I'll be there right away.

MATRYONA. The bird that rules the night puts the day bird t'flight. He
didn't listen t'me, but went along with his wife right away. (MATRYONA
and ANISYA *turn to go.*) Well, yuh comin'?

NIKITA. Be there right away. You go on, I'll follow. I'll come, I'll give my
blessin'... (*The women stop.*) Go on... an' I'll follow. Well, go! (*The women
exit.* NIKITA *follows them with his eyes, lost in thought.*)

SCENE 10

NIKITA *alone, then* MITRICH.

NIKITA (*sits down and takes off his boots*). Don't hold yer breath! No way!
No, you go on an' look, see if I'm not on the crossbeam. I might just tie
a noose an' jump from the crossbeam, then look for me. An' the reins're
here, what luck. (*Becomes thoughtful.*) I'd get over it. Whatever kind o'
trouble, I'd get over it. But this one's right here—deep in my heart, can't
get it out nohow. (*Looks toward the yard.*) Looks like she's comin' again.
(*Mimics* ANISYA.) "It's nice, it's so nice! I'd lay with yuh a bit!" Ugh! yuh
ol' bag! Here's what yuh'll get, hug me when they take me off the crossbeam. Yuh only die once. (*Grabs the rope and pulls it.*)

MITRICH (*drunk, gets up, not letting go of the rope*). I won't let yuh. Won't
let no one. I'll get it myself. Said I'd get some straw—so I'll get it! Mikita,
that you? (*Laughs.*) Ah, dammit! Come for straw?

NIKITA. Gimme the rope.

MITRICH. No, just take it easy. The men sent me. I'll get it... (*Gets up on
his feet, begins to gather straw, but staggers, rights himself, and finally
falls.*) It's got the best o' me. Done me in...

NIKITA. Gimme them reins.

MITRICH. I said I won't. Ah, Mikishka, yuh got pig-shit for brains. (*Laughs.*) I like yuh, but yuh're dumb. Yuh're lookin' cuz I'm drunk. I don't care, yuh can go t'hell! Yuh think I need yuh... Look at me. I'm a noncom! Dummy, yuh can't even say: noncommissioned officer of Her Majesty's Own First Regiment of Grenadiers. Served tsar and country true-blue. But who'm I? Yuh think I'm a soldier? No, I ain't no soldier, I'm the last of all men, I'm an orphan, a stray. Swore off drinkin'. An' now I've hit the bottle again!... So, yuh think I'm 'fraid o' yuh? No way! Ain't 'fraid o' no one. Started drinkin', so I'm gonna drink! Now for 'bout two weeks I'll really hit it, gonna get totally blitzed. I'll drink my hat away, drink everythin' away but the cross roun' my neck; I'll hock my ID, an' I ain't 'fraid o' no one. They used t'flog me in the regiment so's I wouldn't drink. They lashed an' lashed... "So," they says, "yuh gonna?" "Yeah," I says. What's this shit, bein' afraid? That's how I am! I'm the way God made me. Swore off drinkin'. Didn't drink. Now I started—I'm gonna drink. An' I ain't 'fraid o' no one. Cuz I don't lie, just tell it like it is... What's this shit, bein' afraid? "There yuh go," I says, "that's how I am." A priest was tellin' me: "The Devil—now he's a braggart. Soon's yuh might begin braggin'," he says, "right away yuh get scared. An' soon's yuh got scared o' people, right away he, the hoof-footed son of a bitch, right away he's got yuh nabbed an' stuck where he wants." But since I ain't 'fraid o' people, it's easy for me. I spit in his face, the spade-bearded bastard, an' on him, the motherfucker. He won't do me nothin. There, I says, shove it!

NIKITA (*crosses himself*). What's with me, really? (*Throws down the rope.*)

MITRICH. What?

NIKITA (*gets up*). Yuh tellin' me not t'be 'fraid o' people, ain't yuh?

MITRICH. What's this shit, t'be afraid! Take a look at 'em in a bathhouse. They're all made from the same mold. One's got a bigger gut, the other's smaller, that's the whole difference in 'em. So there! Who's there t'be 'fraid of, cocksuckers!

SCENE 11

NIKITA, MITRICH, *and* MATRYONA (*coming from the yard*).

MATRYONA (*calls*). Well, are yuh comin'?
NIKITA. Oh! It's sure betta this way. Comin'. (*Walks toward the yard.*)

Curtain.

PART 2

Change of scene. The cottage of Act I is full of people, some sitting at tables, others standing. AKULINA *and the* GROOM *are in the front corner. Bread and icons are on the table. Among the guests are* MARINA, *her* HUSBAND *and the* POLICEMAN. *The women are singing;* ANISYA *is serving liquor. The singing ceases.*

SCENE 1

ANISYA, MARINA, MARINA'S HUSBAND, AKULINA, GROOM, COACHMAN, POLICEMAN, GROOM'S MOTHER, BEST MAN, MA-TRYONA, GUESTS, *and* PEOPLE.

COACHMAN. If we're gonna go, let's go, the church ain't that close.
BEST MAN. Just hold on, let the stepfather bless 'em. So where's he?
ANISYA. He's comin'. He's comin' now, dear friends. Have another drink, don't hurt our feelins.
GROOM'S MOTHER. What's takin' 'im so long? We've been waitin' forever.
ANISYA. He's comin'. Comin' right away. He'll be here 'fore yuh can bat an eye. Have a drink, dear friends. (*Offers them liquor.*) Comin' right away. In the meantime, sweethearts, sing some mo'.
COACHMAN. They've sung all their songs already while waitin'. (*The women sing. Enter* NIKITA *and* AKIM *in the middle of the song.*)

THE SAME, NIKITA, *and* AKIM.

NIKITA (*holds* AKIM *by the hand and pushes him in front of himself*). Go on, Pa, can't do it widout yuh.

AKIM. I don't like it, I mean, d'ya...

NIKITA (*to the women*). Nuff, be quiet. (*Looks around at everyone in the cottage.*) Marina, yuh here?

GROOM'S MOTHER. Go on, take the icon, an' bless 'em.

NIKITA. Wait, just hold on. (*Looks around.*) Akulina, yuh here?

GROOM'S MOTHER. Whacha callin' everyone for? Where else'd she be? He's kind o' weird...

ANISYA. Saints alive! What's he doin' barefoot!

NIKITA. Pa! Yuh here? Look at me. Christian people, yuh're all here, an' I'm here! Here I am! (*Falls down on his knees.*)

ANISYA. Mikitushka, what's with yuh? Oh, my achin' head!

GROOM'S MOTHER. Gee!

MATRYONA. That's what I'm sayin': he's had too much o' that French stuff, too much. Come t'yer senses, will yuh? (*They try to lift him, but he does not pay attention to anyone, and looks straight ahead.*)

NIKITA. Christian people! I'm in the wrong, an' I wanna confess.

MATRYONA (*pulls him by the shoulder*). What's with yuh, are yuh crazy? Dear friends, he's gone outta his mind. Gotta take 'im away.

NIKITA (*pushes her away with his shoulder*). Leave me alone! An' you, Pa, listen. First thing: Marinka, look here. (*Bows down to her feet and gets up.*) I've wronged yuh; promised t'marry yuh, had my way with yuh. I lied t'yuh, dumped yuh, forgive me, for God's sake! (*Bows down to her feet again.*)

ANISYA. Whacha runnin' off at the mouth for? It ain't at all becomin'. Nobody's askin yuh. Get up, whacha carryin' on for?

MATRYONA. O-oh, somethin's been done to 'im. What's happened? He's under a spell. Get up. Whacha blabbin' nonsense for! (*Pulls him.*)

NIKITA (*shakes his head*). Don't touch me! Forgive my sins 'gainst yuh, Marina. Forgive me, for God's sake. (MARINA *covers her face with her hands in silence.*)

ANISYA. Get up, I tell yuh, whacha carryin' on for! What a thing t'think of. Cut yer clownin'. For shame! Oh, my achin' head! What's this, he's gone completely nuts.

NIKITA (*pushes his wife away and turns to* AKULINA). Akulina, now I'm talkin' t'you. Listen, Christian people! I am a sinner. Akulina! I wronged yuh. Yer father didn't just die. He was poisoned.

ANISYA (*screams*). My achin' head! What's with 'im?

MATRYONA. The man's not 'imself. Take 'im away, will yuh! (PEOPLE *come up to him and try to seize him.*)

AKIM (*waves them off with his hands*). Stop! You guys, d'ya, just stop, I mean.

NIKITA. Akulina, I gave 'im the poison. Forgive me, for God's sake.

AKULINA (*jumps up*). He's lyin'! I know who did.

GROOM'S MOTHER. What's with yuh? You sit still.

AKIM. Oh, Lord! What a sin, what a sin.

POLICEMAN. Seize 'im! An' send for the elder an' witnesses. Gotta draw up an indictment. You get up, come here.

AKIM (*to the* POLICEMAN). Now you, I mean, d'ya, tin badge,[20] d'ya, I mean, just wait. Let 'im, d'ya, tell it, I mean.

POLICEMAN (*to* AKIM). Watch out, old man, don't butt in. I hafta draw up an indictment.

AKIM. Yuh're really somethin', d'ya. Wait, I tell yuh. Don't talk, I mean, 'bout, d'ya, no 'ditement. Here yuh got, d'ya, God's work goin' on... the man's confessin', I mean, an' you, d'ya, 'bout 'ditement...

POLICEMAN. Send for the elder!

AKIM. Let God's work be done, I mean, then, I mean, yuh can, d'ya, do yers too, I mean.

NIKITA. I've done another great sin 'gainst yuh, Akulina: I had my way with yuh, forgive me, for God's sake! (*Bows down to her feet.*)

AKULINA (*comes out from behind the table*). Lemme go, I ain't gettin' married. He told me to, but now I ain't gonna.

POLICEMAN [*to* NIKITA]. Repeat what yuh said.

NIKITA. Wait, Mr. Policeman, lemme finish.

AKIM (*with religious fervor*). Speak, my child, tell it all, yuh'll feel betta. Confess t'God, don't be 'fraid o' people. God, God! He is here!..

NIKITA. I poisoned the father, no good dog that I am, an' ruined the daughter. Had 'er in my power, ruined 'er, an' killed the baby.

AKULINA. That's true, it's true.

NIKITA. I smothered her baby in the cellar with a board. Sat on it... smothered it... an' its little bones crunched. (*Cries.*) An' I buried it in the ground. I did it, I alone!

AKULINA. He's lyin'. I told 'im to.

NIKITA. Don't you defend me. I ain't 'fraid o' nobody now. Forgive me, Christian people! (*Bows down to the ground. Silence.*)

POLICEMAN. Tie 'im up; looks like yer weddin's been upset. (PEOPLE *come up with their belts.*)

NIKITA. Wait, yuh'll have time... (*Bows down to his father's feet.*) My dear Pa, you also forgive me, a sinner! Yuh told me at the beginnin' when I started this whorin' nasty life, yuh told me: "If a claw gets stuck, the bird is lost." I didn't listen t'yer words, no good dog that I am, an' it turned out like yuh said. Forgive me, for God's sake.

AKIM (*with religious fervor*). God'll forgive yuh, my dear child. (*Hugs him.*) Yuh didn't spare yuhself, He'll spare yuh. God, God! He is here!..

SCENE 3

THE SAME *and the* ELDER.

ELDER (*enters*). There's plenty o' witnesses here.

POLICEMAN. We'll hold the inquest now. (*They tie* NIKITA *up.*)

AKULINA (*comes up and stands beside him*). I'll tell the truth. Question me also.

NIKITA (*tied up*). Ain't no need to. I did it all by myself, alone. It was my idea, it was my doin'. Take me you know where. I won't say nothin' mo'.

Curtain.

The Fruits of Enlightenment

A Comedy in Four Acts

Leonid Fyodorovich Zvezdintsev

a retired lieutenant of the horse guards and owner of sixty five thousand acres in various districts; a gentleman, around 60, spry, mild-mannered, and congenial; believes in spiritualism and likes to surprise people with his tales

Anna Pavlovna Zvezdintseva [Annette]*

his wife, a plump woman who tries to appear young, is preoccupied with social decorum, despises her husband, and blindly believes her doctor; an irritable woman

Betsy [Lizaveta Leonidovna]

their daughter, a society girl, around 20, undisciplined and manly in her manners, wears a pince-nez, a flirt and a giggler; speaks very rapidly and very precisely, compressing her lips like a foreigner

Vasily Leonidych [Vovó]

their son, 25, has a law degree but no specific occupation, member of a Cycling Club, Jockey Club, and a Club for Promoting Hounds; a robust young man with indomitable self-confidence; speaks loud and curtly; is either very serious, almost glum, or boisterously cheerful and laughs loudly

Professor Aleksey Vladimirovich Krugosvetlov

a scholar, around 50, with a calm, congenially self-satisfied disposition and equally deliberate, lilting speech; likes to talk; is benignly disdainful of those who do not agree with him; smokes a great deal; a lean, vibrant man

Doctor [Pyotr Petrovich]

around 40, a vigorous, stout, ruddy man; a loudmouth, rude and always grinning complacently

Marya Konstantinovna

a girl of 20, a graduate of the conservatory, a music teacher, wears a fringed band around her forehead, hyperfashionably dressed, servile and shy

---

*Although in the text of the play she is referred to as the mistress, we refer to her as she appears here in the dramatis personae.

Petrishchev

around 28, has a degree in philology and is seeking a position, a member of the same clubs as Vasily Leonidych as well as a Club for Arranging Informal Balls;[1] is bald, quick in movement and speech, and very polite

Baroness

a distinguished lady, around 50, lethargic, speaks in a monotone voice

Princess

a society lady, a guest

Young Princess

a society girl, makes faces, a guest

Countess

an aged lady with a wig and false teeth, moves with difficulty

Grossman [Anton Borisovich]

a swarthy Jewish type, very vibrant, nervous, speaks very loud

Fat Lady: Marya Vasilyevna Tolbukhina

a very distinguished, wealthy and good-natured lady, acquainted with all the important people, past and present; very fat, speaks rapidly, trying to outtalk the others; smokes

Baron Klingen (Kokó)

a graduate of Petersburg University, a Gentleman of the Emperor's Bedchamber, attached to the embassy; very correct and therefore composed and quietly cheerful

Lady

Gentleman

no speaking part

Sakhatov, Sergey Ivanovich [Ivanych]

around 50, a former deputy minister, an elegant gentleman with a broad European education, engaged in nothing and interested in everything; is proper and even somewhat rigid

Fyodor Ivanych

a valet, nearing 60; an educated man, likes education, overuses his pince-nez and handkerchief, which he unfolds slowly; follows politics; an intelligent and kind man

Grigory [Mikhailych]

a footman, around 28, handsome, dissolute, envious and audacious

Yakov [Ivanych]

a butler, around 40, restless, good-natured, cares only about his family
interests in the country

Semyon [Syomka, Syoma, Syomochka]

a butler's assistant, around 20; a robust, unspoiled country boy, fair-
haired, as yet beardless, calm and smiling

Coachman [Timofey]

around 35; a dashing man with a mustache but no beard, rude, and
determined

Former cook [Pavel Petrovich]

around 45, a disheveled, unshaven, swollen, sallow, and trembly man,
wearing a torn cotton summer overcoat, dirty trousers, and cutoff boots;
speaks in a hoarse voice with words breaking out of him as if through a
barrier

Lukerya**

around 30, the [servants'] cook, a talkative and dissatisfied woman

Doorman

a retired soldier

Tanya [Tatyana Markovna]

a maid, around 19, an energetic, strong, cheerful girl with quickly
changing moods; squeals with delight when really excited

First peasant [Yefim Antonych]

around 60, used to be the village elder, thinks he knows how to treat the
gentry, and likes to listen to himself

Second peasant [Zakhar Trifonych]

around 45, an efficient man, rude and truthful, does not like to talk too
much; Semyon's father

Third peasant [Mitry Vlasyevich Chilikin]

around 70, wears bast shoes, nervous, restless, anxious, and timid, tries to
hide his timidity by talking

First footman of the countess

an old man of the old stamp with a footman's pride

**In the original text she is listed in the dramatis personae as the cook. We learn her
name (Lukerya) later on in the play (II, 3). That name will be utilized for this
character.

Second footman
  huge, robust, and rude
Delivery man from a store
  wears a dark blue jacket, has a fresh, rosy face; speaks firmly, effectively, and clearly

The action takes place in the capital, in the Zvezdintsevs' home.

ACT I

The set depicts the hall of a wealthy home in Moscow. There are three doors: an outside one, another to LEONID FYODOROVICH's *study, and a third to* VASILY LEONIDYCH's *room. A staircase goes up to the interior rooms; behind it is a passageway to the pantry.*

SCENE 1

GRIGORY, *a young, handsome servant, is looking at himself in the mirror and preening.*

GRIGORY. I'm real sorry 'bout the mustache. A mustache, she says, won't do for a servant! An' why not? So's everyone can see yuh're a servant. Then I might just outshine her darlin' sonny boy. An' who's he anyway! Even widout my mustache, he's got a long way t'go... (*Stares at himself with a smile.*) There's a bunch of 'em runnin' after me! Only I don't like none of 'em as much as that Tanya! She's just a maid! Yeah! But she's betta than any young miss. (*Smiles.*) She's so nice! (*Listens.*) An' here she comes! (*Smiles.*) Look how she taps her little heels... Wow!..

SCENE 2

GRIGORY *and* TANYA (*with a fur coat and boots*).

GRIGORY. My compliments, Tatyana Markovna!
TANYA. What, still lookin' in the mirror? Think yuh're so fine, don't yuh?
GRIGORY. What, I'm that bad-lookin'?
TANYA. Well, yuh're not bad-lookin' an' not good, but somewhere in the middle halfway. Why d'ya have those coats hangin' there?
GRIGORY. I'll take 'em away right now, ma'am. (*Takes off a fur coat, covers* TANYA *with it, and hugs her.*) Tanya, got somethin' t'tell yuh...
TANYA. Cut it out! What's that all about! (*Tears herself away angrily.*) I'm tellin' yuh, lemme go!

GRIGORY (*looks around*). Gimme a kiss.

TANYA. Why're yuh botherin' me, really? I'll give yuh a kiss aw right!.. (*Raises her hand.*)

VASILY LEONIDYCH. (*A bell is heard behind the scene and then a shout.*) Grigory!

TANYA. There, get goin', Vasily Leonidych's callin'.

GRIGORY. He'll wait, he's just opened his peepers. Listen, why don't yuh love me?

TANYA. What kind of love is it you're thinkin' of! I don't love anyone.

GRIGORY. That's not true, yuh love Syomka. Yuh really found someone there, a clod, butler's assistant!

TANYA. He's what he is, an' yuh're jealous of 'im.

VASILY LEONIDYCH (*behind the scene*). Grigory!

GRIGORY. Yuh have time!... Jealous o' what? Yuh've just started out in the world, an' who'd yuh tie yuhself up with? It'd be different if yuh loved me... Tanya...

TANYA (*angrily and sternly*). I'm tellin' you, you'll get nowhere.

VASILY LEONIDYCH (*behind the scene*). Grigory!!!

GRIGORY. Yuh're way too hard.

VASILY LEONIDYCH (*behind the scene, shouts persistently, regularly and with all his might*). Grigory! Grigory! Grigory! (TANYA *and* GRIGORY *laugh.*)

GRIGORY. Yuh should only know the girls that loved me! (*The bell rings.*)

TANYA. So go to them, and leave me alone.

GRIGORY. I can see yuh're a fool. I'm not Semyon, yuh know.

TANYA. Semyon wants t'marry me, not some monkey business.

SCENE 3

GRIGORY, TANYA, *and the* DELIVERY MAN (*carries a big cardboard box with a dress*).

DELIVERY MAN. Good mornin'!

GRIGORY. Hello! Who from?

DELIVERY MAN. From Burdey's,[2] with a dress, an' here's a note for Madam.

TANYA (*takes the note*). Wait here, I'll deliver it. (*Exits.*)

SCENE 4

GRIGORY, DELIVERY MAN, *and* VASILY LEONIDYCH (*steps out of the door in his shirt and slippers*).

VASILY LEONIDYCH. Grigory!

GRIGORY. Right away!

VASILY LEONIDYCH. Grigory! Don't you hear me?

GRIGORY. I've only just come.

VASILY LEONIDYCH. Some warm water and tea.

GRIGORY. Semyon'll bring 'em at once.

VASILY LEONIDYCH. What's this? From Bourdier's?

DELIVERY MAN. Yes, sir. (VASILY LEONIDYCH *and* GRIGORY *exit. The bell rings.*)

SCENE 5

DELIVERY MAN *and* TANYA (*runs in at the sound of the bell and opens the door*).

TANYA (*to the* DELIVERY MAN). Just wait.

DELIVERY MAN. I'm doin' that already.

SCENE 6

DELIVERY MAN, TANYA, *and* SAKHATOV (*enters through the door*).

TANYA. I'm sorry, the servant just stepped out. Come in, please. Allow me! (*Helps him take off his coat.*)

SAKHATOV (*straightening himself out*). Is Leonid Fyodorovich at home? Is he up and about? (*The bell rings.*)

TANYA. Why certainly, for quite some time now!

SCENE 7

DELIVERY MAN, TANYA, *and* SAKHATOV. *Enter the* DOCTOR.

DOCTOR (*looks for the servant; sees* SAKHATOV *and addresses him casually*). Oh? My regards!

SAKHATOV (*stares at him*). The doctor, I presume?

DOCTOR. I thought you were abroad. Come to see Leonid Fyodorovich?

SAKHATOV. Yes. What about you? Is anyone sick?

DOCTOR (*laughing softly*). Not exactly sick, but, you know, there's always something with these ladies! She's up every night till three playing whist, and tries to look like an hourglass. But the lady is flaccid, fat, and kind of up in years.

SAKHATOV. Is that how you express your diagnosis to Anna Pavlovna? She is not pleased, I suspect.

DOCTOR (*laughing*). Well, you're right. They pull all these stunts, and then they have indigestion, pressure on the liver, a case of nerves, and what not—and go patch her up. Always something with them! (*Laughs softly.*) And what about you? Aren't you also a spiritualist?

SAKHATOV. I? No, I'm not also a spiritualist... Well, my regards! (*Wants to leave but the* DOCTOR *stops him.*)

DOCTOR. No, I don't reject it entirely either, when a man such as Krugosvetlov takes part in it. How can I! He's a professor, a European celebrity. There has to be something to it. I would like to see for myself someday, but I never have the time. I have other things to do.

SAKHATOV. Yes, yes. My regards! (*Exits with a slight bow.*)

DOCTOR (*to* TANYA). Is she up and about?

TANYA. She's in her bedroom. Come up, please. (SAKHATOV *and the* DOCTOR *exit in different directions.*)

SCENE 8

DELIVERY MAN, TANYA, *and* FYODOR IVANYCH (*enters with a newspaper in his hand*).

FYODOR IVANYCH (*to the* DELIVERY MAN). What are you doing here?

DELIVERY MAN. I'm from Burdey's, brought a dress and a note. They told me t'wait.

FYODOR IVANYCH. Oh, from Burdey's! (*To* TANYA.) Who came in?

TANYA. It was Sergey Ivanych Sakhatov, and the doctor. They stood here awhile talking. All about spiritchism.

FYODOR IVANYCH (*correcting her*). Spiritualism.

TANYA. That's what I said, spiritchism. Did you hear how well it went last time, Fyodor Ivanych? (*Laughs.*) There were knocks and things were flyin' around.

FYODOR IVANYCH. And how do you know?

TANYA. Lizaveta Leonidovna told me.

SCENE 9

TANYA, FYODOR IVANYCH, DELIVERY MAN, *and* YAKOV, *the butler* (*runs in with a glass of tea*).

YAKOV (*to the* DELIVERY MAN). Hello!

DELIVERY MAN (*despondently*). Hello. (YAKOV *knocks on* VASILY LEONIDYCH*'s door.*)

SCENE 10

THE SAME *and* GRIGORY.

GRIGORY. Gimme.

YAKOV. Yuh still haven't brought back yesterday's glasses, an' the tray Vasily Leonidych had. An' they'll hold me responsible.

GRIGORY. The tray's bein' used, his cigars are on it.

YAKOV. So put 'em someplace else. It's me that's responsible.

GRIGORY. I'll bring it back, I'll bring it back!

YAKOV. Yuh say yuh'll bring it back, but it ain't back. T'other day we needed it, an' there's nothin' t'serve on.

GRIGORY. I'll bring it back, I tell yuh. What a fuss!

YAKOV. It's aw right for you t'talk that way, but here I'm servin' tea for the third time an' still gotta get breakfast ready. All livelong day yuh rush aroun' an' rush aroun'. Is there anyone in the house who's got mo' t'do than me? An' still I'm no good!

GRIGORY. What betta can there be? That's how good yuh are!

TANYA. Nobody's good enough for you, only you yourself...

GRIGORY (*to* TANYA). No one asked yuh! (*Exits.*)

SCENE 11

TANYA, YAKOV, FYODOR IVANYCH, *and the* DELIVERY MAN.

YAKOV. Well, I ain't bothered. Tatyana Markovna, did the Mistress say somethin' 'bout yesterday?

TANYA. Yuh mean 'bout the lamp?

YAKOV. God knows how it fell outta my hands! Just as I began wipin' it an' was gonna switch hands—out it slipped somehow...an' it's all in pieces! Just my bad luck! It's aw right for that Grigory Mikhailych t'talk, he's single. But what if yuh're a family man? Yuh gotta think 'bout things an' provide. I don't mind workin' hard. So she didn't say nothin'? Well, thank God! Say, how many tea spoons d'ya have, Fyodor Ivanych, one or two?

FYODOR IVANYCH. One, just one. (*Reads the newspaper.* YAKOV *exits.*)

SCENE 12

TANYA, FYODOR IVANYCH, *and the* DELIVERY MAN. *The bell rings. Enter* GRIGORY *with a tray and the* DOORMAN.

DOORMAN (*to* GRIGORY). Inform the master, peasants from the village are here.

GRIGORY (*pointing to* FYODOR IVANYCH). Inform the steward here, I don't have time. (*Exits.*)

SCENE 13

TANYA, FYODOR IVANYCH, DOORMAN, *and* DELIVERY MAN.

TANYA. Where're the peasants from?

DOORMAN. From the Kursk District, I guess.

TANYA (*squeals*). It's them... It's Semyon's father, about the land. I'll go meet them. (*Runs off.*)

SCENE 14

FYODOR IVANYCH, DOORMAN, *and* DELIVERY MAN.

DOORMAN. So what d'ya say: should I let 'em in here, or what? They say it's 'bout the land, the master knows.

FYODOR IVANYCH. Yes, about the purchase of land. Right, right. He's with a visitor now. Here's what you do: tell them to wait.

DOORMAN. T'wait where?

FYODOR IVANYCH. Let them wait outside, I'll send for them afterward. (*Exit* DOORMAN.)

SCENE 15

FYODOR IVANYCH, TANYA *followed by three* PEASANTS, GRIGORY, *and the* DELIVERY MAN.

TANYA. To the right. Over here, over here!

FYODOR IVANYCH. I didn't want them let in here.

GRIGORY. There, yuh busybody.

TANYA. It'll be all right, Fyodor Ivanych, they'll be here on the side.

FYODOR IVANYCH. They'll bring dirt in.

TANYA. They've wiped their feet off, an' I'll clean up after 'em also. (*To the* PEASANTS.) Just stay here. (*The* PEASANTS *enter carrying presents wrapped in handkerchiefs: Easter cake, eggs, towels. They look around for an icon before which to cross themselves. They cross themselves at the stair-case, bow to* FYODOR IVANYCH, *and stand still.*)

GRIGORY (*to* FYODOR IVANYCH). Fyodor Ivanych! Now they say gaiters from Pironey's[3] are pretty stylish, but what's betta than that one's? (*Points to the* THIRD PEASANT, *wearing bast shoes.*)

FYODOR IVANYCH. You always have to make fun of people! (*Exit* GRI-GORY.)

SCENE 16

TANYA, FYODOR IVANYCH, *and three* PEASANTS.

FYODOR IVANYCH (*rises and goes up to the* PEASANTS). So you're the ones from the Kursk District, about the purchase of land?

FIRST PEASANT. Yes, sir. Turns out, fr'instance, we're 'bout completin' the sale o' the land. How 'bout gettin' us announced?

FYODOR IVANYCH. Yes, yes, I know, I know. Wait here, I'll inform him immediately. (*Exits.*)

SCENE 17

TANYA *and the three* PEASANTS. VASILY LEONIDYCH *behind the scene. The peasants look around, do not know where to put their presents.*

FIRST PEASANT. Whacha, I mean, that, don't know whacha call it, put 'em on? Somethin' t'make the things look nice. A dish, maybe?

TANYA. Right away, right away. Give 'em to me; this'll do for the time bein'. (*Puts the presents on a small sofa.*)

FIRST PEASANT. That worthy who came up t'us, what's his callin', fr'instance?

TANYA. That's the valett.

FIRST PEASANT. Clear nuff, the volett. I mean, he's also servin'. (*To* TANYA.) Would you also be in service, fr'instance?

TANYA. I'm a maid, yuh know, I'm also from Demenka.[4] I know you, an' you, but I don't know that ol'timer. (*Points to the* THIRD PEASANT.)

THIRD PEASANT. Them yuh know, but me yuh don't know?

TANYA. Yuh're Yefim Antonych?

FIRST PEASANT. 'Solutely.

TANYA. An' yuh're Semyon's dad, Zakhar Trifonych?

SECOND PEASANT. Correct!

THIRD PEASANT. An' I'm, lemme tell yuh, Mitry Chilikin. D'ya know me now?

TANYA. Now I'll know you too.

SECOND PEASANT. An' who may you be?

TANYA. I'm the orphan girl o' the late Aksinya, the soldier's wife.

FIRST AND THIRD PEASANTS (*surprised*). Really?!

SECOND PEASANT. No wonder they say: Put a piglet out in rye, it'll get sleek by and by.

FIRST PEASANT. 'Solutely . Looks like a young lady.

THIRD PEASANT. That's really so. Oh, Lord!

VASILY LEONIDYCH (*behind the scene: rings, and then shouts*). Grigory! Grigory!

FIRST PEASANT. Now who's that in a fret, fr'instance?

TANYA. That's the young master.

THIRD PEASANT. Oh, Lord! I said we'd be betta off waitin' outside in the meanwhile. (*Silence.*)

SECOND PEASANT. Is it you Semyon wants t'marry?

TANYA. Why, has he been writin'? (*Covers her face with her apron.*)

SECOND PEASANT. It's plain he has. Only he's not doin' the right thing. I can see the kid's gotten spoilt.

TANYA (*excitedly*). No, he ain't gotten spoilt at all. Should I send 'im t'yuh?

SECOND PEASANT. No point to. You just wait. We'll have time!

VASILY LEONIDYCH (*behind the scene: cries out in despair*). Grigory! Damn you!

SCENE 18

THE SAME. VASILY LEONIDYCH *at the door in a shirt, putting on his pince-nez.*

VASILY LEONIDYCH. Are you all dead?

TANYA. He's not here, Vasily Leonidych... I'll send him right away. (*Moves toward the door.*)

VASILY LEONIDYCH. Well I hear someone talking. What are these scarecrows doing here? Huh?

TANYA. They're peasants from our Kursk village, Vasily Leonidych.

VASILY LEONIDYCH (*to the* DELIVERY MAN). And who's this? Ah, yes, from Bourdier's! (*The* PEASANTS *bow.* VASILY LEONIDYCH *pays no attention to them,* GRIGORY *meets* TANYA *at the door.* TANYA *remains.*)

SCENE 19

THE SAME *and* GRIGORY.

VASILY LEONIDYCH. I told you—the other shoes. I can't wear these!

GRIGORY. Well the others are there too.

VASILY LEONIDYCH. But where's there?

GRIGORY. In the same place.

VASILY LEONIDYCH. Bull!

GRIGORY. Well, you'll see for yuhself. (VASILY LEONIDYCH *and* GRIGORY *exit.*)

SCENE 20

TANYA, *the three* PEASANTS, *and the* DELIVERY MAN.

THIRD PEASANT. Say, maybe now ain't the right time, an' we should go t'our lodgins an' wait meanwhile.

TANYA. No, it's all right, just wait. I'll go bring you plates for the presents. (*Exits.*)

SCENE 21

THE SAME, SAKHATOV, *and* LEONID FYODOROVICH *followed by* FYODOR IVANYCH. *The* PEASANTS *take their presents and strike a pose.*

LEONID FYODOROVICH (*to the* PEASANTS). In a minute, in a minute, just wait. (*To the* DELIVERY MAN.) Who's this?

DELIVERY MAN. I'm for Burdey's.

LEONID FYODOROVICH. Ah, from Bourdier's!

SAKHATOV (*smiling*). Well, I'm not denying it; but you will agree that without seeing all of which you speak, it's difficult for us, the uninitiated, to believe.

LEONID FYODOROVICH. You say: "I can't believe." But we don't require belief. We require investigation. I cannot help believing in this ring, you know. For I received this ring from there.

SAKHATOV. What do you mean *from there*? From where?

LEONID FYODOROVICH. From the other world. Yes.

SAKHATOV (*smiling*). Very interesting, very interesting!

LEONID FYODOROVICH. Well, let's assume you think I'm a person who's easily carried away and imagines things that don't exist, but what about Aleksey Vladimirovich Krugosvetlov, he's certainly not just anyone, but a professor, and he also acknowledges it. And he's not the only one. What about Crookes?[5] What about Wallace?[6]

SAKHATOV. Well, I'm not denying it, you know. All I'm saying is that it's very interesting. It would be interesting to know, how does Krugosvetlov explain it?

LEONID FYODOROVICH. He has his own theory! Then come this evening; he'll be here for sure. First we'll have Grossman... you know, the famous mind reader.

SAKHATOV. Yes, I have heard of him, but never happened to see him.

LEONID FYODOROVICH. So do come. First Grossman, and then

Kapchich and our mediumistic seance... (*To* FYODOR IVANYCH.) Hasn't the messenger returned from Kapchich?

FYODOR IVANYCH. Not yet.

SAKHATOV. So how am I to know?

LEONID FYODOROVICH. You just come, come anyway. If Kapchich can't come, we'll find our own medium. Marya Ignatyevna is a medium; not as good as Kapchich, but still...

SCENE 22

THE SAME *and* TANYA (*enters with the plates for the presents; listens to the conversation*).

SAKHATOV (*smiling*). Yes, yes. But there is one thing: why are mediums always from the so-called educated circle? Both Kapchich and Marya Ignatyevna are. If it's a special power, it should be found everywhere, among the people, among the peasants.

LEONID FYODOROVICH. And so it is. It happens quite often that we have a peasant in the house who turns out to be a medium. The other day we called him in during a seance. A sofa had to be moved—and we forgot all about him. He had apparently fallen asleep. And just imagine, our seance was over, Kapchich came to, and suddenly we notice in another part of the room, near the peasant, mediumistic phenomena begin to happen: the table moved and kept going.

TANYA (*aside*). That was when I was crawling out from under the table.

LEONID FYODOROVICH. Evidently, he's also a medium. Especially since he looks a lot like Home.[7] Do you remember Home? He's fair-haired, naive.

SAKHATOV (*shrugging his shoulders*). Is that so. It's very interesting! Then you should try him.

LEONID FYODOROVICH. We certainly will. And he's not the only one. There are no end to mediums. We just don't know them. Why only the other day a sick old woman moved a stone wall.

SAKHATOV. Moved a stone wall?

LEONID FYODOROVICH. Yes, yes, she was lying in bed and had no idea that she was a medium. She leaned her arm against the wall, and the wall moved.

SAKHATOV. And it didn't fall down?

LEONID FYODOROVICH. And it didn't fall down.

SAKHATOV. Strange! Well then, I'll come this evening.

LEONID FYODOROVICH. Come, do come! We'll have a seance in any event. (SAKHATOV *puts on his overcoat.* LEONID FYODOROVICH *sees him off.*)

SCENE 23

THE SAME *without* SAKHATOV.

DELIVERY MAN (*to* TANYA). Would yuh please inform the mistress! Do I have t'spend the whole night here?

TANYA. Just wait. She's goin' t'go out with the young lady, so she'll be out herself soon. (*Exits.*)

SCENE 24

THE SAME *without* TANYA.

LEONID FYODOROVICH (*goes up to the* PEASANTS; *they bow and offer him their presents*). That's not necessary!

FIRST PEASANT (*smiling*). Turns out, that's our first duty. That's what the village preposed t'us.

SECOND PEASANT. That's the way it's done.

THIRD PEASANT. Don't mention it! Cuz we're satisfied a lot... Just like our fathers, let's say, served yer fathers, let's say, we also wish with all our hearts, as is proper... (*Bows.*)

LEONID FYODOROVICH. Well, what is it? What is it you want specifically?

FIRST PEASANT. I mean, we've come t'Yer Lordship.

SCENE 25

THE SAME *and* PETRISHCHEV (*runs in quickly, wearing his overcoat*).

PETRISHCHEV. Is Vasily Leonidych awake? (*Seeing* LEONID FYODOROVICH, *he nods to him.*)

LEONID FYODOROVICH. You've come to see my son?

PETRISHCHEV. I? Yes, to see Vovó for a moment.

LEONID FYODOROVICH. Go on, go on. (PETRISHCHEV *takes off his overcoat and quickly exits.*)

SCENE 26

THE SAME *without* PETRISHCHEV.

LEONID FYODOROVICH (*to the* PEASANTS). Well. So, what do you want?

SECOND PEASANT. Accept the presents.

FIRST PEASANT (*smiling*). I mean, the village's offerins.

THIRD PEASANT. Don't mention it—no matter! We wish yuh like t'our own father. Don't mention it.

LEONID FYODOROVICH. Very well... Fyodor, take them.

FYODOR IVANYCH. Okay, give them here. (*Takes the presents.*)

LEONID FYODOROVICH. So what's this all about?

FIRST PEASANT. We've come t'Yer Lordship.

LEONID FYODOROVICH. I can see that; so what do you want?

FIRST PEASANT. T'make a move 'bout completin' the sale o' the land. Turns out...

LEONID FYODOROVICH. So, you're buying land, is that it?

FIRST PEASANT. 'Solutely, that's it. Turns out... I mean, 'bout the purchase o' ownership o' the land. So the village, fr'instance, inpowered us t'go on up, I mean, as is proper, through the state bank,[8] by enclosin' a note with the legalized date.

LEONID FYODOROVICH. In other words, you want to buy land through the mediation of the bank—is that it?

FIRST PEASANT. That's it. Just like yuh made the preposal t'us last year.

Turns out, I mean, the whole amount in full is 32,864 roubles for the purchase o' ownership o' the land.

LEONID FYODOROVICH. That's right, but what about my money?

FIRST PEASANT. As for yer money, the village preposes, just as was said last year, so as t'pay installments, I mean, in reception o' cash, by the laws o' regulations, four thousand roubles in full.

SECOND PEASANT. Take four thousand cash now, I mean, an' the rest yuh're t'wait for.

THIRD PEASANT (*while he unwraps the money*). Don't yuh worry, we'll sooner hock ourselves so's not t'fail yuh, let's say, somehow, so that, let's say, I mean, like it should be.

LEONID FYODOROVICH. But I wrote you that I would agree only if you could raise the full amount.

FIRST PEASANT. 'Solutely, that would be mo' nice, but it's not in our possibilities, I mean.

LEONID FYODOROVICH. So what's there to do?

FIRST PEASANT. The village, fr'instance, was in hope that the preposal yuh made last year 'bout postponin' payment...

LEONID FYODOROVICH. That was last year. I agreed then, but now I can't...

SECOND PEASANT. But how come? Yuh gave us hope, so we got the paper ready, an' collected the money.

THIRD PEASANT. Have mercy, Master. We've so little land there's no room, so t'say, t'even let a chicken out, t'say nothin' 'bout livestock. Don't wrong us, Master. (*Bows.*)

LEONID FYODOROVICH. That's of course true, last year I agreed to postpone payment, but a certain circumstance has arisen... So that now it's inconvenient for me.

SECOND PEASANT. Widout this land our life's as good as finished.

FIRST PEASANT. 'Solutely, widout this land our livin's gotta weaken an' turn into decline.

THIRD PEASANT (*bows*). Master! We've so little land there's no room, so t'say, t'even let a chicken out, t'say nothin' 'bout livestock. Master! Have mercy. Take the cash, Master.

LEONID FYODOROVICH (*while looking over the paper*). I understand, I myself would like to do you a favor. Just wait. I'll give you my answer in half an hour. Fyodor, see that I'm not disturbed.

FYODOR IVANYCH. Very good. (LEONID FYODOROVICH *exits.*)

SCENE 27

THE SAME *without* LEONID FYODOROVICH. *The* PEASANTS *are dejected.*

SECOND PEASANT. How d'ya like this business! "Give it all," he says. An' where're we gonna get it from?

FIRST PEASANT. If he just didn't give us hope last year. As it is we were, 'solutely, in hope it'd be like was said last year.

THIRD PEASANT. Oh, Lord! I even begun t'unwrap the money. (*Wraps up the money.*) What're we gonna do now?

FYODOR IVANYCH. What's your business about?

FIRST PEASANT. Our business, sir, depends, fr'instance, on just this: Last year he preposed t'us t'pay installments. The village took him up on it an' inpowered us; an' comes now, fr'instance, he preposes so's the whole amount in full. The way things are, we can't no way.

FYODOR IVANYCH. How much do you have?

FIRST PEASANT. The whole amount in readiness is four thousand roubles, I mean.

FYODOR IVANYCH. Well, so what? Make an effort, collect more.

FIRST PEASANT. As is collectin' was tough. There ain't no muscle as far as that goes, sir.

SECOND PEASANT. If it ain't there, yuh can't dig it up.

THIRD PEASANT. We'd wish with all our hearts, but, so t'say, we cleaned 'em all out.

SCENE 28

THE SAME, VASILY LEONIDYCH, *and* PETRISHCHEV (*in the doorway, both smoking cigarettes*).

VASILY LEONIDYCH. But I already said, I'll try. I'll do my level best. Huh?

PETRISHCHEV. Understand now, if you don't come up with it, it'll get real nasty!

VASILY LEONIDYCH. But I already said—I'll try and I will. Huh?

PETRISHCHEV. Okay. I'm only saying be sure to come up with it. I'll wait. (*Exits, locking the door.*)

SCENE 29

THE SAME *without* PETRISHCHEV.

VASILY LEONIDYCH (*waving his arm*). What the hell's going on. (*The* PEASANTS *bow.*)

VASILY LEONIDYCH (*looks at the* DELIVERY MAN; *to* FYODOR IVANYCH.) Why don't you send this guy from Bourdier's away? It's as though he's moved in with us. Look, he's fallen asleep. Huh?

FYODOR IVANYCH. Well, his note has been delivered, and he has been told to wait till Anna Pavlovna comes out.

VASILY LEONIDYCH (*looks at the* PEASANTS *and stares at the money*). And what's this? Money? For whom? Is it for us? (*To* FYODOR IVANYCH). Who're they?

FYODOR IVANYCH. Peasants from the Kursk district, they're buying land.

VASILY LEONIDYCH. So has it been sold?

FYODOR IVANYCH. No, they haven't come to terms yet. They're being stingy.

VASILY LEONIDYCH. Huh? We must persuade them. (*To the* PEASANTS.) So you are buying, huh?

FIRST PEASANT. 'Solutely, we prepose so's t'acquire ownership o' the possession o' the land.

VASILY LEONIDYCH. Don't be stingy now. You know, do I have to tell you how a peasant needs land! Huh? Really needs it.

FIRST PEASANT. 'Solutely, land's undubiteable the main thing for a peasant. That's true.

VASILY LEONIDYCH. Then don't be so stingy. Know what land is? I'll tell you, you can plant rows of wheat on it. You can get twelve hundred bushels; at a quarter of a rouble per bushel, that's three hundred roubles. Huh?... And then there's mint, and you can get more than three hundred roubles per acre, I tell you!

FIRST PEASANT. 'Solutely, that's true, all perducts can be put into action if yuh have understandin'.

VASILY LEONIDYCH. It has to be mint then. I studied this, you know. It's printed in books. I'll show you. Huh?

FIRST PEASANT. 'Solutely, what that concerns is clearer t'yuh through books. That's learnin', I mean.

VASILY LEONIDYCH. So buy it, don't be stingy and hand over the money. (*To* FYODOR IVANYCH.) Where's Papá?

FYODOR IVANYCH. He's here. He asked not to be disturbed now.

VASILY LEONIDYCH. Well, he's probably asking a spirit whether to sell the land or not? Huh?

FYODOR IVANYCH. I can't say. I only know he went off undecided.

VASILY LEONIDYCH. What do you think, Fyodor Ivanych, does he have any money? Huh?

FYODOR IVANYCH. I really don't know. Doubt it. What's it for? Just last week you got a tidy little sum.

VASILY LEONIDYCH. Well I spent that on dogs. And now, you know, there's our new club, Petrishchev has been elected, and I borrowed money from Petrishchev and now have to pay dues for him and for myself. Huh?

FYODOR IVANYCH. What's this new club of yours? Of cyclists?

VASILY LEONIDYCH. No, let me tell you: it's a new club. It's a very serious club, I tell you. And do you know who the president is? Huh?

FYODOR IVANYCH. So what's this new club about?

VASILY LEONIDYCH. It's a Club for Promoting the Breeding of Old Russian Thick-Coated Hounds. Huh? And let me also tell you: today is the first meeting and a luncheon. And I have no money! I'll go to him and give it a try. (*Exits through the door.*)

SCENE 30

The PEASANTS, FYODOR IVANYCH, *and the* DELIVERY MAN.

FIRST PEASANT (*to* FYODOR IVANYCH). And who would that be, sir?

FYODOR IVANYCH (*smiling*). The young master.

THIRD PEASANT. The heir, so t'say. Oh, Lord! (*Tucks away the money.*) Seems I should put it away meanwhile.

FIRST PEASANT. And we were told he's in the military, serves in the cavalry, fr'instance.

FYODOR IVANYCH. No, as an only son he's exempt from military service.

THIRD PEASANT. Left t'sepport his parents, so t'say. That's right.

SECOND PEASANT (*shaking his head*). This one'll give some sepport.

THIRD PEASANT. Oh, Lord!

SCENE 31

FYODOR IVANYCH, *the three* PEASANTS, *and* VASILY LEONIDYCH *followed in the doorway by* LEONID FYODOROVICH.

VASILY LEONIDYCH. It's always that way. It's really amazing. First I'm asked why I don't do anything, and now when I've found something to do and I am busy—there's this serious club with noble aims—I can't even have a measly three hundred roubles!...

LEONID FYODOROVICH. I said I can't, so I can't. I don't have it.

VASILY LEONIDYCH. But you've just sold land.

LEONID FYODOROVICH. In the first place, I haven't sold it, and above all—leave me in peace. Look, you were told I don't have time now. (*Slams the door.*)

SCENE 32

THE SAME *without* LEONID FYODOROVICH.

FYODOR IVANYCH. I told you it's the wrong time now.

VASILY LEONIDYCH. I tell you, isn't this a real fix, huh? I'll go to Mamá, that's my only hope. He's going mad with his spiritualism and forgets everyone. (*Goes upstairs.* FYODOR IVANYCH *sits down and is about to read his newspaper.*)

SCENE 33

THE SAME. BETSY *and* MARYA KONSTANTINOVNA *come downstairs, followed by* GRIGORY.

BETSY. Is the carriage ready?

GRIGORY. It's comin'.

BETSY (*to* MARYA KONSTANTINOVNA). Let's go, let's go! I saw, it is he.

MARYA KONSTANTINOVNA. Who's he?

BETSY. You know very well it's Petrishchev.

MARYA KONSTANTINOVNA. So where is he?

BETSY. He's with Vovó. You'll see.

MARYA KONSTANTINOVNA. What if it's not him? (*The* PEASANTS *and the* DELIVERY MAN *bow.*)

BETSY (*to the* DELIVERY MAN). Ah, you're from Bourdier's, with the dress?

DELIVERY MAN. Yes, ma'am. Please lemme go.

BETSY. Well I don't know. That's up to Mamá.

DELIVERY MAN. I don't know who it's for. I was told t'bring it and collect the money.

BETSY. So just wait.

MARYA KONSTANTINOVNA. It's still about the outfit for the charade?

BETSY. Yes, a charming outfit. But Mamá won't take it and doesn't want to pay for it.

MARYA KONSTANTINOVNA. Why not?

BETSY. Go ask Mamá. For Vovó's dogs it's not too much to pay five hundred roubles, but a dress for a hundred is too much. And I can't act looking like a scarecrow! (*Pointing at the* PEASANTS.) And who are these people?

GRIGORY. Peasants, they're buyin' some piece o' land or other.

BETSY. I thought they were the beaters. You aren't the beaters?

FIRST PEASANT. No, not at all, ma'am. We've come t'Leonid Fyodorovich 'bout completin' the sale o' the deed t'the land.

BETSY. How come, beaters should have come to Vovó? Are you sure you're not the beaters? (*The* PEASANTS *are silent.*) How dumb they are! (*Goes up to the door.*) Vovó! (*Laughs.*)

MARYA KONSTANTINOVNA. But we just now met him.

BETSY. Why do you want to remember!... Vovó, are you there?

SCENE 34

THE SAME *and* PETRISHCHEV.

PETRISHCHEV. Vovó isn't here, but I'm ready to do for him whatever needs to be done. How do you do! How do you do, Marya Konstantinovna! (*Gives* BETSY *and then* MARYA KONSTANTINOVNA *a long and firm handshake.*)

SECOND PEASANT. Look, it's like he's pumpin' water.

BETSY. You can't take his place, still you're better than nothing. (*Laughs.*) What kind of business do you have with Vovó?

PETRISHCHEV. Business? Fi-nancial business, that is, our business is fie! And it's also nancial, besides being financial.

BETSY. What does nancial mean?

PETRISHCHEV. That's a good question! And that's just the point, it doesn't mean anything!

BETSY. Now that was a loser, a real loser! (*Laughs.*)

PETRISHCHEV. Well, it's impossible to win every time, you know. It's like a lottery. You play and you play, and at last you hit. (FYODOR IVANYCH *goes into* LEONID FYODOROVICH's *study.*)

SCENE 35

THE SAME *without* FYODOR IVANYCH.

BETSY. Well, that one was a loser; but tell me, were you at the Mergasovs' yesterday?

PETRISHCHEV. Not so much at *mère* Gasov's as at *père* Gasov's, and not even at *père* Gasov's but at *fils* Gasov's.

BETSY. Can't you get along without a *jeu de mots*? That's a disease. Were there Gypsies too? (*Laughs.*)

PETRISHCHEV (*sings*). On their aprons roosters red, golden combs upon their head!...

BETSY. Lucky you! We were bored at Fofó's.

PETRISHCHEV (*continues to sing*). And she swore and did say—she'd come to me ... What's next? Marya Konstantinovna, what's next?

MARYA KONSTANTINOVNA. To me for a day...

PETRISHCHEV. What? What is it, Marya Konstantinovna? (*Laughs.*)

BETSY. *Cessez, vous devenez impossible!*

PETRISHCHEV. *J'ai cessé, j'ai bébé, j'ai dédé...*

BETSY. I see the only way to be spared from your witticisms is to make you sing. Let's go to Vovó's room, he has a guitar there. Let's go, Marya Konstantinovna, let's go! (BETSY, MARYA KONSTANTINOVNA, *and* PETRISHCHEV *exit to* VASILY LEONIDYCH's *room.*)

SCENE 36

GRIGORY, *the three* PEASANTS, *and the* DELIVERY MAN.

FIRST PEASANT. Who they be?

GRIGORY. One's the young mistress, an' the other's the mamzel that teaches music.

FIRST PEASANT. Means, she makes studies. An' she's so neat, a genuin' piture!

SECOND PEASANT. Why don't they get 'er married? Ain't she plenty old nuff?

GRIGORY. What, marry at fifteen like you do?

FIRST PEASANT. An' that little guy, fr'instance, he a musicalist?

GRIGORY (*mimicking him*). A musicalist!... You don't know nothin'!

FIRST PEASANT. 'Solutely, we're dumb, I mean, noneducated.

THIRD PEASANT. Oh, Lord! (*The sound of a guitar and Gypsy songs are heard from* VASILY LEONIDYCH*'s room.*)

SCENE 37

GRIGORY, *the three* PEASANTS, *and the* DELIVERY MAN. *Enter* SEMYON, *followed by* TANYA. TANYA *watches the meeting between father and son.*

GRIGORY (*to* SEMYON). What d'ya want?

SEMYON. I was sent t'Mr. Kapchich.

GRIGORY. Well, what?

SEMYON. He told me t'say these words: there's no way he can get here tonight.

GRIGORY. Aw right, I'll tell 'im. (*Exits.*)

SCENE 38

THE SAME *without* GRIGORY.

SEMYON (*to his father*). Howdy, Dad! Pa Yefim, Pa Mitry—regards! All well at home?

SECOND PEASANT. Howdy, Semyon.

FIRST PEASANT. Howdy, pal.

THIRD PEASANT. Howdy, kid. Doin' aw right?

SEMYON (*smiling*). So, Dad, let's have some tea, huh?

SECOND PEASANT. Wait, let's get finished—don't yuh see we ain't got time now?

SEMYON. Well, okay, I'll wait by the porch. (*Starts to exit.*)

TANYA (*runs after him*). Why didn't you say something?

SEMYON. How could I in front o' all those people? Gimme time, we'll go have some tea, an' then I'll tell 'im. (*Exits.*)

SCENE 39

THE SAME *without* SEMYON. FYODOR IVANYCH *enters and sits down by the window with his newspaper.*

FIRST PEASANT. Well now, sir, how's our business turnin' out?

FYODOR IVANYCH. Just wait, he'll be out in a moment, he's almost finished.

TANYA (*to* FYODOR IVANYCH). An' how d'ya know he's almost finished, Fyodor Ivanych?

FYODOR IVANYCH. I just know that when he's finished with the questions, he reads the questions and answers over again out loud.

TANYA. Is it really true that you can talk with spirits with a saucer?

FYODOR IVANYCH. Seems to be so.

TANYA. So if they'll tell him to sign—will he really sign?

FYODOR IVANYCH. Sure he will.

TANYA. But they don't speak through words?

FYODOR IVANYCH. Through the alphabet. He watches what letter it stops by.

TANYA. Eh, but if at a seence?...

SCENE 40

THE SAME *and* LEONID FYODOROVICH.

LEONID FYODOROVICH. Well, my friends, I can't. I would like to very much, but I just can't. If you had all the money, it would be different.

FIRST PEASANT. 'Solutely, it'd be betta. But the folks got little means, 'tain't at all possible.

LEONID FYODOROVICH. I can't, I just can't. Here's your paper. I can't sign it.

THIRD PEASANT. Have pity, Master, be merciful!

SECOND PEASANT. How can yuh do it? That's wrong.

LEONID FYODOROVICH. It's not wrong, friends. I told you then, in the summer: if you want it, do it. You didn't want to, and now I can't.

THIRD PEASANT. Master, have mercy! How're we gonna get along now? We've so little land there's no room, so t'say, t'even let a chicken out, t'say nothin' 'bout livestock. (LEONID FYODOROVICH *walks off and stops in the doorway.*)

SCENE 41

THE SAME. ANNA PAVLOVNA, *and the* DOCTOR *come downstairs. Behind them* VASILY, *in a happy, playful mood, is putting money into his wallet.*

ANNA PAVLOVNA (*tightly laced and wearing a hat*). So should I take it?

DOCTOR. If the symptoms recur, be sure to take it. But above all, behave yourself. How can you expect thick syrup to pass through a hair-thin little tube, especially when we squeeze that little tube? You can't. It's the same with the bile duct. It's all very simple, you know.

ANNA PAVLOVNA. Well, all right, all right.

DOCTOR. All right she says, but goes on in the same old way. But you just can't, madam, you cannot. Well, good-bye.

ANNA PAVLOVNA. Not good-bye, but see you. I still expect you this evening; I won't dare do it without you.

DOCTOR. Okay, okay. If I have time, I'll drop by. (*Exits.*)

SCENE 42

THE SAME *without the* DOCTOR.

ANNA PAVLOVNA (*seeing the* PEASANTS). What's this? What's this. Who are these people? (*The* PEASANTS *bow.*)

FYODOR IVANYCH. They're peasants from the Kursk District, come to Leonid Fyodorovich about the purchase of land.

ANNA PAVLOVNA. I can see they're peasants, but who let them in?

FYODOR IVANYCH. Leonid Fyodorovich told us to. He was just talking with them about the sale of land.

ANNA PAVLOVNA. What sale? There's absolutely no need to sell. But above all—how could you let people from the street into the house! How could you let in people from the street! You can't let people into the house, who spent the night God knows where... (*Getting more and more excited.*) I imagine every fold in their clothes is full of microbes: scarlet fever microbes, smallpox microbes, diphtheria microbes! They're from the Kursk District, you know, the Kursk District where there's a diphtheria epidemic!.. Doctor, doctor! Get the doctor back! (LEONID FYODOROVICH *exits, closing the door.* GRIGORY *exits to go for the* DOCTOR.)

SCENE 43

THE SAME *without* LEONID FYODOROVICH *and* GRIGORY.

VASILY LEONIDYCH (*exhales smoke on the* PEASANTS). That's all right, Mamá, would you like me to fumigate them so that all the microbes'll be kaput? Huh? (ANNA PAVLOVNA *keeps a strict silence, waiting for the* DOCTOR *to return.*)

VASILY LEONIDYCH (*to the* PEASANTS). Do you run a feedlot for pigs? Now that's profitable.

FIRST PEASANT. 'Solutely, we go in for the pig line sometimes.

VASILY LEONIDYCH. Like this... Onk, onk! (*Grunts like a young pig.*)

ANNA PAVLOVNA. Vovó, Vovó! Stop it!

VASILY LEONIDYCH. Is that close? Huh?

FIRST PEASANT. 'Solutely, pretty close.

ANNA PAVLOVNA. Vovó, stop it, I tell you!

SECOND PEASANT. What's he doin' that for?

THIRD PEASANT. I told yuh, we'd betta go t'our lodgins meanwhile.

SCENE 44

THE SAME, *the* DOCTOR, *and* GRIGORY.

DOCTOR. Well, what is it now? What is it?

ANNA PAVLOVNA. So you tell me not to get upset. Well how can I stay calm? I don't see my sister for two months, I'm cautious of every dubious visitor, and all of a sudden there are people from Kursk, right from Kursk where there's a diphtheria epidemic, in the middle of my house!

DOCTOR. You mean these guys here?

ANNA PAVLOVNA. Yes, right from a diphtheria zone!

DOCTOR. Well, if they are from a diphtheria zone, then of course, it's careless; nevertheless, there isn't much reason to get upset.

ANNA PAVLOVNA. But didn't you yourself advise caution?

DOCTOR. Well yes, I did, but there isn't much reason to get upset.

ANNA PAVLOVNA. How can I help it? We'll have to disinfect completely.

DOCTOR. No, why completely? That's too expensive, maybe three hundred roubles, or even more. I'll get it done for you cheaply and thoroughly. To a large bottle of water add...

ANNA PAVLOVNA. Boiled water?

DOCTOR. Makes no difference. Boiled is better. So to a bottle of water add a tablespoon of salicylic acid, and have everything that they have as much as touched washed, and, of course, get these guys out of here. And that's all. Then there's nothing to be afraid of. Also spray the air with two, three glassfuls of the same solution, and see how nice it works. Absolutely safe!

ANNA PAVLOVNA. Where's Tanya? Call Tanya!

SCENE 45

THE SAME *and* TANYA.

TANYA. Yes, ma'am.

ANNA PAVLOVNA. Do you know the big bottle in my dressing room?

TANYA. From which we sprayed the laundry maid yesterday?

ANNA PAVLOVNA. Of course, what else! Well then, take that bottle, and first wash off the place where they are with soap, and then with this...

TANYA. Yes, ma'am, I know how.

ANNA PAVLOVNA. And then take the spray... No, when I get back I'll do it myself.

DOCTOR. So do this, and don't be afraid. Well, till tonight, see you. (*Exits.*)

SCENE 46

THE SAME *without the* DOCTOR.

ANNA PAVLOVNA. Now get them out of here, out, away with them. Out, out. Go on, what are you looking at?

FIRST PEASANT. 'Solutely, we sort o' outta stupidity, like we're supposed to...

GRIGORY (*seeing the* PEASANTS *off*). Well, go on, go on.

SECOND PEASANT. Gimme my handkerchief!⁹

THIRD PEASANT. Oh, Lord! I told yuh—we shoulda went t'our lodgins meanwhile. (GRIGORY *pushes him out.*)

SCENE 47

ANNA PAVLOVNA, GRIGORY, FYODOR IVANYCH, TANYA, VASILY LEONIDYCH, *and the* DELIVERY MAN.

DELIVERY MAN (*has tried to speak several times*). Will there be any answer?

ANNA PAVLOVNA. Ah, is this from Bourdier's? (*Irritated.*) None, none, and take it back. I told her I didn't order such an outfit, and I won't allow my daughter to wear it.

DELIVERY MAN. I know nothing about it, I was sent.

ANNA PAVLOVNA. Go, go and take it back. I'll stop by myself.

VASILY LEONIDYCH (*solemnly*). Mr. Ambassador from Bourdier, go away!

DELIVERY MAN. You should've told me that long ago. Why did I spend five hours here?

VASILY LEONIDYCH. Ambassador of Bourdier, go away!

ANNA PAVLOVNA. Stop it, please. (*The* DELIVERY MAN *exits.*)

SCENE 48

THE SAME *without the* DELIVERY MAN.

ANNA PAVLOVNA. Betsy! Where is she? I always have to wait for her.

VASILY LEONIDYCH (*shouts at the top of his voice*). Betsy! Petrishchev! Come quick! Quick! Quick! Huh?

SCENE 49

THE SAME, PETRISHCHEV, BETSY, *and* MARYA KONSTANTI-NOVNA.

ANNA PAVLOVNA. I always have to wait for you.

BETSY. On the contrary, I'm waiting for you. (PETRISHCHEV *nods and kisses* ANNA PAVLOVNA*'s hand.*)

ANNA PAVLOVNA. How do you do! (*To* BETSY.) You always have to answer back!

BETSY. If you are not in a good mood, Mamá, I'd better not go.

ANNA PAVLOVNA. Are we going or not?

BETSY. Yes, let's go, what can you do?

ANNA PAVLOVNA. Did you see what came from Bourdier's?

BETSY. Yes I did, and I was very happy. I ordered the outfit and will wear it when it's paid for.

ANNA PAVLOVNA. I won't pay for it, and won't allow you to wear an indecent outfit.

BETSY. Why is it indecent now? It used to be decent, and suddenly you're overcome by *pruderie.*

ANNA PAVLOVNA. It's not *pruderie.* If the entire bodice is altered, you can wear it.

BETSY. Mamá, really, I can't take it anymore.

ANNA PAVLOVNA. Well, get dressed. (*They sit down.* GRIGORY *puts on their galoshes.*)

VASILY LEONIDYCH. Marya Konstantinovna! Do you see how empty the hall is?

MARYA KONSTANTINOVNA. Why? (*Laughs in anticipation.*)

VASILY LEONIDYCH. Bourdier's man is gone. Huh? Is that good? (*Laughs loudly.*)

ANNA PAVLOVNA. Well, let's go. (*Exits through the door but returns immediately.*) Tanya!

TANYA. Yes, ma'am?

ANNA PAVLOVNA. Don't let Fifka get cold while I'm away. If she wants to be let out, be sure to put on her little yellow coat. She's not altogether well.

TANYA. Yes, ma'am. (ANNA PAVLOVNA, BETSY [MARYA KONSTANTINOVNA], *and* GRIGORY *exit.*)

SCENE 50

PETRISHCHEV, VASILY LEONIDYCH, TANYA, *and* FYODOR IVANYCH.

PETRISHCHEV. Well, did you get it?

VASILY LEONIDYCH. I tell you it was tough. First I tried my father—he gave a growl and kicked me out. So on to mother—and I got it. It's here! (*Taps his pocket.*) Once I start something, I won't let go... It's a death grip. Huh? And today, you know, they're bringing my wolfhounds. (PETRISHCHEV *and* VASILY LEONIDYCH *get dressed and exit.* TANYA *follows them.*)

SCENE 51

FYODOR IVANYCH *alone.*

FYODOR IVANYCH. Yes, nothing but troubles. Why is it they can't live in peace? To tell the truth, the younger generation isn't what it should be. And a women's kingdom? When just before Leonid Fyodorovich was going to take their part but saw that she was excited, he just slammed the door. He's a man of rare kindness! Yes, of rare kindness... What's this? It's Tanya bringing them back again.

SCENE 52

FYODOR IVANYCH, TANYA, *and the three* PEASANTS.

TANYA. That's aw right, ol'timers, go on, go on.

FYODOR IVANYCH. Why did you bring them back again?

TANYA. I can't help it, Fyodor Ivanych, sir, I've gotta do somethin' for 'em. I'll be washin' it all off anyhow.

FYODOR IVANYCH. But nothing will come of the deal, I can see that.

FIRST PEASANT. Sir, how can we get the deal t'be put into action? Yuh might, Yer Prominence, take a little trouble 'bout it, an' we, in reward for yer troubles, can offer thanks in full from the village.

THIRD PEASANT. Do yer best, my dear sir, we can't get along otherwise. We've so little land there's no room, so t'say, t'even let a chicken out, t'say nothin' 'bout livestock. (*They bow.*)

FYODOR IVANYCH. I feel sorry for you, but I really don't know, my friends. I understand it all very well. But, you know, he refused. Now what can you do? And what's more the mistress is also against it. I doubt it'll work! Well, give me the paper anyway—I'll go and try, I'll ask him. (*Exits.*)

SCENE 53

TANYA *and the three* PEASANTS (*sighing*).

TANYA. Now tell me, ol'timers, what's the problem?

FIRST PEASANT. If only he'd be applyin' his hand with a signature.

TANYA. You just want the master to sign the paper, is that it?

FIRST PEASANT. Just that, t'apply his hand an' take the money, an' that'd be the end.

THIRD PEASANT. If only he'd write: as, let's say, the peasants wish, so, let's say, I also wish. And that's the whole thing: take it, sign it, finished.

TANYA. Just sign? Just have the master sign the paper? (*Becomes thoughtful.*)

FIRST PEASANT. 'Solutely, the whole deal depends on that. Let 'im sign, I mean, an' nothin' mo'.

TANYA. Just wait an' see what Fyodor Ivanych'll say. If he can't convince 'im, I'll try somethin'.

FIRST PEASANT. Yuh gonna fool 'im?

TANYA. I'll try.

THIRD PEASANT. Atta girl, wants t'help us. Just get the deal done, we'll guarantee, so t'say, the village'll take care o' yuh for life. That's it!

FIRST PEASANT. If yuh get this here deal t'be put into action, we'll 'solutely make yuh rich.

SECOND PEASANT. That goes widout sayin'!

TANYA. I'm not promisin' for sure; but as the sayin' goes: no harm in tryin', and...

FIRST PEASANT. An' nothin' ventured, nothin' gained. 'Solutely.

SCENE 54

THE SAME *and* FYODOR IVANYCH.

FYODOR IVANYCH. No, my friends, your deal won't go, he didn't agree, and he won't agree. Take your paper. Get going, go on.

FIRST PEASANT (*takes the paper, to* TANYA). So, fr'instance, we'll be countin' on yuh.

TANYA. In a minute, in a minute. You go ahead, wait outside. I'll be out in a minute, an'll have somethin' t'say. (*The* PEASANTS *exit.*)

SCENE 55

FYODOR IVANYCH *and* TANYA.

TANYA. My dear Fyodor Ivanych, ask the master to come out for a moment. I've gotta have a word with him.

FYODOR IVANYCH. What's going on?

TANYA. I've got to, Fyodor Ivanych. Please ask him, it's nothin' bad, I swear.

FYODOR IVANYCH. What's your business with him?

TANYA. That's my little secret. I'll tell you later. Just ask him.

FYODOR IVANYCH (*smiling*). I don't get what you're up to. All right, I'll ask him, I'll ask him. (*Exits.*)

SCENE 56

TANYA *alone.*

TANYA. Really, I'll do it. Now he himself said that Semyon has the power, and I do know how to do it all. Nobody caught on then. And now I'll teach Semyon. And if it doesn't work out, no big deal. Where's the harm?

SCENE 57

TANYA, LEONID FYODOROVICH, *followed by* FYODOR IVANYCH.

LEONID FYODOROVICH (*smiling*). So this is the petitioner! What's your business?

TANYA. A little secret, Leonid Fyodorovich. Allow me to tell yuh in private.

LEONID FYODOROVICH. What is it? Fyodor, step out for a moment.

SCENE 58

LEONID FYODOROVICH *and* TANYA.

TANYA. Because I've lived and grown up in your house, Leonid Fyodorovich, and because I'm grateful to you for everything, I'll open my heart to you like to my own father. There's Semyon; he's livin' in your house, and wants to marry me.

LEONID FYODOROVICH. So that's it!

TANYA. I'm openin' my heart to you like to God. I've no one to ask for advice; I'm an orphan.

LEONID FYODOROVICH. Well, why not! He seems to be a nice fellow.

TANYA. That's right; he'd be all right, but there's one thing I have my doubts 'bout. So I wanted to ask you, there's one thing about him that I don't understand... maybe it's something bad.

LEONID FYODOROVICH. What is it, does he drink?

TANYA. No, God forbid! Because I know there's this spiritchism...

LEONID FYODOROVICH. You do?

TANYA. Sure! I understand it real well. Naturally, because of ignorance, others don't understand this...

LEONID FYODOROVICH. Well, so what?

TANYA. So, I'm frightened about Semyon. Things happen with him.

LEONID FYODOROVICH. What happens?

TANYA. Well, something like spirit...chism. Just ask the others. As soon as he dozes at the table, right away the table begins to shake and creak like: eek, ee...eek! All the others heard it.

LEONID FYODOROVICH. Now that's just what I was talking about to Sergey Ivanovich this morning. Well?...

TANYA. And then...when was it? Yes, on Wednesday. We sat down to dinner. Soon as he sat down by the table, the spoon by itself went jump, right into his hand!

LEONID FYODOROVICH. Ah, that's interesting. The spoon just went jump into his hand? Was he dozing then?

TANYA. I didn't notice. I think he was.

LEONID FYODOROVICH. So?

TANYA. So, I'm frightened, and I wanted to ask you if there's any harm in it? I'll have to live my life with him, and he's got this thing.

LEONID FYODOROVICH (*smiling*). No, don't be afraid, there's nothing bad here at all. It only means that he's a medium—simply a medium. I knew he was a medium before this.

TANYA. That's what it is... And just think, I was afraid!

LEONID FYODOROVICH. No, don't be afraid, it's all right. (*Aside.*) That's great! Kapchich won't be here, so we'll test him tonight... No, my dear, don't be afraid, he'll make a good husband, and all that. This is a special power and everyone has it. Only it's weaker in some, stronger in others.

TANYA. Thank you very much. I won't think about it anymore. I was so afraid... That's what comes from our bein' uneducated!

LEONID FYODOROVICH. No, no, don't be afraid. Fyodor!

SCENE 59

THE SAME *and* FYODOR IVANYCH.

LEONID FYODOROVICH. I'm going out. Get everything ready for the seance tonight.

FYODOR IVANYCH. But Mr. Kapchich isn't coming.

LEONID FYODOROVICH. That's all right, it doesn't matter. (*Puts on his overcoat.*) We'll have a trial seance with our own medium. (*Exits.* FYODOR IVANYCH *sees him out.*)

SCENE 60

TANYA *alone.*

TANYA. He believed it, he believed it! (*Squeals and jumps.*) By God, he believed it! That's a miracle! (*Squeals.*) Now I'll do it, if only Semyon don't chicken out.

SCENE 61

TANYA *and* FYODOR IVANYCH (*returning*).

FYODOR IVANYCH. So, did you tell your secret?

TANYA. I did. I'll tell you too, only later... But I want to ask you a favor, Fyodor Ivanych.

FYODOR IVANYCH. What favor do you want of me?

TANYA (*bashfully*). You've been like a second father to me, and I'll open my heart to you like to God.

FYODOR IVANYCH. Don't beat about the bush. Come to the point.

TANYA. What's the point? The point is Semyon wants to marry me.

FYODOR IVANYCH. So that's it! I kind of noticed...

TANYA. Why should I hide it? I'm an orphan, and you yourself know how things are here in town: everyone gives you the old come-on. Just take Grigory Mikhailych, there's no gettin' rid of him. And that other one also... you know? They think I don't have a soul, that I'm only here for them to play with...

FYODOR IVANYCH. Good girl, I'm proud of you! Well, so what now?

TANYA. Well, Semyon wrote his father, and soon as he, his father, saw me today, he says: "He's spoilt"—that's about his son. Fyodor Ivanych! (*Bows.*) Take the place o' my father, speak to the old man, Semyon's father. I could take 'im into the kitchen, an' you could drop in an' talk t'the old man.

FYODOR IVANYCH (*smiling*). Does that mean you want me to be a matchmaker? Well, I can do that.

TANYA. My dear Fyodor Ivanych, be a father to me, and I'll pray for you the rest of my life.

FYODOR IVANYCH. All right, all right, I'll stop by. I promise I'll do it. (*Takes the newspaper.*)

TANYA. You'll be a second father to me.

FYODOR IVANYCH. All right, all right.

TANYA. Then I'll count on you... (*Exits.*)

SCENE 62

FYODOR IVANYCH *alone.*

FYODOR IVANYCH (*shaking his head*). She's a nice, sweet girl. And to think how many of them get ruined! Just make one mistake—and she's everyone's toy... Then she'll just sink in muck. Just like that Natalya, poor dear... She was also nice, also brought into the world, pampered and cared for by a mother... (*Takes the newspaper.*) Well now, how's our Ferdinand going to get out of this mess?...[10]

Curtain.

ACT II

The set depicts the interior of the servants' kitchen. The PEASANTS, *with their coats off and perspiring, are sitting at a table and drinking tea.* FYODOR IVANYCH *is smoking a cigar on the other side of the stage. On the stove lies the* FORMER COOK, *who is not visible during the first four scenes.*

SCENE 1

The three PEASANTS *and* FYODOR IVANYCH.

FYODOR IVANYCH. My advice is, don't stand in his way. If he wants to and she wants to also, then may God be with them. She's a nice, honest girl. Never mind that she's on the dressy side. That's the way in town, you can't get along without it. And she's a smart girl.

SECOND PEASANT. Well, if he wants t'. It's him who's got t'live with 'er, not me. Only she's a might too neat. How can yuh bring her into a cottage? She won't let her mother-in-law so much as pat 'er on the back.

FYODOR IVANYCH. That doesn't depend on neatness, my friend, but on character. If she has a good character, she'll be obedient and respectful.

SECOND PEASANT. Well I'll take 'er, if the kid's that hooked that he's gotta have 'er. It sure ain't no good livin' with someone yuh don't love! I'll talk it over with my ol' lady, an' then good luck to 'em.

FYODOR IVANYCH. Well then, let's shake on it.

SECOND PEASANT. Yep, looks like we oughta.

FIRST PEASANT. Yuh're really lucky, Zakhar: yuh've come t'complete business, an' look—what a queen of a wife yuh got for yer son. Means, we just hafta drink t'it, t'make it okeydokey.

FYODOR IVANYCH. That's not at all necessary. (*An awkward silence.*) I understand your way of life very well, you know. I'll tell you, I myself am thinking of buying a piece of land. I'd build a little house, and work the land. Maybe in your area.

SECOND PEASANT. That's a nice thing t'do!

FIRST PEASANT. 'Solutely, with money yuh can get all kinds of pleasure for yuhself in the country.

THIRD PEASANT. You said it! Country life, so t'say, is free in every way, not like it's in town.

FYODOR IVANYCH. So would you accept me in your community if I would move among you?

SECOND PEASANT. Why not? Treat the elders t'some liquor an' they'll accept yuh right away.

FIRST PEASANT. An' if yuh'll open a drinkin' establishment, fr'instance, or an inn, yer life'll be such that there'd be no need t'die. Live like a king, an' that's it.

FYODOR IVANYCH. We'll see. I would just like to live nice and peaceful in my old age. I have a good life here too—I'm even sorry to leave: Leonid Fyodorovich is a man of rare kindness, you know.

FIRST PEASANT. 'Solutely. But why'd he do this t'our business? So's there really gonna be no consequences?

FYODOR IVANYCH. He'd be glad to go along.

SECOND PEASANT. Looks like he's 'fraid o' his wife.

FYODOR IVANYCH. No he's not, but they don't agree either.

THIRD PEASANT. It'd be nice if yuh'd try, sir, otherwise how're we gonna get along? We've so little land...

FYODOR IVANYCH. Let's see what comes of Tanya's efforts. She sure took a hand in it.

THIRD PEASANT (*drinking tea*). Have mercy, sir! We've so little land there's no room, so t'say, t'even let a chicken out, t'say nothin' 'bout livestock.

FYODOR IVANYCH. If only the business was in my hands. (*To the* SECOND PEASANT.) So, my friend, we're going to be like in-laws, you and me. It's all settled with Tanya, right?

SECOND PEASANT. If I said so, I won't back out even if we don't drink t'it. If only our business worked out.

SCENE 2

THE SAME. *Enter* LUKERYA, *looks up on the stove, makes gestures in that direction and immediately begins to speak animatedly to* FYODOR IVANYCH.

LUKERYA. Semyon was just called upstairs from the main kitchen; the master an' that guy that calls up spirits with 'im, the bald one, told 'im t'sit down an' take Kapchich's place.
FYODOR IVANYCH. You're talking nonsense!
LUKERYA. No, Yakov just told Tanya.
FYODOR IVANYCH. That's weird!

SCENE 3

THE SAME *and the* COACHMAN.

FYODOR IVANYCH. What do you want?
COACHMAN (*to* FYODOR IVANYCH). Just tell 'em I wasn't hired t'live with dogs. Let someone else live with 'em, but I don't agree t'live with dogs.
FYODOR IVANYCH. What dogs?
COACHMAN. Vasily Leonidych had three dogs brung t'the coachmen's quarters. They've messed all over, they're howlin', an' yuh can't come near 'em—they bite. The vicious devils!—if yuh don't watch out they'll eat yuh alive. I'd like t'take a stick an' break their legs.
FYODOR IVANYCH. When did that happen?
COACHMAN. They just brung 'em today from the show; they cost a lot, they're the slick-coated kind or somethin', who the hell knows! Yuh either have dogs livin' in the coachmen's quarters or coachmen. Just tell 'em that.
FYODOR IVANYCH. No, that's not right. I'll go and ask.
COACHMAN. Maybe we should bring 'em here, t'Lukerya.
LUKERYA (*excitedly*). We've got people eatin' here, an' you wanna lock the dogs in. As it is...

COACHMAN. An' I have coats, covers, harnesses. An' they expect 'em t'be clean. Well, maybe at the yardman's place.

FYODOR IVANYCH. I have to tell Vasily Leonidych.

COACHMAN (*angrily*). Let 'im hang those dogs aroun' his neck, an' go aroun' with 'em; but he sure likes t'go horseback ridin' 'imself. He ruined Beauty for nothin'. Now that was a horse!... Ah, what a life! (*Exits, slamming the door.*)

SCENE 4

THE SAME *without the* COACHMAN.

FYODOR IVANYCH. No, it's not right, it's not right. (*To the* PEASANTS.) Well, boys, so it is, in the meantime, good-bye!

PEASANTS. So long. (FYODOR IVANYCH *exits.*)

SCENE 5

THE SAME *without* FYODOR IVANYCH. *As soon as* FYODOR IVANYCH *leaves, groaning is heard from the top of the stove.*

SECOND PEASANT. Ain't he sleek, just like a genteral.

LUKERYA. You said it! A room for 'imself, the washin's done for 'im, gets sugar, tea—it's all from the masters, even his food's from their table.

FORMER COOK. Why the hell shouldn't he live good—he's stolen nuff!

SECOND PEASANT. Who's that there, up on the stove?

LUKERYA. Just some guy. (*Silence.*)

FIRST PEASANT. Well, I saw when yuh et supper a while ago that yuh got it made, mighty good too.

LUKERYA. We can't complain. She ain't stingy as far as that goes: white bread on Sundays, fish on fast days durin' the holidays, an' whoever wants can even have meat.

SECOND PEASANT. Do people gobble meat on fast days?

LUKERYA. Eh, I'd say just 'bout everyone. The only ones that fast are the coachman (not the one that was just here but the old one), an' Syoma, an' me, an' the housekeeper; but all the rest stuff 'emselves with meat.

SECOND PEASANT. An' what about him?

LUKERYA. Eh, of all people t'think of! He can't even remember that there's such a thing like fastin'.

THIRD PEASANT. Oh, Lord!

FIRST PEASANT. That's the masters' way, they got it from their books. Cuz it's intelligence!

THIRD PEASANT. I guess they have white bread evey day, huh?

LUKERYA. White bread! They've got no use for yer white bread! Yuh should see their food: what don't they have!

FIRST PEASANT. The masters' food, naturally's light like air.

LUKERYA. It may be light like air—but they're sure good at stuffin' 'emselves.

FIRST PEASANT. Means they've got good appekites.

LUKERYA. Cuz they wash it down. Lots o' these sweet wines, vodkas, an' fizzy liquors, each course a different one. It's eat an' drink, eat an' drink.

FIRST PEASANT. Means, it helps the food go through in preportion.

LUKERYA. Yeah, they're really good at stuffin' 'emselves, an' how! They don't just sit down, eat, cross 'emselves an' get up; they eat nonstop.

SECOND PEASANT. Like pigs with their feet in the trough. (*The PEAS- ANTS laugh.*)

LUKERYA. Soon's they open their peepers, God love 'em, right away it's the samovar, tea, coffee, chickolate. Soon's they've emptied two samovars, put on a third one. An' then breakfast, an' then dinner, an' then coffee again. Soon's they're done, right away tea again. An' then comes snacks: candies, pastries—there's no end t'it. They even eat in bed.

THIRD PEASANT. So that's how it is. (*Bursts out laughing.*)

FIRST AND SECOND PEASANTS. What's with you?

THIRD PEASANT. I'd like t'live just one day like that!

SECOND PEASANT. So when do they do work?

LUKERYA. What work? Playin' cards an' the pieano's all they do. Soon's the young mistress opens her peepers, she'd make for the pieano an' go at it! An' the one that lives here, the teacher, stands an' waits t'see when she'll be done; soon's the first one's finished, this one gives it a go. Or they'd put two pieanos side by side, an' there'd be two at each an' the four of 'em bang away. An' they bang away so that yuh can even hear it in here.

THIRD PEASANT. Oh, Lord!

LUKERYA. Well, that's all the work they do: the pieano an' cards. Soon's they get together, it's cards, drinkin' an' smokin'—an' it goes on all night long. Soon's they're up—eatin' again!

SCENE 6

THE SAME *and* SEMYON.

SEMYON. Hope yuh're enjoyin' yer tea!

FIRST PEASANT. Sit down, have some tea.

SEMYON (*comes up to the table*). Thank you very much. (*The* FIRST PEASANT *pours tea for him.*)

SECOND PEASANT. Where've yuh been?

SEMYON. Upstairs.

SECOND PEASANT. So what's goin' on up there?

SEMYON. Yuh got me. I don't know how t'explain it.

SECOND PEASANT. Well, what's goin' on?

SEMYON. But I don't know how t'explain it; they've been testin' some kind o' power in me. I don't get it. Tanya says: "Do it," she says, "We'll get the land for our people, he'll sell it."

SECOND PEASANT. An' how's she gonna do it?

SEMYON. I don't get it an' she ain't sayin'. She says: "Just do as I tell yuh!"

SECOND PEASANT. Do what?

SEMYON. Right now, nothin'. They sat me down, put out the lights, an' told me t'go t'sleep. An' Tanya hid close by. They didn't see 'er, but I did.

SECOND PEASANT. Why, what for?

SEMYON. God only knows—yuh got me.

FIRST PEASANT. It's clear, t'while away the time.

SECOND PEASANT. Well, looks like you an' me ain't gonna make nothin' outta this business. Tell me now, how much money have yuh taken?

SEMYON. Nothin', saved it all. Must be, twenty-eight roubles.

SECOND PEASANT. That's good. Well, if God grants that we come t'terms 'bout the land, I'll take yuh home, Syomka.

SEMYON. I'd like that.

SECOND PEASANT. Yuh've been spoilt, I suppose. Wouldn't wanna plough, huh?

SEMYON. Plough? I'd do it right now. Plough, mow, yuh don't forget all that.

FIRST PEASANT. Still, it don't seem appealin' after life in town, fr'instance.

SEMYON. It's aw right, one can live in the county too.

FIRST PEASANT. Now Pa Mitry here's after yer place, yer softy life.

SEMYON. Well, Pa Mitry, yuh'd get tired of it. It looks easy, but there's a lot o' runnin' aroun'. It knocks yuh out.

LUKERYA. Yuh should see the parties they have, Pa Mitry. Then you'd be amazed!

THIRD PEASANT. What, do they keep on eatin'?

LUKERYA. What d'ya know! Yuh should see what was goin' on! Fyodor Ivanych let me come along. So I had a look: the ladies are somethin'! So dressed up, so dressed up, what d'ya know! Naked down t'here, an' bare arms.

THIRD PEASANT. Oh, Lord!

SECOND PEASANT. Phew, nasty!

FIRST PEASANT. Means, the climmate allows it.

LUKERYA. So, ol'timer, I took a look: what's this?—all of 'em naked. Would yuh believe it, even the old ones—like our mistress, an' she's got grandchildren, yuh know—were naked.

THIRD PEASANT. Oh, Lord!

LUKERYA. An what next? Soon's the music starts, soon's they start playin'—right away the gentlemen go up t'their ladies, put their arms aroun' 'em an' off they go whirlin' aroun'.

SECOND PEASANT. The old women too?

LUKERYA. Them too.

SEMYON. No, the old women just sit.

LUKERYA. Whacha talkin' about, I saw it myself!

SEMYON. No yuh didn't.

FORMER COOK (*sticking his head out, hoarsely*). That's the polka-mazurka. Yuh dummy, what d'ya know!—that's the way they dance...

LUKERYA. Why don't yuh shut up, twinkle toes. There, someone's comin'.

SCENE 7

THE SAME *and* GRIGORY. *The* FORMER COOK *hides hurriedly.*

GRIGORY (*to* LUKERYA). Gimme some sourkrout!

LUKERYA. I just got back from the cellar, an' now I gotta go again. Who's it for?

GRIGORY. The young ladies, for bread soup. Quick! Have Semyon bring it, I don't have time.

LUKERYA. They eat so much sweets, they can't take no more so they get the hungries for sourkrout.

FIRST PEASANT. Means, for purgin'.

LUKERYA. Sure, they're makin' room t'go at it again. (*Takes a cup and exits.*)

SCENE 8

THE SAME *without* LUKERYA.

GRIGORY (*to the* PEASANTS). Look at yuh, made yuhself comfortable. Watch out: the mistress'll find out, an' she'll give yuh a goin' over just like this mornin'. (*Laughs and exits.*)

SCENE 9

The three PEASANTS, SEMYON, *and the* FORMER COOK (*on the stove*).

FIRST PEASANT. 'Solutely, she raised a ruckus then—terrible.

SECOND PEASANT. Seems he wanted t'step in then, but when he saw 'er tearin' the roof down, he slammed the door: like, the hell with yuh.

THIRD PEASANT (*waving his arm*). It's the same old story. My ol' lady, so t'say, flares up sometimes too—red hot! I just get outta the way. The hell with 'er! Yuh betta watch out, so t'say, or else she'll get yuh with the prongs. Oh, Lord!

SCENE 10

THE SAME *and* YAKOV (*runs in with a prescription in his hand*).

YAKOV. Syoma, quick, run t'the druggist, get these powders for the mistress!

SEMYON. But he told me not t'leave.

YAKOV. Yuh've plenty o' time. They'll need yuh later, after tea... Hope yuh're enjoyin' yer tea.

FIRST PEASANT. Come, sit down. (*Exit* SEMYON.)

SCENE 11

THE SAME *without* SEMYON.

YAKOV. I don't have time, but aw right, I'll join yuh for a cup.

FIRST PEASANT. We've been holdin' a disgussion here 'bout how highfalutin yer mistress was a while ago.

YAKOV. Oh, that hothead—terrible! She's so hotheaded, she comes unglued. Sometimes she even bursts out cryin'.

FIRST PEASANT. An' what was I gonna, fr'instance, ask? She said somethin' 'bout macrobes then. "They brought in macrobes," she says, "macrobes." What does it apply to, these here macrobes?

YAKOV. Oh, yuh mean macroves. They say there are such bugs; all diseases come from 'em, they say. So she means you have 'em on yuh. After yuh left, how they washed an' how they sprayed where you were standin'. There's a solution, these bugs croak from it.

SECOND PEASANT. So where are they on us, these here bugs?

YAKOV (*drinking tea*). They say they're so tiny yuh can't even see 'em through a glass.

SECOND PEASANT. So how does she know they're on me? Maybe there's more o' that filth on 'er than on me.

YAKOV. Well go an' ask 'er!

SECOND PEASANT. I think it's baloney.

YAKOV. Of course it's baloney; but doctors gotta think somethin' up or else what would yuh pay 'em for? There's one comin' t'us every day. Comes, talks a bit—here's a tenner.

SECOND PEASANT. Yuh're kiddin'?...

YAKOV. An' there's one that takes a hundred.

FIRST PEASANT. Cut it out! A hundred?

YAKOV. A hundred? You say a hundred—he takes a thou if he's gotta go outta town. "Gimme a thou," he says, "or yuh can kick the bucket!"

THIRD PEASANT. Oh, Lord!

SECOND PEASANT. So does he know some magic word?

YAKOV. He must. I used t'work at a general's place near Moscow: he was real bad-tempered, proud, that general—terrible! So, his daughter took sick. Right away they sent for this doctor. "A thousand roubles an' I'll come..." Well, they made a deal an' he came. Then, somehow the general did somethin' he didn't like. Well, goodness gracious, the way he yelled at 'im. "Ah," he says, "is this how you show me respect, is this how? Then I won't treat her!" So what d'ya know! The general forgot all his pride an' started sweet-talkin' 'im in every way. "Sir! Please, don't leave us!"

FIRST PEASANT. So did he give 'im the thou?

YAKOV. You bet he did!...

SECOND PEASANT. That's easy money. What couldn't a peasant do with that kinda money!

THIRD PEASANT. An' I think it's all baloney. Like that time I had a bad foot. I had it treated an' treated, an' treated it, so t'say, t'five roubles. I stopped havin' it treated, an' it wen' away. (*On the stove the FORMER COOK coughs.*)

YAKOV. He's here again, poor thing!

FIRST PEASANT. Who might that little man be?

YAKOV. He used t'be our master's cook, now he comes t'Lukerya.

FIRST PEASANT. Means, chef master. So, does he live here?

YAKOV. No... They don't let 'im. It's a day here, a day there. If he got three kopecks, he goes t'a flop house; if he drinks it all away, he comes here.

SECOND PEASANT. How did he come t'this?

YAKOV. Simple, he's got weak. An' what a man he used t'be, like a gentleman! Wore a gold watch, made forty roubles a month. An' now he'd die o' hunger if not for Lukerya.

SCENE 12

THE SAME *and* LUKERYA (*carrying sauerkraut*).

YAKOV (*to* LUKERYA). I see Pavel Petrovich's here again.

LUKERYA. Where's he gonna go—freeze t'death?

THIRD PEASANT. What liquor does! Liquor, so t'say... (*Clicks his tongue sympathetically.*)

SECOND PEASANT. That's how it is, a strong man's stronger than stone; a weak one's weaker than water.

FORMER COOK (*climbs down from the stove, his hands and legs shaking*). Lukerya, gimme a shot, I tell yuh.

LUKERYA. Where're you off to? I'll give yuh a shot aw right!...

FORMER COOK. D'ya believe in God? I'm dyin'. Brothers, lemme have five kopecks...

LUKERYA. Get back on the stove, I tell yuh.

FORMER COOK. Cook! Half a shot. For Christ's sake, I tell yuh, d'ya understand—I beg yuh in the name o' Christ!

LUKERYA. Go, go on. Here's some tea for yuh!

FORMER COOK. What's tea? What's tea? A worthless, weak drink. A little liquor, just a swallow... Lukerya!

THIRD PEASANT. Poor guy, he's really sufferin'.

SECOND PEASANT. Go on an' give 'im some.

LUKERYA (*gets a small glass from the cupboard and fills it*). Here, that's all yuh'll get.

FORMER COOK (*grabs it and drinks, trembling*). Lukerya! Cook! I'm drinkin', an' yuh should understand...

LUKERYA. Well, nuff talk! Get up on the stove, an' not another word. (*The* FORMER COOK *submissively climbs up, and keeps on mumbling something to himself.*)

SECOND PEASANT. That's what it is when a man's got weak!

FIRST PEASANT. 'Solutely, human weakness.

THIRD PEASANT. You said it. (*The* FORMER COOK *lies down and keeps on mumbling. Silence.*)

SECOND PEASANT. Well, I wanted t'ask: there's Aksinya's girl workin' here, the one that comes from our village. What's with 'er? How's she? How does she live, I mean, she honest?

YAKOV. She's a nice girl, gotta give 'er credit.

LUKERYA. I'll tell yuh the truth, ol'timer, cuz I sure know how things are here: if yuh wanna have Tatyana for yer son—get 'er outta here quick 'fore she goes bad, or else she's had it.

YAKOV. Yes, that's true. Last year that was a girl here, Natalya. She was also a nice girl. An' she got ruined for nothin', just like this guy... (*Points to the* FORMER COOK.)

LUKERYA. There's so many o' us women gettin' ruined here, yuh can't keep count. Everyone's tempted by the easy life an' sweet stuff. An' cuz o' this sweet stuff, just look how quick she's gone wrong. An' once she's gone wrong, they don't want 'er no more. Out she goes, an' a fresh one's there in 'er place. That's how it was with poor Natalya: she went wrong, an' right away they kicked 'er out. She had a baby, got sick, an' died in the hospital last spring. An' what a girl she was!

THIRD PEASANT. Oh, Lord! They're a weak lot. Yuh hafta feel sorry for 'em.

FORMER COOK. Them bastards feel sorry! (*Hangs his legs down from the stove.*) I roasted myself by the oven for thirty years. An' now they don't want me no more—so croak like a dog!... Them feel sorry!

FIRST PEASANT. 'Solutely, that's the satuation.

SECOND PEASANT. When they'd drink an' eat, yuh were curly head; once they'd finish, get out, mangy mutt!

THIRD PEASANT. Oh, Lord!

FORMER COOK. A lot you know. What's sautey a la bamon? What's bavasari?[11] The things I could make! Just think! The emperor ate my work! An' now the bastards don't want me no more. But I won't give up!

LUKERYA. Now, now, yuh talk too much. I'll let yuh have it!... Get into the corner so's no one can see yuh, or Fyodor Ivanych'll come by, or someone else, and they'll kick me an' you out for good. (*Silence.*)

YAKOV. So, d'ya know my village, Voznesenskoe?

SECOND PEASANT. Sure do. It's no more'n twelve miles from us, an' even less 'cross the ford. So got any land there?

YAKOV. My brother does, an' I send 'im money. I've got t'be here, but I'm dyin' t'go home.

FIRST PEASANT. 'Solutely.

SECOND PEASANT. Means, Anisim's yer brother?

YAKOV. Yep, my flesh'n blood! He's on the far end.

SECOND PEASANT. I know—the third house.

SCENE 13

THE SAME *and* TANYA (*runs in*).

TANYA. Yakov Ivanych! What're you goofin' off here for? She's callin'!

YAKOV. Comin'. What's up?

TANYA. Fifka's barkin', wants to eat; and she's in a tizzy about you: "He's so mean," she says. "He has no feelings," she says. "It's long past her dinner time, and he hasn't brought it!..." (*Laughs.*)

YAKOV (*about to leave*). Oh, she's angry? Hope it don't turn out bad!

LUKERYA (*to* YAKOV). Take the sourkrout.

YAKOV. Give it here! (*Takes the sauerkraut and exits.*)

SCENE 14

THE SAME *without* YAKOV.

FIRST PEASANT. Who's gonna have dinner now?

TANYA. The dog. This dog of hers... (*Sits down and takes the teapot.*) Is there any tea left? I've brought some just in case. (*Puts tea into the teapot.*)

SECOND PEASANT. Dinner for a dog?

TANYA. Sure enough! They prepare a special cotlet for 'er, one that's not fatty. An' I wash this dog's laundry.

THIRD PEASANT. Oh, Lord!

TANYA. Like that gentleman who buried his dog.

SECOND PEASANT. How's that?

TANYA. This's what happened—a man was tellin' us 'bout it—this gentleman's dog croaked. It was in winter, an' he drove out t'bury it. Well, he buried it, an' on the way back the gentleman sits an' cries. It's bitter cold, an' the coachman's nose is runnin', an' he's wipin' it... Lemme me pour. (*Pours the tea.*) His nose keeps runnin', an' he keeps on wipin' it. The gentleman sees 'im an' says: "what are you crying about?" And the coachman says: "I can't help cryin', sir, what a dog it was!" (*Laughs.*)

SECOND PEASANT. I guess he 'imself was thinkin': "I wouldn't cry even if you yuhself'd croaked..." (*Laughs.*)

FORMER COOK (*from the stove*). That's right, true!

TANYA. Well, the gentleman gets home and says t'his wife: "What a kind man our coachman is: he felt so sorry for Bowser, he cried all the way home. Call him in: here, have a drink," he says, "and here's a rouble for you." So that's how she is 'bout Yakov havin' no feelings for her dog. (*The* PEASANTS *laugh.*)

FIRST PEASANT. 'Xactly!

SECOND PEASANT. Now that's a story!

THIRD PEASANT. Yuh sure made us laugh, girl!

TANYA (*pours more tea*). Have some more!... So, it only looks like our life is good, but sometimes it's disgustin' t'clean up all the filth after 'em. Phew! It's better in the country. (*The* PEASANTS *turn their cups upside down* [*as a sign that they have had enough*]. TANYA *pours more tea.*) Please have some more, Efim Antonych! I'll pour yuh some, Mitry Vlasyevich!

THIRD PEASANT. Aw right, go on'n pour.

FIRST PEASANT. Well, bright eyes, how's our business turnin' out?

TANYA. Okay, it's goin'.

FIRST PEASANT. Semyon told us...

TANYA (*quickly*). He did?

SECOND PEASANT. But there's no makin' 'im out!

TANYA. I can't tell you now, but I'm doin' my best, really. Your paper's right here! (*Points to the paper under her apron.*) If only this one thing works out... (*Squeals.*) It'd be great!

SECOND PEASANT. Watch out, don't lose the paper. We paid good money for it.

TANYA. Don't worry. You just want him to sign, right?

THIRD PEASANT. What else? Sign, so t'say, an' finished. (*Turns his cup upside down.*) That's nuff.

TANYA (*aside*). He'll sign, You'll see, he will. Have some more. (*Pours the tea.*)

FIRST PEASANT. Just arrange completin' the sale o' land, an' the village'll marry yuh off. (*Refuses the tea.*)

TANYA (*pours tea and hands it to him.*) Do have some more.

THIRD PEASANT. You just do it: we'll marry yuh off, an' I'll, so t'say, dance at yer weddin'. I've never danced in my life, but I will then!

TANYA (*laughs*). I'll hope for it. (*Silence.*)

SECOND PEASANT (*Looks TANYA over*). That's all aw right, but yuh ain't fit for peasant's work.

TANYA. Who, me? You think I'm not strong? You should see how I lace up the mistress. Not every man'll do it as tight.

SECOND PEASANT. What d'ya mean lace 'er up?

TANYA. There's this thing with bones, like a jacket, up t'here. Well, you spit in your hands, and lace up the cords, just like you saddle a horse.

SECOND PEASANT. Means, yuh pull in the girth?

TANYA. Yes, yes, I pull it in. An' you can't put your foot up against her, you know. (*Laughs.*)

SECOND PEASANT. Why d'ya lace 'er up?

TANYA. Because.

SECOND PEASANT. Did she make a vow?

TANYA. No, it's for beauty's sake.

FIRST PEASANT. Means, yuh draw in her belly for her shape's sake.

TANYA. You'll draw 'er in till her eyes pop out, and she says: "More." You do it till yer hands blister, and you say I'm not strong. (*The PEASANTS laugh and shake their heads.*) Well, I've been talkin' too much. (*Runs away, laughing.*)

THIRD PEASANT. How that girl made us laugh!

FIRST PEASANT. She's so neat!

SECOND PEASANT. Not bad.

SCENE 15

The three PEASANTS, LUKERYA, *and the* FORMER COOK *on the stove. Enter* SAKHATOV *and* VASILY LEONIDYCH. SAKHATOV *has a teaspoon in his hand.*

VASILY LEONIDYCH. Not exactly a dinner but a *déjeuner dînatoir.* And it was an excellent breakfast, I tell you: suckling-pig ham—delicious! Roulier really feeds you well. I've just come back. (*Sees the* PEASANTS.) Ah, the peasants are here again?

SAKHATOV. Yes, yes, that's all very well, but we came here to hide something. So where are we going to hide it?

VASILY LEONIDYCH. Sorry, just a moment. (*To* LUKERYA.) Where are the dogs?

LUKERYA. They're at the coachman's place. Can yuh really keep 'em in the kitchen?

VASILY LEONIDYCH. Oh, at the coachmen's place? Well, good.

SAKHATOV. I'm waiting.

VASILY LEONIDYCH. Sorry, sorry. Huh? Hide it? Yes, Sergey Ivanovich, I'll tell you what: put it into the pocket of one of these peasants. This one here. Listen you. Huh? Where's your pocket?

THIRD PEASANT. Whacha need my pocket for? How d'ya like that, my pocket! I've got money in my pocket.

SAKHATOV. Where's your sack then?

THIRD PEASANT. What's it t'yuh?

LUKERYA. What's the matter with yuh! That's the young master.

VASILY LEONIDYCH (*laughs*). Do you know why he's so scared? I'll tell you why: he's got a pile of money. Huh?

SAKHATOV. Yes, yes, I understand. Well, this is what we'll do: you talk to them, and in the meantime I'll quietly slip it into that bag over there so that they don't notice and can't point it out to him. Talk to them.

VASILY LEONIDYCH. All right, all right. Well, boys, how about it, are you going to buy the land? Huh?

FIRST PEASANT. We prepose t' with all our hearts. But the business ain't bein' put into action.

VASILY LEONIDYCH. Don't be so stingy. Land is an important thing. I told you about mint. Or else you can also try tobacco.

FIRST PEASANT. 'Solutely, yuh can with all kinds o' perducts.

THIRD PEASANT. Please, sir, ask your father. Or else how're we gonna get along? We've so little land, there's no room, so t'say, t'even let a chicken out.

SAKHATOV (*after putting the spoon into the* THIRD PEASANT*'s bag*). *C'est fait.* Done. Let's go. (*Exits.*)

VASILY LEONIDYCH. Don't be stingy. Huh? Well, good-bye. (*Exits.*)

SCENE 16

The three PEASANTS, LUKERYA, *and the* FORMER COOK (*on the stove*).

THIRD PEASANT. I told yuh: go t'the lodgin'. We'd give, let's say, ten kopecks apiece an' at least be left alone, but here—my God! "Gimme the money," he says. What's it for?

SECOND PEASANT. Must be drunk. (*The* PEASANTS *turn their cups upside down, rise, and cross themselves.*)

FIRST PEASANT. D'ya remember how he threw out the idea 'bout sowin' mint? Yuh sure hafta know how t'understand that.

SECOND PEASANT. Yeah, sow mint, what next! Go on an' try, bust yer ass—then yuh won't likely ask for mint... Well, thanks much!... So, my good woman, where can we lie down here?

LUKERYA. One can lie on the stove, the others on the benches.

THIRD PEASANT. God help us. (*Prays.*)

FIRST PEASANT. If only God'd help complete the deal. (*Lies down.*) Tomorrow after dinner we'd jump on the train, an' be home by Tuesday.

SECOND PEASANT. Are you gonna put the light out?

LUKERYA. Put what out! They'll keep runnin' in here, now for one thing, now for another... Go ahead, lie down, I'll turn it down.

SECOND PEASANT. How can yuh get along on so little land? This year I've been buyin' grain ever since Christmas. An' my straw's all used up. Otherwise, I'd plant ten acres, an' take Syomka home.

FIRST PEASANT. Yuh're a family man. Yuh've got no problems! Yuh'll work the land, if yuh get it. If we could only complete the deal!

THIRD PEASANT. We hafta turn t'the Holy Virgin. Maybe, She'll have mercy.

SCENE 17

Silence, sighs. Then footsteps and voices are heard, the doors open wide and in rush GROSSMAN *blindfolded, holding* SAKHATOV *by the hand, the* PROFESSOR *and the* DOCTOR, *the* FAT LADY *and* LEONID FYODOR-OVICH, BETSY *and* PETRISHCHEV, VASILY LEONIDYCH *and* MARYA KONSTANTINOVNA, ANNA PAVLOVNA *and the* BARONESS, FYODOR IVANYCH *and* TANYA. *The three* PEASANTS, LUKERYA, *and the* FORMER COOK (*unseen; the* PEASANTS *jump up;* GROSSMAN *enters quickly and stops*).

FAT LADY. Don't worry: I'm watching, I promised to watch, and I am conscientiously fulfilling my duty. Sergey Ivanych, you aren't leading him, are you?

SAKHATOV. Of course not.

FAT LADY. Don't lead him, but don't resist him either. (*To* LEONID FYO-DOROVICH.) I know all about these experiments, I've done them myself. I would feel an ectoplasm, and as soon as I felt it...

LEONID FYODOROVICH. May I ask you to observe complete silence.

FAT LADY. Ah, I know all about this! I've experienced it myself. As soon as my attention was distracted, I couldn't...

LEONID FYODOROVICH. Sh-h.

(They walk around, search near the FIRST PEASANT *and* SECOND PEASANT, *and then approach the* THIRD PEASANT. GROSSMAN *stumbles over a bench.)*

BARONESS. *Mais dites moi, on le paye?*

ANNA PAVLOVNA. *Je ne saurais vous dire.*

BARONESS. *Mais c'est un monsieur?*

ANNA PAVLOVNA. *Oh! oui.*

BARONESS. *Ça tient du miraculeux. N'est-ce pas? Comment est-ce qu'll trouve?*

ANNA PAVLOVNA. *Je ne saurais vous dire. Mon mari vous l'expliquera.* (*Seeing the* PEASANTS, *looks around and sees* LUKERYA.) *Pardon...* What's this? (*The* BARONESS *approaches the group. To* LUKERYA.) Who let the peasants in?

LUKERYA. Yakov did.

ANNA PAVLOVNA. And who told Yakov to?

LUKERYA. I don't know. Fyodor Ivanych saw 'em.

ANNA PAVLOVNA. Leonid! (LEONID FYODOROVICH *does not hear, being occupied with the search, and says "sh-h."*) Fyodor Ivanych! What is the meaning of this? Didn't you see me disinfect the entire hall, and now you've infected my whole kitchen, the bread, the drinks...

FYODOR IVANYCH. I thought there would be no danger here; and the men have come on business. They have a long way to go, and are from our village.

ANNA PAVLOVNA. That's exactly the problem, they're from the Kursk village where people are dying like flies from diphtheria. But the main point is, I ordered them out of the house!... Did I or did I not? (*Goes over to the group gathered near the* PEASANTS.) Be careful! Don't touch them: they're all infected with diptheria! (*No one pays attention to her; she steps aside with dignity and stands quietly, waiting.*)

PETRISHCHEV (*sniffs loudly*). I don't know about diphtheria, but there is some other infection in the air. Do you smell it?

BETSY. Cut it out! Vovó, which bag?

VASILY LEONIDYCH. That one, over there. He's getting closer, closer.

PETRISHCHEV. What's this, a smell or a spell?

BETSY. Now's when your smokes come in handy. Go ahead, smoke, closer to me. (PETRISHCHEV *leans over and blows smoke at her.*)

VASILY LEONIDYCH. He's getting close, I tell you. Huh?

GROSSMAN (*anxiously gropes around the* THIRD PEASANT). Here, right here. I feel it's here.

FAT LADY. Do you feel an ectoplasm? (GROSSMAN *leans over the bag and takes out the spoon.*)

ALL. Bravo! (*General delight.*)

VASILY LEONIDYCH. Huh? So that's where our little spoon was! (*To the* PEASANT.) So that's how you are?

THIRD PEASANT. Whacha mean how I am? I didn't take yer spoon. What's he mixin' up? I didn't take it, an' that's that, I don't know nothin' 'bout it. He can talk all he wants. I saw he meant no good. "Gimme yer sack," he says. I didn't take it, so help me Christ, I didn't. (*The young people gather around him and laugh.*)

LEONID FYODOROVICH (*angrily to his son*). You're always fooling around! (*To the* THIRD PEASANT.) Don't worry, my friend! We know you didn't take it; it was only an experiment.

GROSSMAN (*removes the blindfold and pretends to be just coming to*). Can I have some water...please. (*Everyone fusses around him.*)

VASILY LEONIDYCH. Let's go to the coachman's place. I'll show you a male I have there. *Epâtant!* Huh?

BETSY. What a nasty word. Can't you just say dog?

VASILY LEONIDYCH. No. Just as you can't say about you: what an *Epâtant* being Betsy is! You have to say: girl; it's the same here. Huh? Marya Konstantinovna, isn't that right? Isn't it nice?

MARYA KONSTANTINOVNA. Well, let's go. (MARYA KONSTANTINOVNA, BETSY, PETRISHCHEV, *and* VASILY LEONIDYCH *exit.*)

SCENE 18

THE SAME *without* BETSY, MARYA KONSTANTINOVNA, PETRISHCHEV, *and* VASILY LEONIDYCH.

FAT LADY (*to* GROSSMAN). So? How are you? Are you rested? (GROSS-

MAN *does not answer. To* SAKHATOV.) Did you feel an ectoplasm, Sergey Ivanovich?

SAKHATOV. I didn't feel a thing. Yes, it was wonderful, wonderful. A complete success.

BARONESS. *Admirable! Ça ne le fait pas souffrir?*

LEONID FYODOROVICH. *Pas le moins du monde.*

PROFESSOR (*to* GROSSMAN). Would you mind? (*Hands him a thermometer.*) At the beginning of the experiment your temperature was ninety-nine. (*To the* DOCTOR.) Isn't that right? Please, check his pulse. Some loss is inevitable.

DOCTOR (*to* GROSSMAN). Now then, sir, your hand, please. We'll check it, we'll check it. (*Takes out his watch and holds his hand.*)

FAT LADY (*to* GROSSMAN). Wait a minute. The state you were in can't be called sleep, can it?

GROSSMAN (*wearily*). Hypnosis, it's the same.

SAKHATOV. Therefore, are we to understand that you hypnotized yourself?

GROSSMAN. And why not? Hypnosis may be induced not only by association, by the beat of a tom-tom, for example, as Charcot[12] did it, but also by merely entering a hypnogenetic zone.

SAKHATOV. Let's assume that is so, but nevertheless it would be desirable to define more specifically what hypnosis is.

PROFESSOR. Hypnosis is a phenomenon that transforms one energy into another.

GROSSMAN. That is not how Charcot defines it.

SAKHATOV. Excuse me, excuse me. That is your definition, but Libò[13] himself told me...

DOCTOR (*lets go of* GROSSMAN's *hand*). Ah, good, good, now for your temperature.

FAT LADY (*interrupting*). No, excuse me! I agree with Aleksey Vladimirovich. And here's the best proof for you. When I was lethargic after my illness, I felt an urge to talk. Generally I am reserved, but then I had this urge to talk and talk, and they tell me that everyone was surprised that I talked so much. (*To* SAKHATOV.) Anyway, I believe I interrupted you?

SAKHATOV (*with dignity*). Not at all. Please go on.

DOCTOR. His pulse is eighty-two, and his temperature has risen half a degree.

PROFESSOR. Now there's proof for you! That's exactly how it should be. (*Takes out his notebook and writes.*) Eighty-two, right? And ninety-nine point five? As soon as hypnosis is induced, invariably the heart's action intensifies.

DOCTOR. As a doctor I can testify that your prognosis is fully confirmed.

PROFESSOR (to SAKHATOV). You were saying?...

SAKHATOV. I wanted to say that Libò himself told me that hypnosis is only a specific psychic state that increases susceptibility to suggestion.

PROFESSOR. That is so, but nevertheless the main factor is the law of equivalents.

GROSSMAN. Furthermore, Libò is far from being an authority, while Charcot has studied the matter from every perspective, and proved that hypnosis produced by shock, trauma...

SAKHATOV. But I'm not at all rejecting Charcot's work. I know him too; I'm only repeating what Libò told me.

GROSSMAN (*excitedly*). There are three thousand patients in the Salpêtrière,[14] and I attended the whole course.

PROFESSOR. Excuse me, gentleman, that's not the point.

FAT LADY (*interrupting*). I'll explain it to you in a couple of words. When my husband was sick, all the doctors refused...

LEONID FYODOROVICH. Why don't we go back to the house. Baroness, if you please! (*Everyone exits talking together and interrupting each other.*)

SCENE 19

The three PEASANTS, LUKERYA, FYODOR IVANYCH, TANYA, *the* FORMER COOK (*on the stove*), LEONID FYODOROVICH, *and* ANNA PAVLOVNA.

ANNA PAVLOVNA (*stops* LEONID FYODOROVICH *by catching hold of his sleeve*). How many times have I asked you not to take charge of things around the house. You only know about your own foolishness, but I'm responsible for the house. You'll infect everyone.

LEONID FYODOROVICH. Who? How? I don't understand what you're talking about.

ANNA PAVLOVNA. How? People sick with diptheria are sleeping in the kitchen, which is in constant contact with the house.

LEONID FYODOROVICH. But I...

ANNA PAVLOVNA. What I?

LEONID FYODOROVICH. I don't know what you're talking about.

ANNA PAVLOVNA. You should, since you're the head of the family. You can't do this.

LEONID FYODOROVICH. But I didn't think... I thought...

ANNA PAVLOVNA. It's sickening to listen to you! (LEONID FYODOR-OVICH *remains silent. To* FYODOR IVANYCH.) Get them out of here! Don't ever let me see them in my kitchen! Its's awful. Nobody listens to me, everything to spite me... I chase them out of one place, and they let them back in another. (*Gets more and more excited, and bursts into tears.*) Everything to spite me! To spite me! And I'm in such pain... Doctor! Doctor! Pyotr Petrovich!... He's also left me! (*Exits sobbing, followed by* LEONID FYODOROVICH.)

SCENE 20

The three PEASANTS, TANYA, FYODOR IVANYCH, LUKERYA, *and the* FORMER COOK (*on the stove; tableau; all stand silent for a long time*).

THIRD PEASANT. They can go t'hell! If yuh don't watch out, the cops'll nab yuh. An' I've never been tried in my life. Let's go to a lodgin', boys!

FYODOR IVANYCH (*to* TANYA). What should we do?

TANYA. No problem, Fyodor Ivanych. They can go to the coachman's place.

FYODOR IVANYCH. How can we do that? As it is the the coachman was complaining that his place is full of dogs.

TANYA. Well then, to the yardman's place.

FYODOR IVANYCH. What if they find out?

TANYA. They won't find out. Don't worry, Fyodor Ivanych. How can we chase them out at night? They won't find anything now.

FYODOR IVANYCH. Well, do what you think best, just get them out of here. (*Exits.*)

SCENE 21

The three PEASANTS, TANYA, LUKERYA, *and the* FORMER COOK. *The* PEASANTS *pack their bags.*

FORMER COOK. Those damn bastards! It's cuz o' fat livin'! Bastards!

LUKERYA. You shut up. Lucky they didn't see yuh.

TANYA. So, ol'timers, let's go to the yardman's place.

FIRST PEASANT. Well, but how's our business goin'? How, fr'instance, 'bout the signature, applyin' his hand? Can we hope for it?

TANYA. We'll know everythin' in an hour.

SECOND PEASANT. Yuh gonna pull it off?

TANYA (*laughing*). God willin'.

Curtain.

ACT III

The action takes place in the evening of the same day in a small parlor where LEONID FYODOROVICH *always conducts his experiments.*

SCENE 1

LEONID FYODOROVICH *and the* PROFESSOR.

LEONID FYODOROVICH. So, shall we risk a seance with our new medium?

PROFESSOR. Certainly. He's undoubtedly a strong medium. Moreover, it's desirable to have a mediumistic seance today with the same people. Grossman will most certainly respond to the influence of the mediumistic energy, and then the connection and unity of the phenomena will be all the more evident. You'll see, if the medium is as strong as he was just now, Grossman will vibrate.

LEONID FYODOROVICH. In that case, I'll tell you what, I'll send for Semyon and invite those who wish to attend.

PROFESSOR. Yes, yes, I'll just make a few notes. (*Takes out his notebook and writes.*)

SCENE 2

THE SAME *and* SAKHATOV.

SAKHATOV. They're over by Anna Pavlovna playing whist, and I, as odd man out...and interested in the seance, am here with you... So, will there be a seance?

LEONID FYODOROVICH. Yes, there certainly will!

SAKHATOV. What, without Mr. Kapchich's mediumistic power?

LEONID FYODOROVICH. *Vous avez la main heureuse.* Just imagine, the peasant I told you about turns out to be a definite medium.

SAKHATOV. Really! Oh, now that's all the more interesting!

LEONID FYODOROVICH. Yes, yes. We conducted a little preliminary experiment with him after dinner.

SAKHATOV. You had time to do that and become convinced?

LEONID FYODOROVICH. Completely, and he turned out to be a remarkably strong medium.

SAKHATOV (*skeptically*). Really!

LEONID FYODOROVICH. It turns out that the servants have been noticing this for quite awhile. When he has tea, the spoon jumps into his hand by itself. (*To the* PROFESSOR.) Have you heard about it?

PROFESSOR. No, as a matter of fact I haven't.

SAKHATOV (*to the* PROFESSOR.) But still, do you think such phenomena are possible?

PROFESSOR. What phenomena?

SAKHATOV. Well, spiritualistic, mediumistic, and supernatural phenomena in general.

PROFESSOR. The point is what do we call supernatural? When a piece of stone, and not an animate being, attracted a nail to itself, how did this phenomenon appear to observers, natural or supernatural?

SAKHATOV. Yes, of course; but only such phenomena as magnetic attraction are continually repeated.

PROFESSOR. It's exactly the same in this case. The phenomenon repeats itself, and we investigate it. Moreover, to the phenomena being investigated, we apply laws common to other phenomena. You see, phenomena seem to be supernatural only because their causes are attributed to a medium. But that is wrong. Phenomena are produced not by a medium, but by psychic energy through a medium, and that's a great difference. The entire matter hinges on the law of equivalents.

SAKHATOV. Yes, of course, but...

SCENE 3

THE SAME *and* TANYA (*enters and stands behind the curtain*).

LEONID FYODOROVICH. You should know one thing, with this medium, just as with Home and Kapchich, you cannot count on anything for certain. There may be a failure, and there may even be a full materialization.

SAKHATOV. A materialization even? What kind of materialization can there be?

LEONID FYODOROVICH. Something like a dead person may appear: your father, or grandfather will take you by the hand, or give you something; or someone will suddenly rise into the air, as happened the last time here with Aleksey Vladimirovich.

PROFESSOR. Of course, of course. But the main thing is to explain the phenomena, and to classify them under common laws.

SCENE 4

THE SAME *and the* FAT LADY.

FAT LADY. Anna Pavlovna allowed me to join you.

LEONID FYODOROVICH. Welcome!

FAT LADY. I must say how tired Grossman is. He can hardly hold a cup. Did you notice (*to the* PROFESSOR) how pale he turned the moment he came close to it? I noticed it immediately, and was the first to tell Anna Pavlovna.

PROFESSOR. Undoubtedly—a loss of vital energy.

FAT LADY. It's just as I say, one should not abuse this. How about this, a hypnotist suggested to a friend of mine, Verochka Konshina—oh you know her—that she should stop smoking, and her back began to ache.

PROFESSOR (*tries to speak*). The temperature and the pulse obviously indicate...

FAT LADY. Just a moment, excuse me. So I said to her: it's better to smoke than to suffer because of your nerves. Of course, smoking is harmful, and I would like to give it up myself, but say what you want, I can't. Once I went two weeks without smoking, but I couldn't stand it any longer.

PROFESSOR (*tries to speak again*). Undoubtedly indicate...

FAT LADY. No, excuse me! Just two more words. You say a loss of strength? I also wanted to say that when I traveled by stage... The roads were terrible then, you don't remember, but I noticed, and say what you want, all our nervousness comes from the railways. For example, I can't sleep while traveling—I can't fall asleep for the life of me!

PROFESSOR (*begins again, but the* FAT LADY *does not let him speak*). A loss of strength...

SAKHATOV (*smiling*). Yes, yes. (LEONID FYODOROVICH *rings a bell.*)

FAT LADY. I'll be up for one, two, three nights, and still I won't fall asleep.

SCENE 5

THE SAME *and* GRIGORY.

LEONID FYODOROVICH. Please tell Fyodor to get everything ready for the seance, and have Semyon come here—the butler's assistant, Semyon, do you hear?

GRIGORY. Yes, sir! (*Exits.*)

SCENE 6

LEONID FYODOROVICH, *the* PROFESSOR, *the* FAT LADY, *and* TANYA (*hidden*).

PROFESSOR (*to* SAKHATOV). The temperature and pulse indicated a loss of vital energy. The same thing will also happen during mediumistic manifestations. The law of the conservation of energy...

FAT LADY. Yes, yes. I just wanted to say that I am very glad that a simple peasant turned out to be a medium. That's wonderful. I always said that the Slavophiles...

LEONID FYODOROVICH. Let's go ino the living room in the meantime.

FAT LADY. Excuse me, just a couple more words... The Slavophiles are right, but I always told my husband that one shouldn't exaggerate anything. The golden mean, you know. How can one assert that everything to do with the peasants is good when I myself have seen...

LEONID FYODOROVICH. Won't you please come into the living room?

FAT LADY. A boy, that little, drinking already. I reprimanded him immediately. And he was grateful afterwards. They are children, and I've always said, children need both love and discipline. (*Everyone exits, talking.*)

SCENE 7

TANYA *alone, comes out from behind the door.*

TANYA. Oh, if it would only work! (*Ties up some string.*)

SCENE 8

TANYA *and* BETSY (*enters hastily*).

BETSY. Isn't Papá here? (*Looks closely at* TANYA.) What are you doing here?

TANYA. Nothing, Lizaveta Leonidovna, I came in, I only wanted... Nothing... (*Embarrassed.*)

BETSY. Isn't there going to be a seance here soon? (*Notices that* TANYA *is gathering the strings, stares at her and suddenly bursts out laughing.*) Tanya! You're doing it all, aren't you? Now don't deny it. And the last time you did it too? You did it, right?

TANYA. Lizaveta Leonidovna, dear!

BETSY (*delighted*). Oh, that's great! I had no idea! But why did you do it?

TANYA. Dear Miss Lizaveta, don't give me away!

BETSY. I won't, not for anything. I'm so glad! But how do you do it?

TANYA. Well, like this. I hide, and then, when they put out the lights, I come out and do it.

BETSY (*pointing to the strings*). And what's that for? But don't tell me, I understand, you pull...

TANYA. Lizaveta Leonidovna, dear, you're the only one I'll tell. Before this I was just havin' fun, but now I need to do something.

BETSY. Oh, what? What's something?

TANYA. Well you saw the peasants that came, that want to buy some land, but your dad won't sell it, an' didn't sign the paper an' gave it back to 'em. Fyodor Ivanych says the spirits have fobidden him. So this is what I thought up.

BETSY. Ah, how clever you are! Go ahead, do it. But how will you do it?

TANYA. This is what I thought of: when they put out the lights, right away I'll start to knock and throw things around, touch their heads with the strings, and finally I'll take the paper about the land—I have it right here—and throw it on the table.

BETSY. And what then?

TANYA. Then? They'll be surprised. The peasants had the paper and now it's suddenly here. And now I'll tell them ...

BETSY. But Semyon is the medium today!

TANYA. So I'll tell him... (*Laughs so that she can't speak*) I'll tell him to squeeze whoever he can get hold of—only not your dad, he won't dare—and let him squeeze any of the others until the paper's signed.

BETSY (*laughing*). But that's not the way it's done. A medium doesn't do anything himself.

TANYA. That's all right, it's all the same—I hope it'll work.

SCENE 9

TANYA *and* FYODOR IVANYCH. BETSY *makes a sign to* TANYA *and exits.*

FYODOR IVANYCH (*to* TANYA). What are you doing here?

TANYA. I came to see you, Fyodor Ivanych, dear!...

FYODOR IVANYCH. What about?

TANYA. About the thing I've been askin' you.

FYODOR IVANYCH (*laughing*). I made the match, I sure did, we even shook on it. We didn't drink to it though.

TANYA (*squeals*). Really?

FYODOR IVANYCH. I'm telling you it is. He says: "I'll talk it over with the old lady, and then, God willing."

TANYA. Is that what he said?... (*Squealing.*) Oh, Fyodor Ivanych, dear, I'll pray for you the rest o' my life!

FYODOR IVANYCH. Well, okay, okay. Now's not the time. I was told to arrange things for the seance.

TANYA. Let me help you. How's it to be arranged?

FYODOR IVANYCH. How? Well, the table in the middle of the room, chairs, the guitar, the accordion. No lamp—just candles.

TANYA (*places the things with* FYODOR IVANYCH). Is this right? The guitar here, the inkwell here... (*puts it down.*) Like this?

FYODOR IVANYCH. Will they really have Semyon here?

TANYA. Probably. They had him before, you know.

FYODOR IVANYCH. I wonder! (*Puts on his pince-nez.*) But is he clean?

TANYA. How should I know!

FYODOR IVANYCH. Then this is what you do...

TANYA. What, Fyodor Ivanych?

FYODOR IVANYCH. You go, get the nailbrush and some Tridas soap—you can even take mine... And cut his nails and wash his hands real good.

TANYA. He'll do it himself.

FYODOR IVANYCH. Well then just tell him to. And tell him to put on clean clothes too.

TANYA. All right, Fyodor Ivanych. (*Exits.*)

SCENE 10

FYODOR IVANYCH *alone, sits down in an armchair.*

FYODOR IVANYCH. Educated as they are—just take Aleksey Vladimirovich, he's a professor—and yet sometimes you really wonder. They're putting an end to popular superstitions, crude superstitions about house demons, wizards and witches... And come to think of it, this is exactly the same supersision. Is it really possible for the souls of the dead to speak and play the guitar? Someone's fooling them, or they're fooling themselves. As for this business with Semyon, you just can't make it out. (*Looks through an album.*) Here's their spiritualistic album. How's it possible to take a picture of a spirit? Now here's a picture—a Turk and Leonid Fyodorovich sitting together. I just wonder at human weakness!

FYODOR IVANYCH *and* LEONID FYODOROVICH.

LEONID FYODOROVICH (*entering*). So, is everything ready?

FYODOR IVANYCH (*rises slowly*). Yes. (*Smiling.*) Only I'm afraid your new medium may let you down, Leonid Fyodorovich.

LEONID FYODOROVICH. No, Aleksey Vladimirovich and I tested him. He's an amazingly strong medium!

FYODOR IVANYCH. I don't know about that. But is he clean enough? You didn't bother to tell him to wash his hands. It might be embarrassing.

LEONID FYODOROVICH. His hands? Oh, yes, you think they're dirty?

FYODOR IVANYCH. What else, he's a peasant. And there'll be ladies present, and Marya Vasilyevna.

LEONID FYODOROVICH. Well, that's all right.

FYODOR IVANYCH. And there's something else I wanted to tell you: Timofey, the coachman, came to complain that he can't keep the place clean with dogs around.

LEONID FYODOROVICH (*arranging the things on the table, absentmindedly*). What dogs?

FYODOR IVANYCH. They brought three hounds for Vasily Leonidych today, and put them in the coachman's place.

LEONID FYODOROVICH (*irritably*). Tell Anna Pavlovna, let her do what she wants, I don't have time.

FYODOR IVANYCH. But you know how he is...

LEONID FYODOROVICH. Well, let her do what she wants. I have nothing but trouble from him... Anyway, I don't have time.

SCENE 12

THE SAME *and* SEMYON (*enters, wearing a jacket, smiles*).

SEMYON. Did you ask for me?

LEONID FYODOROVICH. Yes, yes. Let me see your hands. Just fine, fine.

Look here, my friend, you do just as you did last time, sit down and give yourself up to your senses. But don't think about anything.

SEMYON. What would I think about? It's worse when yuh think.

LEONID FYODOROVICH. That's it, that's it. The less conscious one is, the stronger it'll be. Don't think, just give yourself up to your mood: if you feel like sleeping—sleep, if you feel like walking—walk. Do you understand?

SEMYON. What's there t'understand? Nothin' tricky 'bout it.

LEONID FYODOROVICH. But the main thing is, don't get confused. Or you may wonder yourself. You understand that just as we live here, so does an invisible world of spirits also.

FYODOR IVANYCH (*correcting him*). Unseen beings, understand?

SEMYON (*laughs*). What's there t'understand? As you said, it's all very simple.

LEONID FYODOROVICH. You may rise up in the air or something else may happen, just don't be afraid.

SEMYON. What's there t'be 'fraid o'? I can do it.

LEONID FYODOROVICH. Well then, I'll go and get everyone. Is everything ready?

FYODOR IVANYCH. Seems to be.

LEONID FYODOROVICH. What about the blackboards?

FYODOR IVANYCH. They're downstairs, I'll get them right away. (*Exits.*)

SCENE 13

LEONID FYODOROVICH *and* SEMYON.

LEONID FYODOROVICH. Well then, all right. So don't get confused, and be relaxed.

SEMYON. Maybe I should take my jacket off: It'll be more relaxin'.

LEONID FYODOROVICH. Your jacket? No, no don't take it off. (*Exits.*)

SCENE 14

SEMYON *alone.*

SEMYON. She told me t'do the same thing again, an' she'll do what she does again. How come she's not afraid?

SCENE 15

SEMYON *and* TANYA (*enters without shoes, and in a dress the same color as the wallpaper.*) SEMYON *laughs.*

TANYA (*hushes him*). Sh-h!... They'll hear! Here, stick these matches onto your fingers like last time. (*Sticks them on.*) So, do you remember everything?

SEMYON (*counting on his fingers*). First of all, wet the matches. Wave my hands about—that's one. The second thing—chatter my teeth, like this... That's two. Now I forgot the third thing.

TANYA. But the third's the most important one. Now remember: soon as the paper falls on the table—I'll ring the bell—right away you do like this with your arms... Stretch them out as wide as you can an' grab. Whoever it is sitting near you, grab that one. And when yuh got that one, squeeze. (*Laughs.*) A gentleman or a lady—squeeze, just squeeze and don't let go, just as if yuh was asleep, and chatter yer teeth or growl, like this... (*Growls.*) And when I start playin' the guitar, make as if yuh're wakin' up, stretch, yuh know, like this, an' wake up... Do yuh remember everythin'?

SEMYON. I do, but it's so funny.

TANYA. Now don't you laugh. But even if you do, it won't do no harm. They'll think yuh're doin' it in yer sleep. Just one thing, don't really fall asleep when they put the lights out.

SEMYON. Don't worry, I'll pinch my ears.

TANYA. So watch out, Syomochka darling. Just do everything, don't be afraid. He'll sign the paper. You'll see. They're comin'... (*Gets under the sofa.*)

SCENE 16

SEMYON *and* TANYA. *Enter* GROSSMAN, *the* PROFESSOR, LEONID FYODOROVICH, *the* FAT LADY, *the* DOCTOR, SAKHATOV, *and* ANNA PAVLOVNA. SEMYON *stands by the door.*

LEONID FYODOROVICH. Please come in, all you nonbelievers! Although we have a new, unexpected medium, I anticipate very significant manifestations tonight.

SAKHATOV. That's very, very interesting.

FAT LADY (*about* SEMYON). *Mais il est très bien.*

ANNA PAVLOVNA. As a butler's assistant, yes, but...

SAKHATOV. Wives never believe in their husbands' doings. You don't think it at all possible, do you?

ANNA PAVLOVNA. Of course not. True, there is something special about Kapchich, but this one is God knows what!

FAT LADY. No, excuse me, Anna Pavlovna, you must not judge this way. Before I was married, I once had a remarkable dream. You know, there are such dreams that you don't know when they begin and when they end; so I had just such a dream...

SCENE 17

THE SAME. VASILY LEONIDYCH *and* PETRISHCHEV *enter.*

FAT LADY. And that dream revealed a lot to me. Nowadays these young people (*points to* PETRISHCHEV *and* VASILY LEONIDYCH) reject everything.

VASILY LEONIDYCH. But I tell you I never reject anything. Huh?

SCENE 18

THE SAME. *Enter* BETSY *and* MARYA KONSTANTINOVNA *and they begin to talk with* PETRISHCHEV.

FAT LADY. How can you reject the supernatural? They say it's irrational. But the rationale may be stupid, what then? Just take this thing at Sadovaya Street—have you heard?—it appeared every evening. My husband's brother—what do you call him?... Not *beau frère*, but in Russian... some other name.[15] I can never remember the names of the different relations in Russian—well, he went over there three nights in a row, and still didn't see anything, so that's why I say...

LEONID FYODOROVICH. Well now, who's staying?

FAT LADY. I am, I am!

SAKHATOV. I am!

ANNA PAVLOVNA (*to the* DOCTOR). Are you really going to stay?

DOCTOR. Yes, I have to see for once what it is that Aleksey Vladimirovich finds here. It's wrong to reject it without proof, you know.

ANNA PAVLOVNA. So shall I definitely take it tonight?

DOCTOR. Take what?... Oh, yes, the pill. Yes, why don't you take it. Yes, yes, take it... I'll drop by.

ANNA PAVLOVNA. Please do. (*Loudly.*) When you're finished, *messieurs et mesdames*, you are welcome to come over to me to relax from your emotions, and we'll also finish our game of whist.

FAT LADY. Certainly.

SAKHATOV. Yes, yes! (ANNA PAVLOVNA *exits.*)

SCENE 19

THE SAME *without* ANNA PAVLOVNA.

BETSY (*to* PETRISHCHEV). I'm telling you, stay. I promise you something extraordinary. Do you want to bet?

MARYA KONSTANTINOVNA. Do you really believe in this?

BETSY. Today I do.

MARYA KONSTANTINOVNA (*to* PETRISHCHEV). And do you?

PETRISHCHEV. "I can't, no I can't believe thy artful vows." But if Elizaveta Leonidovna bids me...

VASILY LEONIDYCH. Let's stay, Marya Konstantinovna. Huh? I'll think of something *épâtant*.

MARYA KONSTANTINOVNA. No, don't make me laugh. You know I can't help it.

VASILY LEONIDYCH (*loudly*). I'm staying!

LEONID FYODOROVICH (*sternly*). I ask those who stay not to make a joke out of this. It's a serious matter.

PETRISHCHEV. Do you hear that? Well then, let's stay. Vovó, sit here, but look out, don't get scared.

BETSY. You laugh now, but wait and see what happens.

VASILY LEONIDYCH. And what if it really does? That'll be something! Huh?

PETRISHCHEV (*trembling*). Oh, I'm scared, I'm scared. Marya Konstantinovna, I'm scared!.... my treet femble.

BETSY (*laughs*). Hush! (*All sit down.*)

LEONID FYODOROVICH. Sit down, sit down. Semyon, sit down!

SEMYON. Yes, sir. (*Sits down on the edge of his chair.*)

LEONID FYODOROVICH. Make yourself comfortable.

PROFESSOR. Sit properly, in the middle of the chair, completely at ease. (*Seats* SEMYON.)

(BETSY, MARYA KONSTANTINOVNA, *and* VASILY LEONIDYCH *laugh.*)

LEONID FYODOROVICH (*raising his voice*). I ask those who stay not to fool around, and to treat this matter seriously. The consequences might be bad. Do you hear, Vovó? If you can't be quiet, leave.

VASILY LEONIDYCH. Quiet! (*Hides behind the* FAT LADY.)

LEONID FYODOROVICH. Aleksey Vladimirovich, hypnotize him.

PROFESSOR. No, why should I when Anton Borisovich is here? He has much more practice and power in this regard... Anton Borisovich!

GROSSMAN. Ladies and Gentlemen! I'm not really a spiritualist. I've only studied hypnosis. It's true, I've studied hypnosis in all its known manifestations. But I'm entirely unfamiliar with what's called spiritualism. From the subject's trance I can anticipate certain hypnotic phenomena: lethargy, abulia, anesthesia, analgesia, catalepsy and every kind of susceptibility to suggestion. But here it is not these, but some other phenomena that are being proposed for investigation. Therefore, it would be desirable to know what kind of phenomena to expect, and what is their scientific significance.

SAKHATOV. I fully agree with Mr. Grossman's opinion. Such an explanation would be most interesting.

LEONID FYODOROVICH (*to the* PROFESSOR). Aleksey Vladimirovich, I think you will not refuse to give us a brief explanation.

PROFESSOR. Why not, I can explain if they wish. (*To the* DOCTOR.) Will you please take his temperature and pulse. My expanation will inevitably be superficial and brief.

LEONID FYODOROVICH. Yes, brief, brief...

DOCTOR. Just a moment. (*Takes out a thermometer and hands it over.*) Now then, young man!... (*Inserts it.*)

SEMYON. Yes, sir.

PROFESSOR (*rising and addressing the* FAT LADY, *then sitting down*). Ladies and Gentlemen! The phenomenon that we are investigating usually is, on the one hand, regarded as something new, and, on the other, as something transcending the course of natural conditions. Neither view is correct. This phenomenon is not new, but is as old as the world; nor is it supernatural, but is subject to the same eternal laws to which all that exists is subject. This phenomenon has usually been defined as communication with the spiritual world. This definition is inaccurate. According to this definition the spiritual world is contrasted to the material world, but this is wrong: there is no such contrast. Both worlds are so closely connected that it is not at all possible to draw a line of demarcation, separating one world from the other. We say: matter is composed of molecules...

PETRISHCHEV. Boring matter! (*Whispering, laughter.*)

PROFESSOR (*pausing and then continuing*). Molecules are made up of atoms, but atoms, having no extension, are in essence nothing but points where forces are applied. That is, not forces, strictly speaking, but energy—that same energy which is as indivisible and indestructible as matter. Thus energy is just like matter, which, though one, has diverse forms. Until recently we were aware of only four forms of energy that are convertible into one another. The energies we are aware of are: dynamic, thermal, electrical and chemcial. But four forms of energy fall short of accounting for all the varieties of its manifestations. There are multifarious forms of the manifestation of energy, and one of these new, little-known forms of energy is what we are investigating here. I am speaking about mediumistic energy.

(*Again whispering and laughter from the young people.*)

PROFESSOR (*pauses, looks around sternly, then continues*). Mediumistic energy has been known to mankind for a very long time: prognostications, premonitions, visions, and so on. All of this is nothing but manifestations of mediumistic energy. The phenomena produced by it have been known for a very long time. But the energy itself has not been recognized as such until very recently, when an environment, the vibrations of which produce mediumistic energy, was recognized. And just as the phenomenon of light remained unexplained until the existence of a weightless substance, ether, was recognized, so, too, did mediumistic phenomena seem mysterious until the now indisputable fact was recognized, that between the particles of ether there exists another weightless substance, even more rarefied than ether, that is not subject to the law of three dimensions...

(*Again whispering, laughter, and squealing.*)

PROFESSOR (*looking around again sternly*). And just as mathematical calculations have irrefutably confirmed the existence of weightless ether which produces the phenomena of light and electricity, so, too, have a brilliant series of the most definitive experiments by the ingenious Hermann Schmidt and Josef Schmatzhofen[16] indisputably confirmed the existence of a substance that fills the universe, and can be called psychic ether.

FAT LADY. Yes, now I understand, how grateful I am...

LEONID FYODOROVICH. Yes, but, Aleksey Vladimirovich, couldn't you... make it a bit shorter?

PROFESSOR (*ignoring him*). Thus, a series of strict, scientific experiments and studies have explained the laws of mediumistic phenomena to us, as I have had the honor of informing you. These experiments have explained to us that the immersion of certain individuals into a hypnotic state, which differs from ordinary sleep only in that upon immersion into this sleep, physiological activity not only does not decrease, but always increases—as we have just witnessed—demonstrated that the immersion of any subject whatever into this state invariably results in certain perturbations in the psychic ether—perturbations completely analagous to those produced by the immersion of a solid body into a liquid. These very perturbations are what we call mediumistic phenomena...

(*Laughter, whispering.*)

SAKHATOV. That is completely correct and understandable; but may I ask: if, as you say, the immersion of a medium into a trance produces perturbations of the psychic ether, why, then, do these perturbations always reveal themselves, as is usually presupposed at spiritualistic seances, in the manifestation of activity of spirits of the dead?

PROFESSOR. Because the particles of this psychic ether are nothing other than the spirits of the living, the dead, and the unborn, so that any vibration of this psychic ether inevitably causes a certain movement of its particles. And these particles are nothing other than human spirits which by this movement communicate with each other.

FAT LADY (*to* SAKHATOV). What's there not to understand? It's so simple... Thank you, very, very much!

LEONID FYODOROVICH. I think everything is clear now, and we can begin.

DOCTOR. The young fellow is absolutely in normal condition: temperature ninety-nine, pulse seventy-four.

PROFESSOR (*takes out his notebook and writes*). Confirmation of what I've had the honor of informing you will be the immersion of the medium into a trance, which, as we shall now witness, will inevitably cause a rise in temperature and pulse, just as in hypnosis.

LEONID FYODOROVICH. Yes, yes, excuse me; I only wanted to reply to what Sergey Ivanych asked: how do we know that the spirits of the dead are communicating with us? We know this because the spirit that appears plainly tells us—as plainly as I'm telling you—tells us who it is and why it has appeared, and where it is and whether all is well with it! At the last seance a Spaniard, Don Castillos, appeared, and he told us everything. He told us who he was, and when he died, and that he was miserable because he took part in the Inquisition. Moreover, he related what was happening to him at the very time he was talking to us, specifically, that at the very time he was talking to us he had to be born again on earth, and therefore could not finish the conversation that he had begun with us. But now you'll see for yourselves...

FAT LADY (*interrupting*). Oh, how interesting! Maybe the Spaniard was born in our house, and is a baby now.

LEONID FYODOROVICH. It's very possible.

PROFESSOR. I think it's time to begin.

LEONID FYODOROVICH. I only wanted to mention...

PROFESSOR. It's late already.

LEONID FYODOROVICH. Very well. Then we can begin. Anton Borisovich, please hypnotize the medium...

GROSSMAN. How do you want me to hypnotize the subject? There are many generally used ways. There's Braid's method,[17] there is the Egyptian symbol, and there's Charcot's method.

LEONID FYODOROVICH (*to the* PROFESSOR). I think it makes no difference.

PROFESSOR. It doesn't.

GROSSMAN. Then I'll use my own method, which I demonstrated in Odessa.

LEONID FYODOROVICH. Please do!

(GROSSMAN *waves his hands over* SEMYON. SEMYON *closes his eyes and stretches.*)

GROSSMAN (*looks at him closely*). He's falling asleep, he's asleep. A remarkably quick occurrence of hypnosis. Apparently the subject has already reached an anesthetic state. He's a remarkably and unusually receptive subject, and could be subjected to interesting experiments!... (*Sits down, stands up, sits down again.*) We could prick his hand now. If you wish...

PROFESSOR (*to* LEONID FYODOROVICH). Do you notice how the medium's trance is affecting Grossman? He's beginning to vibrate.

LEONID FYODOROVICH. Yes, yes, can the lights be put out now?

SAKHATOV. But why must there be darkness?

PROFESSOR. Darkness? Because darkness is one of the conditions under which mediumistic energy is manifested, just as a certain temperature is a condition for certain manifestations of chemical or dynamic energy.

LEONID FYODOROVICH. But not always. I and many others have witnessed manifestations both by candlelight and daylight.

PROFESSOR (*interrupting*). Can the lights be put out?

LEONID FYODOROVICH. Yes, yes. (*Puts out the candles.*) Ladies and Gentlemen! Your attention, please.

(TANYA *crawls out from under the sofa and takes hold of a string attached to a sconce.*)

PETRISHCHEV. You know, I liked the Spaniard. The way he went head-first in the middle of the conversation... that's what's called *piquer une tête*.

BETSY. You just wait and see what's next!

PETRISHCHEV. I'm just afraid of one thing: that Vovó will begin to grunt like a pig.

VASILY LEONIDYCH. Do you want me to? I can easily...

LEONID FYODOROVICH. Ladies and gentlemen! No talking, please...

(*Silence.* SEMYON *licks his finger, smears his knuckles and waves.*)

LEONID FYODOROVICH. A light! Do you see the light?

SAKHATOV. A light! Yes, yes, I see it; but wait a minute...

FAT LADY. Where, where? Ah, I didn't see it! There it is. Ah!...

PROFESSOR (*to* LEONID FYODOROVICH *in a whisper, pointing to* GROSSMAN, *who is moving*). Notice how he vibrates. It's the dual force. (*The light appears again.*)

LEONID FYODOROVICH (*to the* PROFESSOR). That is he, you know.

SAKHATOV. Who's he?

LEONID FYODOROVICH. The Greek, Nicholas. It's his light. Isn't that so, Aleksey Vladimirovich?

SAKHATOV. Who's the Greek Nicholas?

PROFESSOR. A Greek who was a monk in Constantinople during the time of Constantine, and who has been visiting us lately.

FAT LADY. Where is he? Where is he? I don't see him.

LEONID FYODOROVICH. He can't be seen yet. Aleksey Vladimirovich, he's always been especially responsive to you. Ask him.

PROFESSOR (*in a distinctive voice*). Nicholas, is that you?

(TANYA *knocks twice on the wall.*)

LEONID FYODOROVICH (*joyfully*). It is he! It is he!

FAT LADY. Oh, oh! I better leave.

SAKHATOV. Why do you assume it is he?

LEONID FYODOROVICH. The two knocks. That's a positive answer; otherwise there would have been silence.

(*Silence. Restrained laughter in the young people's corner.* TANYA *throws a lampshade, pencil, and a penwiper on the table.*)

LEONID FYODOROVICH (*in a whisper*). Notice, ladies and gentlemen, here's a lampshade. And something else. A pencil! Aleksey Vladimirovich, it's a pencil.

PROFESSOR. Good, good. I'm watching him and Grossman. Do you notice?

(GROSSMAN *stands up and looks over the objects that dropped on the table.*)

SAKHATOV. Excuse me, excuse me! I would like to see whether the medium is doing all this himself.

LEONID FYODOROVICH. Do you think so? Then sit down beside him and hold his hands. But be assured he's asleep.

SAKHATOV (*approaches, his head touches the string which* TANYA *lowered, becomes frightened and stoops.*) Yes.. ah-ah!.... Strange, very strange. (*Comes up to* SEMYON, *takes hold of his elbow.* SEMYON *growls.*)

PROFESSOR (*to* LEONID FYODOROVICH). Do you hear how Grossman's presence affects him? This is a new phenomenon, I must make note of it... (*Runs out, notes it down, then returns.*)

LEONID FYODOROVICH. Yes... But we can't leave Nicholas without an answer, we have to begin...

GROSSMAN (*stands up, comes up to* SEMYON, *raises and lowers his arm*). It would be interesting to produce contracture now. The subject is fully under hypnosis.

PROFESSOR (*to* LEONID FYODOROVICH). Do you see, do you see?

GROSSMAN. If you wish...

DOCTOR. Now, my friend, just let Aleksey Vladimirovich handle it, this is a serious thing.

PROFESSOR. Leave him alone. He's talking in his sleep already.

FAT LADY. How glad I am now that I've decided to be present. It's frightening, but still I'm glad, because I always said to my husband...

LEONID FYODOROVICH. Silence, please.

(TANYA *draws the string across the* FAT LADY*'s head.*)

FAT LADY. Aah!

LEONID FYODOROVICH. What? What is it?

FAT LADY. He pulled my hair.

LEONID FYODOROVICH (*in a whisper*). Don't be afraid, it's all right, give him your hand. His hand might be cold, but I like that.

FAT LADY (*hides her hand*). Never!

SAKHATOV. Yes, strange, very strange!

LEONID FYODOROVICH. He's here and is looking to communicate. Does anyone want to ask something?

SAKHATOV. Let me ask.

PROFESSOR. Please do.

SAKHATOV. Do I believe or not?

(TANYA *knocks twice.*)

PROFESSOR. A positive answer.

SAKHATOV. Let me ask again. Do I have a ten-rouble note in my pocket?

(TANYA *knocks many times and draws the string across* SAKHATOV's *head.*)

SAKHATOV. Ah!... (*Grabs the string and breaks it.*)

PROFESSOR. I would ask those present not to ask indefinite or facetious questions. He doesn't like that.

SAKHATOV. No, excuse me, I have a string in my hand.

LEONID FYODOROVICH. A string? Keep it. That often happens; not only a string, but silk laces, very old ones.

SAKHATOV. But where did the string come from?

(TANYA *throws a pillow at him.*)

SAKHATOV. Excuse me, excuse me! Something soft hit me in the head. Let's have some light—there's something here...

PROFESSOR. Please, do not interrupt the manifestations.

FAT LADY. For God's sake, don't interrupt! I also want to ask, may I?

LEONID FYODOROVICH. Yes, of course. Go ahead.

FAT LADY. I want to ask about my stomach. May I? I want to ask, what should I take, aconite or belladonna?

(*Silence, whispers from the young people, and suddenly* VASILY LEONIDYCH *begins to cry like a nursing infant: oo-ah, oo-ah! Laughter. Covering their noses and mouths and snorting, the girls and* PETRISHCHEV *run away.*)

FAT LADY. Ah, evidently this Greek monk is born again too.

LEONID FYODOROVICH (*infuriated, in an angry whisper*). There's nothing but nonsense from you! If you can't behave decently, leave.

(VASILY LEONIDYCH *exits.*)

SCENE 20

LEONID FYODOROVICH, *the* PROFESSOR, *the* FAT LADY, SAKHA-TOV, GROSSMAN, *the* DOCTOR, SEMYON, *and* TANYA. *Darkness and silence.*

FAT LADY. Ah, what a pity! Now I can't ask. He was just born.

LEONID FYODOROVICH. Not at all. That's Vovó's nonsense. *He* is here. Go ahead, ask.

PROFESSOR. That often happens: these jokes and ridicule are a very common phenomenon. I assume *he* is still here. Anyway, we can ask. Leonid Fyodorovich, will you?

LEONID FYODOROVICH. No, will you, please. This has upset me. It's so unpleasant! So tactless!...

PROFESSOR. All right, all right!... Nicholas, are you still here?

(TANYA *knocks twice and rings the bell.* SEMYON *begins to growl and stretches his arms out. He grabs* SAKHATOV *and the* PROFESSOR *and squeezes them.*)

PROFESSOR. What an unexpected manifestation! A repercussion on the medium himself. That has never happened before. Leonid Fyodorovich, keep watch, it's awkward for me. He's squeezing me. And keep an eye on Grossman. You have to be very attentive now.

(TANYA *throws the peasants' paper on the table.*)

LEONID FYODOROVICH. Something fell on the table.

PROFESSOR. See what it is.

LEONID FYODOROVICH. A paper! A folded sheet of paper.

(TANYA *throws a portable inkwell on the table.*)

LEONID FYODOROVICH. An inkwell!

(TANYA *throws a pen on the table.*)

LEONID FYODOROVICH. A pen!

(SEMYON *growls and squeezes.*)

PROFESSOR (*being squeezed*). Wait a moment, wait, this is an entirely new phenomenon: it's not the educed mediumistic energy that's acting, but the medium himself. Then open the inkwell, and put the pen on the paper, he'll write something, he will.

(TANYA *goes behind* LEONID FYODOROVICH *and hits him in the head with the guitar.*)

LEONID FYODOROVICH. He struck my head. (*Looks at the table.*) The pen isn't writing yet, and the paper is folded.

PROFESSOR. See what kind of paper it is, be quick about it; obviously the dual force—his and Grossman's—is producing perturbations.

LEONID FYODOROVICH (*goes out with the paper and immediately returns*). Incredible! This paper is the agreement with the peasants that I refused to sign this morning, and gave back to them. Could *he* want me to sign it?

PROFESSOR. Of course! Of course! But ask him.

LEONID FYODOROVICH. Nicholas! Do you really want...

(TANYA *knocks twice.*)

PROFESSOR. Do you hear? It's obvious, quite obvious!

(LEONID FYODOROVICH *takes the pen and exits.* TANYA *knocks, plays the guitar and accordion, and crawls under the sofa again.* LEONID FYODOROVICH *returns.* SEMYON *stretches and coughs.*)

LEONID FYODOROVICH. He's waking up. We can light the candles.

PROFESSOR (*hurriedly*). Doctor, doctor, please, his temperature and pulse. You'll see that both will have risen.

LEONID FYODOROVICH (*lights the candles*). So what do you say, all you nonbelievers?

DOCTOR (*goes up to* SEMYON *with the thermometer*). Here you are, my boy. So, did you have a nap? Here, insert this and give me your hand. (*Looks at his watch.*)

SAKHATOV (*shrugging his shoulders*). I can assert that the medium could not have done all that has taken place. But the string? I would like an explanation of the string.

LEONID FYODOROVICH. String, the string! There were more serious phenomena.

SAKHATOV. I don't know. In any case, *je réserve mon opinion.*

FAT LADY (*to* SAKHATOV). But how can you say: *je réserve mon opinion?* What about the infant with wings? Didn't you see it? At first I thought it was my imagination; but afterward it was as clear as clear can be, like it was alive...

SAKHATOV. I can only speak of what I saw. I didn't see that, not at all.

FAT LADY. Well, how come? It was absolutely clearly visible. And to the left there was a monk in black habit bending over it...

SAKHATOV (*walking away*). What exaggeration!

FAT LADY (*addressing the* DOCTOR). You must have seen it. It rose up from your side.

(*Not listening to her, the* DOCTOR *continues taking* SEMYON*'s pulse.*)

FAT LADY (*to* GROSSMAN). And the light, the light coming from it, especially around its little face. And the expression, so sweet, so tender, something really heavenly! (*Smiles tenderly herself.*)

GROSSMAN. I saw a phosphorescent light, and moving objects, but I didn't see anything else.

FAT LADY. Oh, stop it! You're just saying so. It's because you, scholars of the Charcot school, don't believe in life after death. But now no one, absolutely no one can shake my faith in a future life.

(GROSSMAN *walks away from her.*)

FAT LADY. No, no, whatever you say, this is one of the happiest moments in my life. When Sarasate played,[18] and now... Yes! (*No one listens to her.*

She goes up to SEMYON.) Now tell me, my friend, what did you feel? Was it very hard for you?

SEMYON (*laughs*). Yes, ma'am.

FAT LADY. Still, not unbearable?

SEMYON. No, ma'am. (*To* LEONID FYODOROVICH.) Can I go?

LEONID FYODOROVICH. Yes, go.

DOCTOR (*to the* PROFESSOR). His pulse is the same, but the temperature is lower.

PROFESSOR. Lower? (*Becomes thoughtful and suddenly conjectures.*) That's right—it should decrease! Dual energy crossing should produce some kind of interference. Yes, yes.

(*Leaving, they all speak together*)

LEONID FYODOROVICH. I'm only sorry that there wasn't a complete materialization. But still... Ladies and gentlemen, to the living room, please.

FAT LADY. I was especially impressed when it flapped its little wings, and you could see it rise.

GROSSMAN (*to* SAKHATOV). If we had stuck to hypnosis alone, we might have produced full-blown epilepsy. We could have succeeded totally.

SAKHATOV. It's interesting, but not entirely convincing! That's all I can say.

SCENE 21

LEONID FYODOROVICH *holding the paper. Enter* FYODOR IVANYCH.

LEONID FYODOROVICH. Well, Fyodor, what a wonderful seance we had! It turns out that I have to let the peasants have the land on their terms.

FYODOR IVANYCH. Is that so!

LEONID FYODOROVICH. What else? (*Shows him the paper.*) Just imagine, the paper I gave back to them turned up on the table. I signed it.

FYODOR IVANYCH. How did it get there?

LEONID FYODOROVICH. It just did. (*Exits.* FYODOR IVANYCH *follows him.*)

SCENE 22

TANYA *alone, crawls out from under the sofa and laughs.*

TANYA. Goodness gracious! My God, how scared I was when he caught the string! (*Squeals.*) But it worked out anyway—he signed!

SCENE 23

TANYA *and* GRIGORY.

GRIGORY. So it's you that's been foolin' 'em?

TANYA. What's it to you?

GRIGORY. D'ya think the mistress'll praise yuh for this? Forget it, now yuh've had it. I'll tell 'em 'bout yer hocus-pocus if yuh don't do what I want.

TANYA. I won't do what you want, and you're not goin' to do anything to me either.

Curtain.

ACT IV

The set is the same as in Act I.

SCENE 1

Two FOOTMEN *in livery,* FYODOR IVANYCH, *and* GRIGORY.

FIRST FOOTMAN (*with gray whiskers*). Yers is the third place today. Lucky the receptions are in the same direction. Yers used t'be on Thursdays before.

FYODOR IVANYCH. Then they changed it to Saturday, to be on the same day as the Golovkins and Grade von Grabes...

SECOND FOOTMAN. It's really great at the Shcherbakovs, whenever there's a ball, there's treats for the footmen.

SCENE 2

THE SAME. *The* PRINCESS *and* YOUNG PRINCESS *come downstairs.* BETSY *is seeing them off. The* PRINCESS *looks at her notebook, her watch, and sits down on a chest.* GRIGORY *helps her put on her galoshes.*

YOUNG PRINCESS. Oh please come. If you won't, Dodó won't—and then nothing will come of it.

BETSY. I don't know. I certainly have to go to the Shubins. Then there's the rehearsal.

YOUNG PRINCESS. You'll make it. Oh, please come. *Ne nous fais pas faux bond.* There'll be Fedya and Kokó.

BETSY. *J'en ai par dessus la tête de votre Cocó.*

YOUNG PRINCESS. I thought I'd find him here. *Ordinairement il est d'une exactitude...*

BETSY. He'll certainly be here.

YOUNG PRINCESS. Whenever I see him with you, it seems to me that he either just proposed, or is about to.

BETSY. Yes, I'll probably have to go through that. It's so unpleasant, too!

YOUNG PRINCESS. Poor Kokó! He's so in love.

BETSY. *Cessez, les gens.*

YOUNG PRINCESS (*sits down on the sofa, talking in a whisper;* GRIGORY *puts on her galoshes*). See you tonight.

BETSY. I'll try.

PRINCESS. So tell your Papá that I don't believe in anything, but I'll come to see his new medium. Ask him to let me know. Good-bye, *ma toute belle.* (*Kisses* [BETSY] *and exits with the* YOUNG PRINCESS. BETSY *goes upstairs.*)

SCENE 3

The two FOOTMEN, FYODOR IVANYCH, *and* GRIGORY.

GRIGORY. I don't like puttin' galoshes on ol' ladies: they can't bend down, can't see over their bellies, an' just poke 'round with their feet. Now it's different with a young one—it's real nice t'hold 'er foot in yer hand.

SECOND FOOTMAN. Look who's bein' fussy!

FIRST FOOTMAN. We can't be none too fussy.

GRIGORY. Why not, ain't we also people? It's them that think we don't understand; like just now, they started talkin' an' then looked at me, an' right away: ley zhan.

SECOND FOOTMAN. An' what's that?

GRIGORY. In Russian that means: don't talk, they'll understand. It's the same at dinner, but I understand. Yuh say there's a difference—but there ain't none.

FIRST FOOTMAN. There's a big difference for those who understand.

GRIGORY. Ain't no difference at all. Today I'm a footman, but tomorrow I may be as well off as them. Hasn't it ever happened that their women marry footmen? I'd better go have a smoke. (*Exits.*)

SCENE 4

THE SAME *without* GRIGORY.

SECOND FOOTMAN. Yuh've got a pretty cocky guy there.

FYODOR IVANYCH. He's worthless, not fit for service; used to be an office boy, got spoilt. I was against taking him, but the mistress liked him—stands out on visits.

FIRST FOOTMAN. I'd like to send 'im t'our count: he'd put 'im in his place. Oh, how he hates such airheads. If yuh're a footman, be a footman, live up to yer callin'; but this kinda pride ain't fittin'.

SCENE 5

THE SAME. PETRISHCHEV *runs downstairs and takes out a cigarette. He meets* KOKÓ KLINGEN, *who enters wearing a pince-nez.*

PETRISHCHEV (*thoughtful*). Yes, yes. My second syllable rhymes with my first. Lo-co-mo-... The whole thing is... Yes, yes... A Kokó-Loco! Where're you coming from?

KOKÓ KLINGEN. From the Shcherbakovs. You're always fooling around...

PETRISHCHEV. No, listen, here's my charade: my first clue is a "title," the second is a "bird," and the third could mean an"opening." The whole thing is something one should not do.

KOKÓ KLINGEN. Oh I don't know. And I don't have time.

PETRISHCHEV. Where else are you going?

KOKÓ KLINGEN. Where? To the Ivins, there's the chorus, must be there. Then to the Shubins, and then to the rehearsal. Don't you have to be there also?

PETRISHCHEV. Yes, certainly. Both to the rehearsal and the traversal.[19] I was a savage, you know, and now I'm both a savage and a general.

KOKÓ KLINGEN. Well how was the seance yesterday?

PETRISHCHEV. It was a riot! There was a peasant; but the main thing— it was all in the dark. Vovó squealed like an infant. The professor gave explanations and Marya Vasilyevna went into details. Really funny! Too bad you weren't there.

KOKÓ KLINGEN. I'm afraid, *mon cher*, somehow you have a way of getting away with things with your jokes; but it seems to me that as soon as I utter the least little word, it's immediately turned into a proposal. *Et ça ne m'arrange pa du tout, du tout. Mais du tout, du tout!*

PETRISHCHEV. Why don't you make a proposal into a disposal,[20] then nothing will come of it. So drop by Vovó's, and we'll go to the reversal together.

KOKÓ KLINGEN. I don't understand how you can hang around with such a fool. He's so stupid—a real good-for-nothing.

PETRISHCHEV. But I love him, I love Vovó, but "with a strange love", "to him the people's path will not be overgrown"...[21] (*Exits into* VASILY LEONIDYCH's *room.*)

SCENE 6

The two FOOTMEN, FYODOR IVANYCH, *and* KOKÓ KLINGEN. BETSY *sees a* LADY *off.* KOKÓ *bows significantly.*

BETSY (*shakes his hand, turned sideways to the* LADY). Aren't you acquainted?

LADY. No.

BETSY. Baron Klingen. Why weren't you here yesterday?

KOKÓ KLINGEN. I couldn't make it, didn't have time.

BETSY. What a pity, it was very interesting. (*Laughs.*) You would have seen the *manifestations* we had. So tell me, is our charade moving along?

KOKÓ KLINGEN. Oh, yes! The verses for *mon second* are ready, Nick wrote them and I did the music.

BETSY. So how does it go? Tell me.

KOKÓ KLINGEN. Wait a second, how does it go?... Yes! A knight sings to Nanna. (*Sings.*)

> "*Na*ture in its splendor,
> A *na*rcotic for my soul...
> *Na*nna, Nanna! Na,na,na!*"

LADY. So *mon second* is *na*, but what is *mon premier*?

KOKÓ KLINGEN. *Mon premier*—is *Aré*, the name of a girl savage.

BETSY. *Aré*, you see, is a girl savage who wants to eat the object of her love... (*Laughs.*) She walks around pining and singing:

> "Ah, my appetite..."

KOKÓ KLINGEN (*interrupting*). "I must fight...

BETSY (*continues*).

> "I want someone to eat
> I roam, I'm out of my mind...

KOKÓ KLINGEN.

> "For I'm not able to find...

BETSY.

> "On whom to dine—I'm daft...

KOKÓ KLINGEN.

> "But look, there's a raft...

BETSY.

> "And here comes this craft,
> With two generals on aft...

KOKÓ KLINGEN.

> "Two generals are we,
> Who by fate's decree,
> To this island must flee."

And again the *refrain:*

> "Who by fate's decree,
> To this island must fle-e-e."

LADY. *Charmant!*

BETSY. Just think how silly it is!

KOKÓ KLINGEN. Yes, but that's the charm of it.

LADY. And who is Aré?

BETSY. I am. I had a costume made, but Mamá says: "It's indecent." But it isn't more indecent than a ball dress. (*To* FYODOR IVANYCH.) Is the man from Bourdier's still here?

FYODOR IVANYCH. Yes, he's in the kitchen.

LADY. Well, how are you going to act out *aréna*?

BETSY. You'll see. I don't want to spoil the fun for you. *Au revoir.*

LADY. Good-bye! (*They curtsy to each other. The* LADY *exits.*)

BETSY (*to* KOKÓ KLINGEN). Let's go to *Maman*. (BETSY *and* KOKÓ KLINGEN *go upstairs.*)

SCENE 7

FYODOR IVANYCH, *the two* FOOTMEN, *and* YAKOV (*enters from the pantry carrying a tray with tea and pastry; walks through the hall out of breath*).

YAKOV (*to the* FOOTMEN). Regards t'yuh, regards!

(*The* FOOTMEN *bow.*)

YAKOV (*to* FYODOR IVANYCH). I wish yuh'd tell Grigory Mikhailych to give me a hand. I'm about t'drop... (*Exits.*)

SCENE 8

THE SAME *without* YAKOV.

FIRST FOOTMAN. That's a hard-workin' guy yuh've got there.
FYODOR IVANYCH. He's a nice guy, but the mistress doesn't like him—says, he doesn't look good enough. And now off they went and snitched on him yesterday that he let peasants into the kitchen. I'm afraid he might get sacked! And he's such a nice guy.
SECOND FOOTMAN. What peasants?
FYODOR IVANYCH. Those that came from our Kursk village to buy land; it was late at night, and we all come from the same area. One is our butler's father. So we let them into the kitchen. It just so happened they were having a mind reading session; they hid something in the kitchen, and all the ladies and gentlemen came in, and the mistress saw them—what an uproar! "How could you," she said, "these peasants may be infected, and you let them into the kitchen!..." She's really afraid of this infection.

SCENE 9

THE SAME *and* GRIGORY.

FYODOR IVANYCH. Grigory, go help Yakov Ivanych, I'll stay here by myself. It's too much for him alone.

GRIGORY. He's a clod, that's why it's too much. (*Exits*).

SCENE 10

THE SAME *without* GRIGORY.

FIRST FOOTMAN. What's this newfangled thing—these infections!... So yers is also afraid?

FYODOR IVANYCH. Worse than fire! The only thing we're doing now is fumigating, washing and spraying.

FIRST FOOTMAN. I thought I could smell somethin' strong. (*Animated.*) It's a cryin' shame how they carry on 'bout these infections. It's real nasty! They've even forgotten God. There's our master's sister, Princess Mosolov, her daughter was dyin'. So what d'ya think? Neither the father nor mother even came into the room t'say good-bye. And the daughter was cryin' an' callin' 'em t'come say good-bye—but they didn't go. The doctor found some kinda infection. But their own maid an' a nurse took care of 'er, an' both are aw right an' alive.

SCENE 11

THE SAME. VASILY LEONIDYCH *and* PETRISHCHEV *enter smoking cigarettes.*

PETRISHCHEV. Let's go then, I just want to get hold of Kokó-Loco.

VASILY LEONIDYCH. Your Kokó is an idiot! I tell you, I can't stand him. Now that's a nothing, a real loafer! Doesn't do a thing, just hangs around. Huh?

PETRISHCHEV. Well, wait then, I still want to say good-bye.

VASILY LEONIDYCH. All right, I'll go the coachman's place, have a look at the dogs. One male is so viscious, the coachman says he almost ate him. Huh?

PETRISHCHEV. Who ate whom? Did the coachman really eat the dog?

VASILY LEONIDYCH. You're always... (*Puts on his overcoat and exits.*)

PETRISHCHEV (*thoughtful*). Co-lo-, lo-co-mo-... Yes, yes. (*Goes upstairs.*)

SCENE 12

The two FOOTMEN, FYODOR IVANYCH, *and* YAKOV (*runs across the stage at the beginning and end of the scene*).

FYODOR IVANYCH (*to* YAKOV). What now?

YAKOV. No hors d'oeuvres! I said... (*Exits.*)

SECOND FOOTMAN. An' then our master's son got sick. So right away they took 'im with a nurse to a hotel, an' there he died widout his mother.

FIRST FOOTMAN. They just ain't 'fraid o' sinin'. I figger, yuh can't get away from God.

FYODOR IVANYCH. I think so too.

(YAKOV *runs upstairs with the hors d'oeuvres.*)

FIRST FOOTMAN. Yuh also hafta consider that if yer afraid o' everyone like that, yuh hafta lock yuhself up between four walls, like in jail, an' just sit.

SCENE 13

THE SAME *and* TANYA, *then* YAKOV.

TANYA (*curtsies to the* FOOTMEN). Hello! (*The* FOOTMEN *bow.*) Fyodor Ivanych, I have something to tell you.

FYODOR IVANYCH. Well what is it?

TANYA. The peasants have come again, Fyodor Ivanych.

FYODOR IVANYCH. So what? I gave the paper to Semyon...

TANYA. I gave them paper. I can't even begin to tell you how grateful they are. The only thing they want now is to pay the money.

FYODOR IVANYCH. But where are they?

TANYA. Here, by the porch.

FYODOR IVANYCH. All right, I'll tell the master.

TANYA. I have another request, dear Fyodor Ivanych.

FYODOR IVANYCH. What now?

TANYA. Well, Fyodor Ivanych, I can't stay here any longer. Please ask them to let me go. (YAKOV *runs in.*)

FYODOR IVANYCH (*to* YAKOV). What do you want?

YAKOV. Another samovar an' some oranges.

FYODOR IVANYCH. Go ask the housekeeper. (YAKOV *runs out.* [*To* TANYA]) Why's that?

TANYA. What else! That's how things are now.

YAKOV (*running in*). There ain't enough oranges.

FYODOR IVANYCH. Serve whatever there is. (YAKOV *runs out.*) You've chosen a bad time. You see what a fuss there is...

TANYA. You know yourself, Fyodor Ivanych, there's no end to this fuss no matter how long you wait—you know yourself—but my business is for the rest of my life. Dear Fyodor Ivanych, you've been very good to me, be like a father to me now, choose a good time and tell her. Otherwise, she'll be angry and won't let me have my papers.

FYODOR IVANYCH. But why are you in such a hurry?

TANYA. Why not, Fyodor Ivanych, everything's been settled now... I'd go to my mother, my godmother, get ready. And we'd have our wedding after Easter.[22] Please tell her, dear Fyodor Ivanych!

FYODOR IVANYCH. Go now—this is not the place!

SCENE 14

An elderly GENTLEMAN *comes downstairs and, without saying a word, exits with the* SECOND FOOTMAN. TANYA *exits.* FYODOR IVANYCH, *the* FIRST FOOTMAN, *and* YAKOV (*enters*).

YAKOV. Yuh know, Fyodor Ivanych, it's really an outrage! She wants t'fire me now. She says: "You break everything, you forgot about Fifka, and you let the peasants into the kitchen against my orders." And you know yuhself, I didn't know nothin' 'bout it! Tatyana's the one that told me: "Take 'em into the kitchen," an' I didn't know whose order it was.

FYODOR IVANYCH. Did she really speak to you?

YAKOV. Just now. Please stick up for me, Fyodor Ivanych! My family has just started t'straighten things out, an' if yuh lose yer place, how long till yuh get another one. Fyodor Ivanych, please!

SCENE 15

FYODOR IVANYCH, FIRST FOOTMAN, *and* ANNA PAVLOVNA *seeing off the* OLD COUNTESS *with the wig and false teeth. The* FIRST FOOTMAN *helps the* COUNTESS *put on her outdoor clothes.*

ANNA PAVLOVNA. Certainly, how else? I am truly moved.

COUNTESS. If it were not for my ill health, I would visit you more often.

ANNA PAVLOVNA. Really, try Pyotr Petrovich. He's brusque, but no one can calm you down like he can. Everything with him is so simple and clear.

COUNTESS. No, I'm used to mine.

ANNA PAVLOVNA. Be careful now.

COUNTESS. *Merci, mille fois merci.*

SCENE 16

THE SAME *and* GRIGORY (*disheveled and excited, barges out of the pantry*). SEMYON *can be seen behind him.*

SEMYON. Yuh better leave 'er alone.

GRIGORY. You bastard, I'll teach yuh t'fight! You good-for-nothin, you!

ANNA PAVLOVNA. What is this? You think you're in tavern, do you?

GRIGORY. My life's miserable cuz o' this cruddy peasant.

ANNA PAVLOVNA (*irritated*). Are you out of your mind, don't you see? (*To the* COUNTESS.) *Merci, mille fois merci. A mardi.* (*The* COUNTESS *and* FIRST FOOTMAN *exit.*)

SCENE 17

FYODOR IVANYCH, ANNA PAVLOVNA, GRIGORY, *and* SEMYON.

ANNA PAVLOVNA (*to* GRIGORY). What is this?

GRIGORY. I may only be a footman but I have my pride an' won't let any peasant push me aroun'.

ANNA PAVLOVNA. But what has happened?

GRIGORY. This here Semyon of yers has gotten pushy cuz he's been with his betters. Wants t'fight.

ANNA PAVLOVNA. Why? What for?

GRIGORY. God only knows.

ANNA PAVLOVNA (*to* SEMYON). What is the meaning of this?

SEMYON. Why don't he leave 'er alone?

ANNA PAVLOVNA. What has happened between you two?

SEMYON (*smiling*). It's just that he keeps on grabbin' Tanya, the maid, an' she don't want 'im to. So I just pushed 'im aside... with my hand, just a bit.

GRIGORY. Aside aw right, nearly broke my ribs. An' he ripped my good coat. An' here's what he says: "I got," he says, "the power I had yesterday," an' begins squeezin' me.

ANNA PAVLOVNA (*to* SEMYON). How dare you fight in my house?

FYODOR IVANYCH. Excuse me, Anna Pavlovna, may I explain? I must tell you that Semyon has certain feelings for Tanya, and they are engaged now; and Grigory—well, I must tell the truth—does not treat her properly, honorably. That is why, I suppose, Semyon took exception to him.

GRIGORY. Not at all; it was outta spite cuz I found out 'bout all their hocus-pocus.

ANNA PAVLOVNA. What hocus-pocus?

GRIGORY. At the seance. It wasn't Semyon but Tanya that pulled all them stunts yesterday. I saw 'er crawl out from under the sofa myself.

ANNA PAVLOVNA. What do mean crawled out from under the sofa?

GRIGORY. On my word o' honor. She's the one that brought the paper an' threw it on the table. If not for her, the paper wouldn't o' been signed, an' the land wouldn't o' been sold t'the peasants.

ANNA PAVLOVNA. Did you see it yourself?

GRIGORY. With my own eyes. Have 'er come, she won't deny it.

ANNA PAVLOVNA. Call her. (GRIGORY *exits.*)

SCENE 18

THE SAME *without* GRIGORY. *There is noise behind the scene, the voice of the* DOORMAN: No, no you can't! *The* DOORMAN *appears, three* PEASANTS *force their way by him. The* SECOND PEASANT *is in front; the* THIRD PEASANT *trips, falls, and grabs his nose.*

DOORMAN. No yuh can't, go 'way!

SECOND PEASANT. So where's the harm! Are we here for some bad thing? We've got money t'hand over.

FIRST PEASANT. 'Solutely, since by the applyin' of his hand with a signature the deal's come t'conclusion, we only wanna present the money with our thanks.

ANNA PAVLOVNA. Just wait, wait with your thanks, it was all a fraud. It's not over yet. Not sold yet. Leonid! Call Leonid Fyodorovich. (*The* DOORMAN *exits.*)

SCENE 19

THE SAME *and* LEONID FYODOROVICH (*enters, but seeing* ANNA PAVLOVNA *and the* PEASANTS, *wants to go back*).

ANNA PAVLOVNA. No, no, come here, please! I told you distinctly not to sell the land on credit, everyone told you so. And you let them cheat you like the stupidest man alive.

LEONID FYODOROVICH. How so? I don't understand, what cheat?

ANNA PAVLOVNA. You should be ashamed of yourself! Your hair is gray, and you let them cheat you like a boy, and laugh at you. You begrudge your son three hundred measly roubles to help his social standing, and you let them trick you like a fool out of thousands.

LEONID FYODOROVICH. Now you calm down, Annette.

FIRST PEASANT. We're only 'bout yer receipt o' the sum, I mean...

THIRD PEASANT (*takes out the money*). Let us go, for God's sake!

ANNA PAVLOVNA. Wait, wait.

SCENE 20

THE SAME, GRIGORY, *and* TANYA.

ANNA PAVLOVNA (*sternly to* TANYA). Were you in the small parlor during the seance last night?

(*Sighing,* TANYA *looks at* FYODOR IVANYCH, LEONID FYODOROVICH, *and* SEMYON.)

GRIGORY. No use hemin' an' hawin', I saw yuh myself...

ANNA PAVLOVNA. Speak up, were you? I know all about it, admit it. I won't do anything to you. I only want to expose him (*pointing to* LEONID FYODOROVICH), the master... Did you throw the paper on the table?

TANYA. I don't know what to say. Only one thing, would you please let me go home?

ANNA PAVLOVNA (*to* LEONID FYODOROVICH). There, you see, they're making a fool of you.

SCENE 21

THE SAME. *Enter* BETSY *unnoticed at the beginning of the scene.*

TANYA. Please let me go, Anna Pavlovna!

ANNA PAVLOVNA. No, my dear! You may have caused us a loss of several thousand roubles. Land was sold which should not have been sold.

TANYA. Please let me go, Anna Pavlovna.

ANNA PAVLOVNA. No, you will answer for this. You can't get away with swindling. I'm going to take you to court.

BETSY (*stepping forward*). Let her go, Mamá. If you want to try her, then you have to try me too—she and I did everything together yesterday.

ANNA PAVLOVNA. Well, if you had anything to do with it, it could be nothing but the nastiest thing.

SCENE 22

THE SAME *and the* PROFESSOR.

PROFESSOR. How are you, Anna Pavlovna! And you, young lady! Leonid Fyodorovich, I've brought you a report from the Thirteenth Congress of Spiritualists in Chicago. There's a wonderful speech by Schmidt.

LEONID FYODOROVICH. Oh, that's very interesting!

ANNA PAVLOVNA. I'll tell you something far more interesting. It turns out that this girl duped both you and my husband. Betsy says she's the one, but that's only to provoke me; however, an illiterate girl duped you, and you believed it! There was none of that mediumistic phenomena of yours yesterday, it was she (*pointing to* TANYA) who did it all.

PROFESSOR (*taking off his overcoat*). What do you mean?

ANNA PAVLOVNA. I mean, she played the guitar in the dark, and struck my husband in the head, and did all that foolishness of yours, and she just admitted it.

PROFESSOR (*smiling*). So what does that prove?

ANNA PAVLOVNA. It proves that your mediumism is nonsense! That's what it proves.

PROFESSOR. Because this girl wanted to deceive us, mediumism is nonsense, as you put it? (*Smiling.*) Strange conclusion! It's quite possible that this girl wanted to deceive us: that often happens; it's possible that she actually did something, but what she did—she did; what was a manifestation of mediumistic energy—was a manifestation of mediumistic energy. It is even very probable that what this girl did, evoked, solicited, so to speak, the manifestation of mediumistic energy, gave it a definite form.

ANNA PAVLOVNA. Another lecture!...

PROFESSOR (*sternly*). You say, Anna Pavlovna, that this girl, and perhaps this charming young lady also, did something; but the light we all saw, and the decrease in temperature in the first instance, and increase in the second, and Grossman's agitation and vibration—did this girl also do that? And these are facts, facts, Anna Pavlovna! No, Anna Pavlovna, there are things which have to be examined and fully understood in order to speak about them—things too serious, too serious...

LEONID FYODOROVICH. And the child that Marya Vasilyevna clearly saw! And I saw it too... This girl couldn't do that.

ANNA PAVLOVNA. You think you're intelligent, but you're a fool!

LEONID FYODOROVICH. Well, I better go. Aleksey Vladimirovich, come with me. (*They begin to exit into his study.*)

PROFESSOR (*shrugging his shoulders, follows him*). Yes, how far behind Europe we still are!

SCENE 23

ANNA PAVLOVNA, *the three* PEASANTS, FYODOR IVANYCH, TANYA, BETSY, GRIGORY, SEMYON, *and* YAKOV (*enters*).

ANNA PAVLOVNA (*to* LEONID FYODOROVICH *as he exits*). They cheated him like a fool, and he sees nothing. (*To* YAKOV.) What do you want?

YAKOV. How many persons should I set the table for?

ANNA PAVLOVNA. How many?... Fyodor Ivanych, take the silver from him! Get out now! It's all his fault. This man will drive me to my grave. Yesterday he nearly let my poor dog starve, and she didn't do him any harm. As if that weren't enough, yesterday he brought these infected peasants into the kitchen, and they are here again. It's all his fault! Get out, get out now! You're fired, fired! (*To* SEMYON.) And if you ever dare to make a commotion in my house again, I'll teach you, you filthy peasant!

SECOND PEASANT. Well now, if he's a filthy peasant, ain't no need t'keep 'im; fire 'im, an' that's it.

ANNA PAVLOVNA (*listening to him, she stares at the* THIRD PEASANT). Just look, he has a rash on his nose, a rash! He's sick, he's a reservoir of infection!! I told you yesterday not to let them in, and here they are again. Get them out of here!

FYODOR IVANYCH. Will you not allow me to accept their money?

ANNA PAVLOVNA. Money? Take the money, but out with them, especially that sick one, out this instant! He's all rotten!

THIRD PEASANT. Yuh're wrong, ma'am, honest t'God, wrong. Just ask, so t'say, my ol' lady. How come I'm rotten? I'm whole like glass, so t'say.

ANNA PAVLOVNA. He talks yet?... Out, out! It's all to spite me!... No, I can't take it, I can't! Send for Pyotr Petrovich. (*Runs out sobbing.* YAKOV *and* GRIGORY *exit.*)

SCENE 24

THE SAME *without* ANNA PAVLOVNA, YAKOV, *and* GRIGORY.

TANYA (*to* BETSY). Miss Lizaveta, dear, what am I to do now?

BETSY. It's all right. Go with them, I'll arrange everything. (*Exits.*)

SCENE 25

FYODOR IVANYCH, *the three* PEASANTS, TANYA, *and the* DOORMAN.

FIRST PEASANT. How 'bout reception o' the sum now, sir?

SECOND PEASANT. Please let us go.

THIRD PEASANT (*hesitating with the money*). If I only knew, I wouldn't o' done it for nothin. It's worse than the plague.

FYODOR IVANYCH (*to the* DOORMAN). Take them to my place, we'll settle up there. And over there I'll accept the money. Go on, go on.

DOORMAN. Come on, come on.

FYODOR IVANYCH. Say thanks to Tanya. If not for her, you'd be without land.

FIRST PEASANT. 'Solutely, just as she made the preposal, so she put it into action.

THIRD PEASANT. She made us into men; what were we otherwise? We've so little land, there's no room, so t'say, t'even let a chicken out, t'say nothin' 'bout livestock. Good-bye, bright eyes! When you come to the village, come an' eat honey with us.

SECOND PEASANT. Soon's I get home, I'll start preparin' for the weddin', brew beer. Be sure an' come!

TANYA. I will, I will! (*Squeals.*) Semyon, isn't it great! (*The* PEASANTS *exit.*)

SCENE 26

FYODOR IVANYCH, TANYA, *and* SEMYON.

FYODOR IVANYCH. Have a good trip. Well now, Tanya, when you have your own house, I'll come and visit. Will you welcome me?

TANYA. My dear Fyodor Ivanych, we'll welcome you like a father! (*Hugs and kisses him.*)

Curtain.

The End.

Notes

INTRODUCTION

1. Gerold Tanquary Robinson, *Rural Russia under the Old Regime* (Berkeley: University of California Press, 1932), p. 116.

2. Quoted in N. K. Gudzy's notes to *The Realm of Darkness* in Lev Tolstoy, *Polnoe sobranie sochinenii v devianosta tomakh* (Moscow, 1928–53), vol. 26, p. 706. All further quotes from the works of Tolstoy will be cited by volume and page number from this edition. All translations from the Russian are mine unless stated otherwise.

3. Aleksei Pisemsky, "Gor'kaia sud'bina," in *Sobranie sochinenii v deviati tomakh* (Moscow, 1959), vol. 9, p. 229.

4. Letter to Druzhinin of December 20, 1859 (Tolstoy, vol. 60, p. 217).

5. Tolstoy, vol. 51, p. 98.

6. While we are making a list of Russian stories that use part or all of this paradigm, it is worth mentioning Nikolai Leskov's "Lady Macbeth of the Mtsensk District." In that story a merchant's wife and her lover (later husband) murder her father-in-law, and seven-year-old nephew, before they are discovered. Although this story lacks the scene of confession (since the last murder is witnessed by townsfolk), it does contain the motif of disposing of the body in the cellar, which Tolstoy will use.

7. Tolstoy, vol. 26, p. 710.

8. Ibid., p. 721.

9. Ibid., p. 722.

10. *L. N. Tolstoy v vospominaniiakh sovremmennikov*, ed. N. N. Gusev, 2 vols. (Moscow, 1960), vol. 1, pp. 450–51.

11. Maria Carlson, *No Religion Higher Than the Truth* (Princeton: Princeton University Press, 1993), p. 22.

12. Ibid., p. 23.

13. *L. N. Tolstoy v vospominaniiakh sovremennikov*, vol. 1, pp. 527–28.

THE REALM OF DARKNESS

1. Its difficult to say whether Tolstoy forgot that Matryona just said that she paid the old man, or whether this is a character trait of Matryona.

2. We are using this form of address to indicate that there is a relationship, though not by blood, between Mavra and Anisya. Specifically, in Russian *kum* or *kuma* indicates a spiritual relationship between the godparents of a child and the child's actual parents. Mavra is the godmother of Anisya's daughter.

3. A dying person is customarily placed under the icons in the home of Orthodox peasants.

4. The tradition among peasants was to hold weddings in the fall, after the harvest.

5. Matryona apparently bowed when she greeted Pyotr, as was the custom.

6. It is customary for a dying person to ask for forgiveness, the anticipated reply to which is "God will forgive you." Nikita's hesitation forces Pyotr to ask for forgiveness a second time.

7. What is understood here is earth piled up around the walls of the cottage, on which one can sit.

8. The gist of the information Matryona receives is that they (the village elders) will not permit her (Anisya) to take an outsider into the family who, as her new husband, could claim control over the estate of her deceased husband; of course, whatever means she has in her possession are not affected.

9. Public wailing was a customary ritual among peasants.

10. The word for "bank" (Russian *bank*) is corrupted throughout the play. Since for the peasants it is an unfamiliar foreign word but sounds like the native word for "jar" (*banka*), the familiar-sounding form is substituted for the foreign one. It is as though the bank is a jar into which or from which money can be put or taken.

11. The Russian expression, literally "pea pie into her/his/their mouth," is an obscenity and used euphemistically for fellatio. Mitrich, a former soldier, employs this expression as an expletive to punctuate his language, as if he were still in the army. This usage is the equivalent of "fuck" and its variants as it is frequently encountered among American servicemen.

12. This garment is an open gown made of silk (*rasstegai*) that is worn by Russian peasant women.

13. Tolstoy is referring ironically to the common saying "matchmaking is boasting" to state the very opposite, viz., that a future marriage should

not be founded on false expectations. Of course this statement is all the more ironic, since it is uttered by Matryona, who purposefully lies. Indeed, the Russian verb *khvastat'*, "to boast, brag," has the additional meaning of "to lie," and a more literal translation of the above should read: "Matchmakin' ain't for lyin'. I've never been one t'lie."

14. Mitrich is corrupting the word for "foundling." He is referring to the Home for Foundlings in Moscow.

15. Tolstoy originally composed this variant when the play was being examined by the censor after rumors had reached him that the censorship found the murder scene in Act IV to be too graphic. Subsequently, however, both variants were approved. Having found out about this, Tolstoy requested that half the edition be printed with one and half with the other variant, but his secretary and advisor, Vladimir Chertkov (who was supervising the printing), decided to include both variants. He told Tolstoy: "It will be interesting and good for readers to read both versions of the end of this act, and, it seems to me that the variant not only does not spoil the overall impression but, to the contrary, adds to the play" (Lev Tolstoy, *Polnoe sobranie sochinenii*, ed. V. Chertkov et. al. [Moscow, 1928–53], 90 vols., vol. 26, p. 717). Ultimately, Tolstoy agreed with Chertkov, and all editions of the play print both variants. In performance, obviously, directors can opt for whichever version they prefer.

16. Mitrich is not related to Anyutka, who simply addresses him in an affectionate manner.

17. The reference appears to be to the Kurds, a name Mitrich associates with the Russian word for "round," *kruglyi*. In order to capture the lost word play, Kurds in the English translation is associated with "crud."

18. This is a reference to the songs sung in praise of the bride and groom at the wedding of Russian peasants.

19. It was customary for a bride to wail over leaving her parental home and joining a family of strangers.

20. In the original text the nickname for the policeman is "bright buttons," which is an allusion to the buttons on his uniform. It is interesting to note that in the slang of American pickpockets during Prohibition, the police were called, among other things, "buttons." However, in order to make the association to the police clearer for the modern reader, we have changed "buttons" to "badge."

1. This is an informal, economical ball because the ladies can wear dresses made of cotton materials.

2. Maria Petrovna Burdey (Bourdier) was the proprietor of a shop in Moscow that custom tailored ladies dresses.

3. Josephine Karlovna Pironey (Pironnet) was the proprietor of a footwear shop in Moscow, and purveyor to the imperial theaters.

4. A village approximately two and half miles from Yasnaya Polyana, Tolstoy's estate. Tolstoy appears simply to have borrowed the name, since, if the peasants are from the Kursk area, they would not know people who lived near Yasnaya Polyana, some one hundred miles away.

5. Sir William Crookes (1832–1919), an English chemist and physicist, who discovered the element thallium. He also devoted some time to the investigation of psychic phenomena, and attempted to find a correlation between them and physical laws.

6. Alfred Russel Wallace (1823–1913), a British naturalist who, independent of Charles Darwin, worked out a theory of the origin of species through natural selection. He also wrote *Miracles and Modern Spiritualism* (1881), in which he explains his reasons (purely experimental and not connected with Christianity) for accepting beliefs that were not shared by many men of science.

7. Daniel Dunglas Home (1833–86), a Scottish spiritualist, who gave seances at several European courts including the Russian court in 1871, before Alexander II. His most famous book was *Lights and Shadows of Spiritualism*.

8. See note 10, *The Realm of Darkness*.

9. That is, the handkerchief in which the presents were wrapped.

10. This is a reference to Prince Ferdinand I (1861–1948), who in 1887 was chosen as ruler of Bulgaria under Turkish sovereignty. He declared independence from the Turks in 1908, and in 1918 abdicated in favor of his son Boris III.

11. The former cook is referring to the French expressions *sauté à la Beaumont* and *bavasari*, respectively.

12. Jean-Martin Charcot (1825–93), a French physician, who is considered the father of modern clinical neurology. His classic work, *Leçons sur*

les maladies du système nerveux, had considerable influence on the development of the science of neurology. He was renowned internationally and attracted many students, among whom was Sigmund Freud. However, his reputation suffered a setback during the final phase of his career as a result of his studies on hysteria and hypnotism that led to many observations that were subsequently discredited.

13. Other translators of this play have rendered this obviously non-Russian name as either Liebault or Libot. Since we were unable to determine who this person is, we did not venture a guess, and simply transliterated the name as it appears in the text.

14. Hospital of the Salpêtrière opened in Paris in the seventeenth century as an asylum-prison for insane women and women convicted of adultery, theft, and murder. It also served as a detention center for old women, beggars, and prostitutes. By 1862, the time Charcot arrived there, it was less a prison and more an institution for displaced unfortunates.

15. The word she uses for the relation given in the text, *svëkor,* is the husband's father or father-in-law to the wife. The word she has forgotten, for the husband's brother, is *dever'*, i.e., brother-in-law to the wife. Russian has numerous terms that express a broad range of relationships which are generally covered by some form of the word "in-law" in English. The terms for these relationships to the husband, i.e., the wife's father and brother, are *test'* and *shurin,* respectively. A similar differentiation is made in the terms for a brother's wife, a sister's husband, a husband's sister, a wife's sister, a brother-in law on the husband's side, etc.

16. We have not been able to determine who these people are, and have simply transliterated their names into their assumed German form.

17. James Braid (1795–1860), a British surgeon whose studies of hypnosis repudiated many of the superstitions associated with it. His experiments demonstrated that the ability to induce hypnotic states is physiological, and not due to the transmission of a supposed "fluidum."

18. Pablo Martin Melitón de Sarasate y Navascuéz (1844–1908), Spanish violinist and composer, who gained renown for his purity of tone and flawless technique. Concert tours, which he began in 1859, spread his fame throughout the world. He performed in Saint Petersburg in 1879, 1883 and again in 1889.

19. The first part of the Russian word for "rehearsal" (*repetitsiya*) is sim-

ilar to the word for "turnip" (*repa*). In his play on words for vegetables, Petrishchev forms another word with the same suffix as the word for rehearsal, but replaces its first part, "turnip," with "carrot" (*morkovetitsiya*). He does this once again in his next to last dialogue with Kokó Klingen in this scene, where he now replaces "turnip" with the word for "horse-radish" (*red'ka*, hence, *red'kotitsya*). We have tried to capture this word play by using words in English with the same suffix as "rehearsal" that are completely out of context.

20. Petrishchev is playing on the other meanings of the Russian noun for "proposal," viz., "sentence" (*predlozhenie*), thus what he says literally is: "Make a sentence with a predicate."

21. Petrishchev is mixing lines from two poems by different authors. The first quotation ("with a strange love") is from the poem "Fatherland" (*Otchizna*) by Mikhail Yuryevich Lermontov (1814–41); the second quotation ("to him the people's path will not be overgrown") is from the poem "Monument" (*Pamyatnik*) by the great Russian poet, Aleksandr Sergeyevich Pushkin (1799–1837).

22. The period mentioned in the original text is between Easter Sunday and the fast prior to Pentecost. It is known in the vernacular as *krasnaya gorka*. It was customary for peasants to marry at this time, before work began in the fields. Otherwise weddings were postponed until fall.